THE ULTIMATE
GOLF
BOOK

THE ESSENTIAL GUIDE TO
PLAYING BETTER GOLF

4955
This material previously appeared in *Improve Your Golf*
Compiled by *Steve Newell*
Copyright © Eaglemoss Publications Ltd 1989, 1990, 1991, 1992
All rights reserved under the Pan-American and International Copyright Conventions.
This edition first published in the United States by Courage Books, an imprint of
Running Press Book Publishers.

Printed in Hong Kong

9 8 7 6 5 4 3 2 1
Digit on the right indicates the number of this printing

Library of Congress Cataloging-in-Publication Number 96-70068
ISBN 0-7624-0116-8

This book was produced by CLB International
Godalming, Surrey, U.K.

Published by Courage Books
an imprint of Running Press Book Publishers
125 South Twenty-second Street
Philadelphia, Pennsylvania 19103-4399

THE ULTIMATE
GOLF
BOOK

THE ESSENTIAL GUIDE TO PLAYING BETTER GOLF

EDITED BY STEVE NEWELL

COURAGE
BOOKS
AN IMPRINT OF RUNNING PRESS
PHILADELPHIA • LONDON

CONTENTS

INTRODUCTION

Golf is a game of tiny fractions acted-out on the largest playing field in the whole of sport. The average golf course may cover tens of acres, but the 18 holes that represent the extent of a golfer's ambitions each measure little more than 4 inches in diameter. Not exactly a needle in a haystack, but nearly.

The statistical realities of the golf swing itself are even more bewildering. The average club possesses an optimum hitting area perhaps only half an inch in diameter. During the full swing the clubhead will travel as far as 15 yards, reaching speeds in excess of 100 miles per hour, ultimately to collide with a golf ball measuring just $1^3/_4$ inches in diameter. If the clubface is just five degrees out of alignment at the moment of impact, then you can probably wave good-bye forever to that golf ball. Two degrees out and you've missed the fairway or the green.

Seldom does the difference between excellence and mediocrity come down to such tiny margins. A bad golf shot is quite literally a case of "so near, and yet so far." Do not fear, however. These facts should provide hope rather than cause despair. Precision may well be the prerequisite of success, but achieving it is not nearly as daunting as the statistics might suggest. Precision stems merely from an understanding of golf's basic fundamentals – the grip, stance, address position, aim and alignment. Once these basics are firmly entrenched in one's approach to the game, the absolute beginner can within a matter of months be hitting shots not so far removed from the realms of professional golf.

When it comes down to the short game, the margin between novice and professional can become even more blurred. Any golfer – irrespective of age, height, sex or build – can hole a chip shot, blast a bunker shot or drain a long putt. This aspirational element is, in essence, the main attraction of the game. Golf's feel-good factor cannot be achieved, though, without sensible and constructive tuition on a long-term basis. That is exactly what this book represents. It is a comprehensive manual packed with in-depth instruction from tee to green. Its user-friendly format enables you to study closely golf's fundamentals and appreciate how the golf swing works, and how best you can apply these principles to your own game. Sections on fault-finding can help you avoid the pitfalls of poor technique and allow you to understand how and why mistakes happen. This book will serve as an invaluable reference manual, something to dip in and out of as and when the need arises, helping you to make the most of your game.

1

THE FUNDAMENTALS

Even the best golfers in the world are meticulous about golf's fundamentals. Someone as dedicated as Nick Faldo will spend probably as much time working on the various elements that make up his address position as he will on the swing itself. That should set the alarm bells ringing inside every golfer's head, because the fact is, the average player just doesn't pay enough attention to what happens before the swing starts. Don't fall into that same trap. Virtually every swing fault stems from a problem at address. Get set correctly and you're well on the way to a better golf swing. This chapter tells you how to do just that.

Clubhead control

Ben Hogan, one of the greatest golfers who ever lived, once said that a golfer with a bad grip doesn't want a good swing. That just about hits the nail on the head. Sure, every tiny detail, every moving part in the golf swing is vitally important. But when it comes to the hands, there's an added significance. Your hands are the only contact with the golf club. Good contact – in other words, a fundamentally correct grip – gives you every chance of playing this game to your full potential. Bad contact, in the shape of a faulty grip, means you will forever struggle. That's a fact – there's no way round it. Holding the club in such a way that your hands work together as a single unit is the only way you can conceivably hope to achieve clubhead control on a consistent basis. And that is basically what hitting good golf shots is all about.

Q **Why do I lose control of the club at impact?**

A Your grip is most probably wrong. The club must be held firmly but with the minimum of effort. A correct grip means your hands can work freely but with utmost control. A sloppy grip – perhaps you hold the club too much in the palms of your hands so your left hand is slightly weak and your right strong (**1**) – can only lead to poor clubhead control.

Impact position

A poor grip can lead to all sorts of problems at impact. As you strike a ball, great force is exerted, and if you haven't a firm grip your hands lose control of the club (**2**) – the blade can either open or close at impact.

With a correct grip your impact position (**4**) should mirror address (**3**), so that the blade returns square with no hint of twisting in the hands.

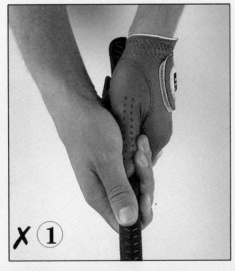

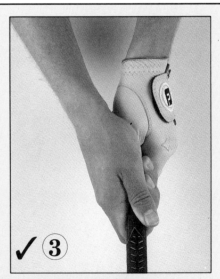

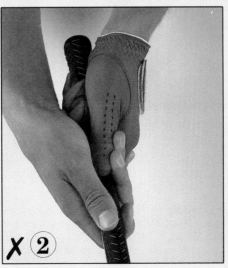

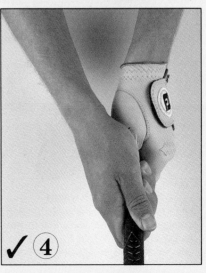

LOOK AGAIN AT YOUR GRIP

Keep practicing this grip time and time again until it becomes automatic.

CLUB DIAGONALLY ACROSS PALM

½-1in (1.5-2.5cm) OVERHANGING

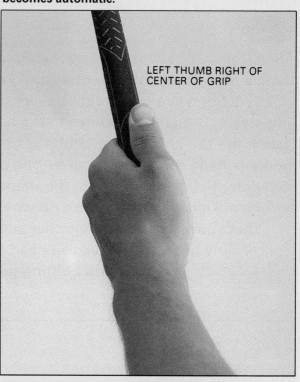

LEFT THUMB RIGHT OF CENTER OF GRIP

① LEFT PALM POSITION
Place the club diagonally across your left palm, starting from the middle joint of your forefinger. Let 1⁄2-1in (1.5-2.5cm) of the butt-end overhang your palm.

② LEFT HAND GRASP
Close your hand around the grip – "shake hands" with it – and place your thumb slightly to the right of center. The clubface should be square when the back of the hand faces the target.

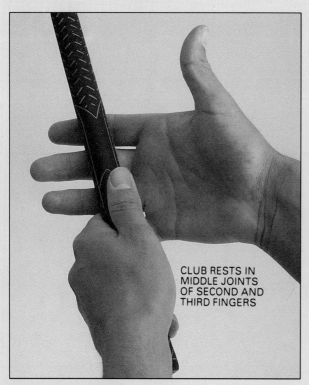

CLUB RESTS IN MIDDLE JOINTS OF SECOND AND THIRD FINGERS

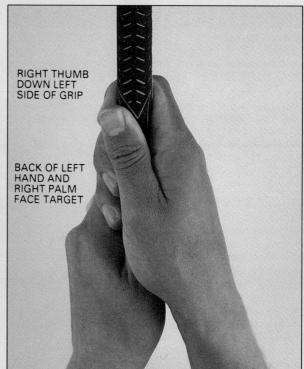

RIGHT THUMB DOWN LEFT SIDE OF GRIP

BACK OF LEFT HAND AND RIGHT PALM FACE TARGET

③ BRING IN RIGHT HAND
Place the underside of the grip in the middle joints of the second and third fingers of your right hand. Either overlap or interlock your little finger with the forefinger of your left hand.

④ FINAL GRIP
Close your hand around the grip and your left thumb. Point your right thumb down the left side of the grip. Your right palm and the back of your left hand should both face the target.

Posture and alignment problems

**It doesn't matter whether you're the height of Faldo or Woosnam – you must adopt the correct stance before you can
make a good swing and deliver the blade square at impact.
Problems start when you believe you're set up
correctly just because you feel comfortable. But you may be too
upright, crouched or poorly aligned – shots
that fly either left or right of target are the result.**

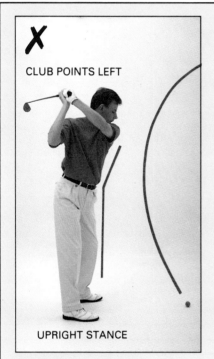

✗

CLUB POINTS LEFT

UPRIGHT STANCE

✗

STANCE TOO CROUCHED

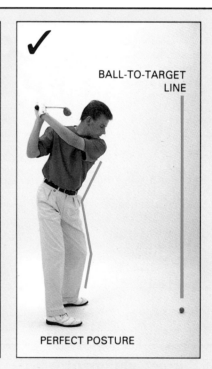

✓

BALL-TO-TARGET LINE

PERFECT POSTURE

Q Why do most of my shots start left then bend sharply right?

A If you're standing too close to the ball you naturally adopt an upright position. This leads you to pick the club up outside the line and it points left of target at the top of the backswing.

From this position you swing down on an out-to-in path and cut across the ball at impact. If your blade is square the ball starts left then curves away to the right.

Q Usually my shots move gently from right to left, but sometimes they become a violent hook. Why?

A When you hit your draw you attack the ball slightly from the inside. But if you swing too far from the inside, too much sidespin is produced and the ball moves wildly from right to left.

Standing too far away from the ball – so you have to stoop and crouch to reach it – is a likely cause. You naturally swing around your body and the plane becomes too flat. You mirror this plane on the downswing and the club attacks the ball from too far on the inside.

Correct posture
A good posture helps you to put the club on the correct takeaway path, which in turn helps you achieve the correct top of backswing position. From here it's easy to swing down and through on the proper path – in-to-in.
Key points:
○ Don't stoop, or stand too upright at address.
○ Knees should be gently flexed, *not* straight or too bent.
○ As you swing, the angle of your back should stay constant.

Q **I'm striking the ball well, but often my shots curve to the right. Why?**

A It may be that you're aligned left. If your feet, hips and shoulders point left, the tendency is to swing along that line and create an out-to-in swing path. If your blade is square to the target the action of cutting across the ball sends it left and then it bends severely right.

A tell-tale sign of a slice is a flat, rounded finish.

Q **I can't understand why suddenly my drives bend left when most of the time I hit the ball straight. What am I doing wrong?**

A You could be aligning right. This makes you swing on an in-to-out path, as you naturally follow the line of your feet. This swing path combined with a square clubface starts the ball slightly right of target, then it curves – often violently – left.

The high-handed finish position is the product of an unwanted in-to-out swing path.

Correct alignment

If your feet, hips and shoulders all align perfectly parallel to the ball-to-target line, you have a good chance of swinging the club on the correct plane and path. The in-to-in swing path combined with a square clubface sends the ball straight, and a balanced finish should be natural.

Key points:
) Feet, hips and shoulders must align parallel to the target line.
) Good alignment must go with a sound set-up for straight hitting.
) Be relaxed for free and rhythmical swinging.

Ball positions

**If you're striking the ball well but still hitting wayward
shots, check your ball placement – even if it's just a
fraction behind or in front of the correct position the blade
doesn't return square at impact. However, there are times
when you must make a deliberate change from the usual position
to help you hit a specialist shot.**

LAY DOWN CLUBS
TO CHECK BALL POSITION

FURTHER BACK IN
STANCE FOR
LOW PUNCH

Placement check

If you are struggling to keep the ball on the fairways
or firing at the flag, it's time to check your ball
positioning. To find out exactly where you place the
ball, lay down a club parallel to the ball-to-target line.
Then lay another perpendicular to the first so that it's
in line with the ball. This gives you an accurate
assessment of whether you have the ball too far
forward or back in your stance.

For a medium to long iron, position the ball
between the center of your stance and the inside of
your left heel.

Q When, if ever, should I change my ball position
from normal?

A When you need to play a specialist shot – like a
low punch into the wind or a high fading driver –
you have to change your normal ball position for the
shot to work.

To play the low, controlled punch shot you must
place the ball further back in your stance. With a
medium to long iron, place the ball in the center of
your stance (above). If you square the blade and
push your hands slightly forward, the clubface is
naturally delofted, which helps you to keep the ball
low. But you must combine this set-up with the
correct technique – a short swing with little wrist
break – for the shot to come off.

Q Why do my shots usually fly straight right, but sometimes hook?

A You probably have the ball too far back in your stance. The club attacks the ball on an in-to-out path and makes contact earlier than normal with the blade slightly open – the result is a push. But if the blade does strike the ball squarely, the effect of the in-to-out path produces a hook.

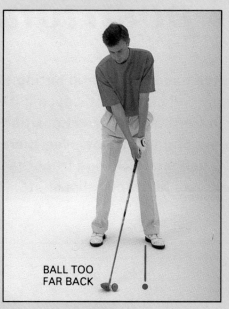

BALL TOO
FAR BACK

PUSHED RIGHT

BALL STRUCK TOO EARLY
IN SWING ON IN-TO-OUT PATH

Q Most of my shots fly off to the left but sometimes I slice. Why?

A These shapes of shot are produced if you have the ball too far forward in your stance. The clubface strikes the ball later than normal and on an out-to-in path. This usually means the clubface is slightly closed at impact and the ball flies straight left – a pull. The shot that curves away to the right is produced by keeping the blade square to the target at impact – this has the effect of cutting across the ball, hence the slice.

BALL TOO
FAR FORWARD

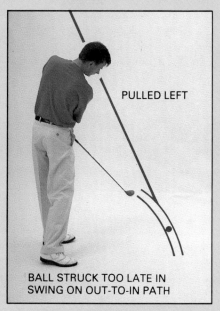

PULLED LEFT

BALL STRUCK TOO LATE IN
SWING ON OUT-TO-IN PATH

Ball basics
Ball positioning is one of the most important fundamentals of golf. Correct placing helps you to build a constant, repeatable swing and enhances your ball striking ability.

If you combine a good posture and swing with the correct ball position – opposite the left heel for the woods – your shots should fly consistently straight and true.

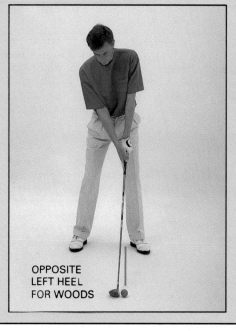

OPPOSITE
LEFT HEEL
FOR WOODS

STRAIGHT SHOT

BALL STRUCK AT
CORRECT POINT

PERFECT PRACTICE
=== FOR ===
PERFECT PLAY

Gary Player used to say that the more he
practiced the luckier he got. That's reason
enough to spend time on the range, but there are
other more tangible benefits to working hard on
your golf game, benefits that are within your grasp
providing you go about your business in an
intelligent and constructive manner. This means
going to the practice green with a clear idea of what
you want to work on, then being disciplined while
you're there. This kind of approach will not only
help your game generally, it can also help you
prepare for a competition more thoroughly. This
chapter reveals some of the elements of a fruitful
practice session.

Faults on the range

**Practice is essential, but you must work on the correct techniques if it's to be of any use.
Building in faults can have devastating effects on your game when you're out on the course.**

Q I always aim at a target on the driving range to help my alignment, and I think I swing well. But I still can't hit shots consistently straight. Why?

A Though it's a good idea always to aim at a target, you must make sure that you're perfectly aligned to it for straight shots.

When you pick out a target make sure that your mat is square to it. If it isn't, it's easy for you to swing along the line of the edge of the mat. However well your feet are aligned, the swing path isn't correct. Take time to square up the mat before you start to play. Your ball-to-target line should be parallel to the edge of the mat.

One other way that you can hit wayward shots – even if you are aligned correctly – is by trying to hit the ball too hard. The balls on a range don't go as far as the top quality ones you use on the course, so forget the yardage markers. Hit a club that comfortably reaches the target even if it means hitting two clubs more than usual.

Don't practice too quickly – take each shot as it comes and go easy. Belting away balls in quick succession naturally quickens your rhythm, and inconsistencies occur.

✗ ALIGNED AT TARGET BUT MAT POINTS LEFT

✗ TEND TO SWING OUT TO IN IN LINE WITH EDGE OF MAT

✓ ALIGN MAT AT YOUR CHOSEN TARGET TO HELP SWING ON CORRECT PATH

✓ SWING ALONG LINE OF MAT – CORRECT IN-TO-IN PATH

Q I strike the ball well at the driving range but out on the course I tend to hit a lot of thinned and topped shots with my irons. How could this be?

A The main reason for this is using the mat incorrectly. Each mat has its own rubber tee and the ball sits invitingly on top. It's easy to hit any club off the tee but it teaches you the wrong principles of iron play.

Though it's fine to hit woods off the peg you can't strike down on the ball with – for instance – a 7 iron. Instead you come up on the shot.

At the range you can get away with it – in fact it can flatter you. Every shot is easy when the ball is sitting up on the tee.

But on the course a shot off a fairway can cause problems, because the lie looks worse than it really is. You tend to use the same swing as on the range, attacking the ball slightly on the up. Either a top or a thin are natural results of this swing.

Bear in mind that too much practice on the range can ingrain faults into your swing. These flaws only show up on the course. Balance your golf between the practice range and the course to gauge a fair reading of your abilities.

X PLAYING IRONS FROM RUBBER TEE INGRAINS WRONG TECHNIQUE – TOP OR THIN ON COURSE

✓ PLAY OFF MAT FOR CORRECT DOWNWARD PATH

IRON OFF TEE

X HIT BALL ON THE UP

PLAYING OFF DECK – CRISP DOWNWARD STRIKE

✓ GOOD TRAJECTORY WITH BACKSPIN

Off the deck

To hit crisp irons both on and off the course fire them directly off the mat at the practice range – it ingrains the correct attack into your swing.

For consistent striking you must attack the ball on a downward path – the more lofted an iron the steeper the angle of attack. If you make sure you strike the ball before the ground the shot should fly on the correct trajectory with a good deal of backspin.

Once you have practiced this on the range, it's easy to go out on the course and hit well struck irons regularly.

Entering a competition

Once you've gained a handicap – and perhaps improved it – you probably want to test your skills in a serious competition against other golfers.

To do this, you must be a member of a club. If you're not a member of a private club – you might also be on an extended waiting list – bear in mind that many public courses have clubs attached. These are mainly for the purpose of providing competitions for members. You can often join such clubs more easily than private ones.

COMPETION DAY
Arrive in plenty of time for a golf event so that you can relax and practice before you tee off. Slight nervousness keeps you on the ball, but don't let nerves ruin your day – enjoy your golf and you're more likely to succeed.

▲SUITABLE SHOES
Good quality footwear is vital to a
successful round of golf – make sure
your shoes are clean and in good
condition. Waterlogged or split
shoes can destroy confidence – as
well as a potential low score.

▶BE READY FOR RAIN
Pack some wet weather clothing –
waterproof jacket, trousers and
umbrella are essential, whatever
the conditions. Even if rain is
unlikely, it's possible you'll need to
play out of a water hazard!

Competitions are normally
posted on the club noticeboard.
Usually you'll also find the results
there, and a yearly schedule.

STROKEPLAY

Monthly medal tee-off times are
shown on the noticeboard. Write
your name next to a starting time
that suits you. You can play with a
friend if you prefer, but competitions provide a fine opportunity
to play a serious round with golfers of different standards.

Medals are usually broken up
into three classes or divisions. Division One may cover scratch
players to those with a handicap
of 11; Division Two might contain
those between 11 and 16, and the
third division 16 to 28. In each
medal competition there is a divi-
sional winner as well as an overall victor.

Women's medals work in the
same way, with Gold, Silver and
Bronze classes. As with the men's

▶LOCAL RULES
Check the noticeboard in
the clubhouse for any
changes in local rules.
Some apply for a short
period of time only so
make sure you're aware of
any solely for your
competition – local rules
almost always work to
your advantage.
While you're there,
double check your
starting time – missing it
is likely to lead to
disqualification.

◄NEW GLOVE
Consider buying a new glove for an important competition. An old one becomes hard and dirty after use – with a new glove, your grip on the club should feel much more comfortable. It provides a psychological boost as well.

▲POCKET ITEMS
Take plenty of tees with you. Have a couple of ball markers as well – you need them for the green. A pitchfork is also necessary – the etiquette of golf states that you should repair all pitchmarks on the green.

▲CLUB COUNT
Have you counted the number of clubs in your bag? Remember that you're allowed 14 at the most – though they can be a mixture of any 14. You lose 2 strokes for every hole at which you break the rule, to a maximum of 4 shots. You can carry less clubs if you prefer.

▶PUTTING PRACTICE
Brush up on your putting stroke and rhythm before your round. Gauging the speed of the practice putting green helps you gain an idea of the speed of the greens on the course. Seeing a few balls drop into the hole gives you confidence too.

medals there is a competition in each class as well as the overall medal.

MATCHPLAY EVENTS

Matchplay competitions are advertised on the club noticeboard – those who enter their names are drawn out of the hat.

Even as a high handicapper you could find yourself facing the club champion on the first tee. Naturally, the chances are you'd receive plenty of strokes to help calm your nerves.

Whatever the event in which you're taking part, prepare for it properly. Follow a set drill before a competition – a positive approach pays rich dividends.

Don't rush to the first tee to meet your starting deadline. Your first swing – vital to set the tone and tempo for the round – is sure to be rushed. As a competition golfer it's important to start off with the proper habits. Make sure you follow all the formalities, such as marking your scorecard correctly.

▲ WARMING UP
No golfer should ever head for the first tee without striking some balls first. Warm up the muscles you use in the swing – hitting cold usually causes a creaky swing and a poor strike. Check your alignment and posture at the same time.

▲ PRIZE GIVING
Although some prizes are awarded on the day of the competition, most clubs have a Finals Day at the end of the season. This is when monthly medals and other trophies are presented. The formalities differ from club to club.

pro tip

Allow for adrenalin
In the excitement of a competition, your adrenalin really flows – especially when it looks as if you're going to post a good score. But sometimes you're so pumped up that the ball flies further than you think.

Club down to allow for this. For instance, if you're a 7 iron from the green and feeling the adrenalin flow, go down to an 8 iron. The chances are that it will send the ball the same distance as you hit in normal conditions with the lower numbered club.

Bear in mind that this strategy is useful only for players in confident mood. Doubt in your mind breeds a duffed shot.

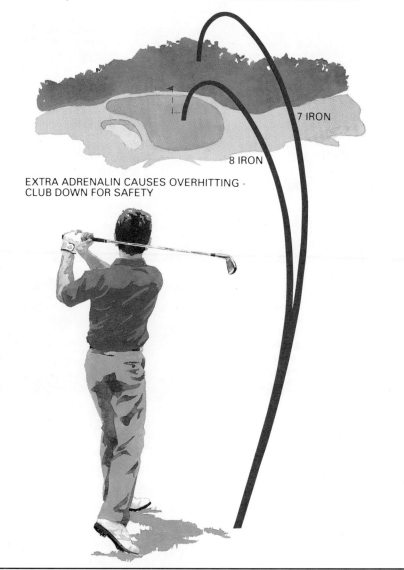

EXTRA ADRENALIN CAUSES OVERHITTING - CLUB DOWN FOR SAFETY

7 IRON

8 IRON

Preparing for a competition

T here's no such thing as a dead certainty in golf. Good rounds crop up when you least expect them, and nightmares can unfold just when you really felt it was going to be your day.

Tour professionals experience similar peaks and troughs. The difference is that pros go through the same pre-tournament routine every week. In many ways, this must make it all the more frustrating, but they at least give themselves a chance of performing to the best of their ability.

Competition preparation is essential if you want to do yourself justice. There's more than one way to get ready for a competition, so try to find an overall approach that works for you. Certain points are a feature of every successful routine. It's a good idea to be aware of them, because at the end of the day it's important to be able to say you did your best – win or lose.

AWAY FROM HOME

Preparation doesn't start on the day itself. There's plenty to do before the day of the competition – particularly if you're playing away from your home club. It's normal for the organizers of any event to grant all competitors courtesy of the course for the week leading up to the event.

Try to take advantage of this whenever possible because it greatly boosts your chances of winning. Most golfers find a course easier when they've seen it before. Club selection is often

GIVE IT YOUR BEST SHOT
Make the most of the hour or so immediately before your tee time. These valuable minutes often make the difference between success and failure. Spend some time on the practice ground. Work your way through the bag building the sort of rhythm into your swing that you can repeat on the 1st tee. Too many club golfers go into battle totally unprepared. When you're not ready, there will be days when your game clicks into place. But there are likely to be many more when your chances of winning are severely dented through making a frustrating poor start.

READY FOR THE BIG EVENT

If a competition matters to you, it makes sense to give yourself the best possible chance of winning. There isn't a single professional golfer in the world who plays a competitive round without first preparing thoroughly. Before you see them thump their first shot straight down the middle, they've probably been peppering the targets on the practice ground.

Most professionals go through the same routine every week. You're unlikely to have as much time on your hands as a professional – and it's almost certain that your club doesn't have the same facilities as a tour venue, but there are ways of making the most of those precious few minutes before you tee off.

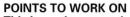

POINTS TO WORK ON

This is no time to make a swing change. Ensure the fundamentals are there, but don't become bogged down with too many theories on the golf swing. The most crucial part of your game to work on is rhythm and tempo – you need to find a pace of swing that you can take on to the course.

Start with some gentle chips to several targets. Try to gain an overall feel for each shot, and don't worry too much if every one doesn't finish stone dead. Then move up gradually through the clubs in your bag. Don't feel you have to hit a shot with every club – select three or four of those you're most comfortable with.

Finish off by hitting a few shots with your driver. Swing within yourself and remember, there are no prizes for trying to smash the cover off the ball. This is likely to upset the rhythm you've developed over the last half hour and entirely defeats the object of practicing before the round.

pro tip

The finishing touch
Round off every practice session with a spot of putting. If possible, try to find a flat area on the putting green and concentrate on the medium length putts and the occasional one from long range. Try to avoid practicing the short

putts – they're easily missed and can undermine your confidence.

Grip the putter lightly in your hands and stand comfortably. Work at building a smooth stroke and trying to gain a good feel for distance. Try not to think too much about technique – this can

often cause tension.

Again, don't be upset if the putts don't drop – you should stroll from the practice green in a relaxed frame of mind. In many ways this is the ideal winding down exercise to a pre-competition practice session.

more accurate second time around and you can also gain a feel for the greens, which may be different to those you're used to.

ROUTE MAP

Pick up a course planner when you're there and study it on the way round. There are several points you need to look out for, such as hidden bunkers or ditches. You also need to identify the danger holes, where you can easily drive into trouble, and those where you feel there's an opportunity to attack.

Often forgotten is the route you intend taking to the course. Make sure you know how to get there and how long it takes – don't rely on a last minute glance at the map and a frantic dash in the car. Struggling to make your tee off time is the worst preparation in the world.

Getting ready for a competition

at your home course – the monthly medal or Captain's Weekend for example – takes on a different form. You should know when to play safe and when to attack – club selection and reading the greens are unlikely to cause problems.

EQUIPMENT INSPECTION

Check that your clubs are clean, particularly if you've recently put in lots of practice. Having hit plenty of balls it's quite possible that your clubs are caked in a layer of dry grass and mud. This looks unsightly and more importantly reduces the amount of spin you can apply on the ball.

Make sure your golf bag is well stocked with balls, tees and anything else you might need. And don't make the mistake of taking more than the regulation maximum 14 clubs on to the course. You also need to make sure that none of your clubs is missing. For

instance, it's easy to leave your putter behind – particularly if you've been working on your stroke at home.

ACCEPT THE BAD DAYS

Even the best preparation in the world is no guarantee of success. When your own worst nightmare unfolds before your eyes, take heart from the fact that you don't earn a living hitting golf balls.

When professionals have their off days they generally accept them more favorably than their on-screen image suggests. Most are seldom as unhappy as they appear.

"Television is the reason golf has this serious image," said Fuzzy Zoeller at the 1990 US Open. "They only show the leaders on television – those guys are tensed up. Those of us in the back of the field, we're having a good time." There lies a message for every amateur having a bad day.

READY, STEADY, GO

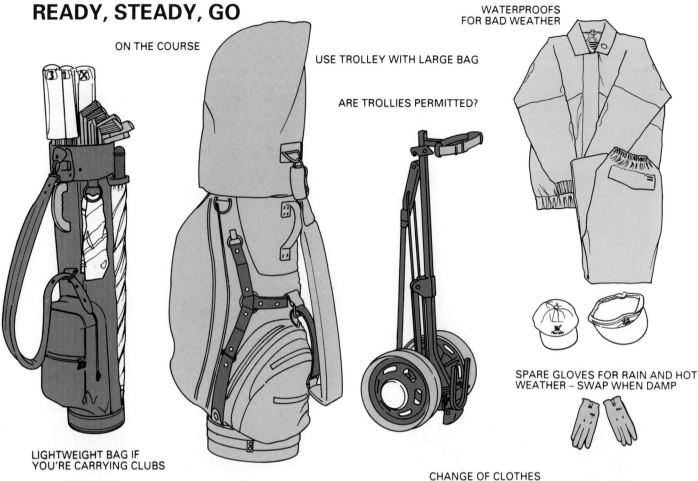

ON THE COURSE

USE TROLLEY WITH LARGE BAG

ARE TROLLIES PERMITTED?

WATERPROOFS
FOR BAD WEATHER

LIGHTWEIGHT BAG IF
YOU'RE CARRYING CLUBS

SPARE GLOVES FOR RAIN AND HOT
WEATHER – SWAP WHEN DAMP

CHANGE OF CLOTHES
HANDY FOR AFTERNOON ROUND

IN THE CLUBHOUSE

ON COURSE TO CONQUER

Doing well at a tournament away from your home club is a truly satisfying experience and there's no greater proof that your game is in good shape. It's generally harder to win away than it is at home, so in many ways it's these tournaments that you need to prepare for most.

If you're used to pulling your clubs rather than carrying them, make a quick call to the secretary or professional at the away club and find out if they allow trollies. Some clubs ban them in winter, or at other times of the year when major re-seeding of the course has taken place. If this is the case and you turn up with your pro size golf bag, you're in for a hard time carrying it for 18 holes, let alone 36. If you haven't managed to persuade a close friend or relative to caddie for you, it's better to pack your lightweight bag just in case. This is also worth doing when you use an electrically powered trolley – you never know when the battery might go flat.

DRESS FOR SUCCESS

Be prepared for changes in the weather. Pack your waterproofs and also bring a change of clothes for the afternoon round. This is worth while whether it's pouring with rain or extremely hot because it's always refreshing to have clean clothes to change into. Pulling on a soaking wet pair of socks and trousers is hardly the most pleasant start to an afternoon of golf.

Most competitions are followed by a dinner and presentation in the evening, so bring along a jacket and tie for the formal part of the day. Always make a point of doing this – there aren't too many clubs around that allow you into the dining room if you're improperly dressed. After all, you should go along to every competition with the attitude that you might be fortunate – and well prepared – enough to collect a prize.

FORMAL WEAR USUALLY
NEEDED FOR DINNER
AND PRESENTATION

GOLF'S SEVEN DEADLY SINS ... CURED

The hook, the slice, the shank – these are just some of the words that send shivers down the spine of any golfer. They describe the most destructive shots in golf, the real card-wreckers...not to mention confidence-wreckers. The surprising thing is, though, that every golfer hits these shots from time to time, even someone like Greg Norman. The difference is, top professionals recover better from a bad situation and, more importantly, are able to recognize the swing-faults which led to the shot. This is the first step to correction and prevention, which is why this chapter is dedicated to helping you understand why you hit such shots and how you can stop them from becoming a nasty habit.

Hooking help

Hooking doesn't have to be a result of an in-to-out swing path.
It can also be caused by poor wrist action – perhaps bad
positioning or excessive use. A wrong top of backswing position
or a whippy action can close the clubface at impact – a
sure route to a hook.

Q I feel as though I'm swinging on the correct plane and path but still hit the occasional hook. What could I be doing wrong?

A If you're not swinging from in to out, the only other way to hit a hook is to have a closed clubface at impact. You're almost certain to return the clubface closed if your blade is shut at the top of your backswing.

If you have an arched wrist at the top – even if your club points parallel to the target line – the blade is shut. From here you naturally swing down and strike the ball with a closed clubface – unless you make drastic changes in your wrist position.

The ball starts straight – as you attack it on the correct in-to-in path – but then curves left.

Flat wristed

To avoid a closed blade attack, your wrist has to be positioned correctly at the top of the backswing. The back of your left hand and your forearm must form a straight line for the blade to be square at the top. From this position you have a great chance of returning the blade square at impact.

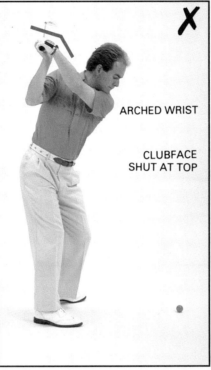

ARCHED WRIST

CLUBFACE
SHUT AT TOP

BLADE CLOSED
INTO IMPACT

FLAT WRIST

CLUBFACE SQUARE

BLADE SQUARE
INTO IMPACT

Q **I'm striking the ball powerfully but keep hitting a snap hook. Why?**

A You're likely to be using your wrists and hands too much. It's important to swing with free wrists to create clubhead speed, but your action should never be too whippy. If your downswing is very wristy the clubhead often overtakes your hands too soon – just before impact – and so is closed when you strike the ball.

This whippy action continues through the ball and your wrists roll and release too early, accentuating the right-to-left spin.

TOO WRISTY – CLOSES CLUB AT IMPACT

RELEASED TOO QUICKLY

Wrist control

You must combine a free wrist action with control if you're to return the blade consistently square. To be controlled through the hitting area, let your wrists be naturally free without them ever becoming too loose. This should automatically find a happy medium between too passive and too active.

On the downswing you should leave the attack with the wrists just late enough to generate good clubhead speed, without the blade ever overtaking your hands before impact.

A controlled downswing with good wrist action naturally leads to a correct release of your hands – essential for straight hitting.

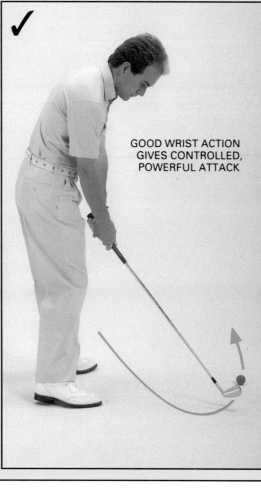

GOOD WRIST ACTION GIVES CONTROLLED, POWERFUL ATTACK

CONTROLLED RELEASE

Slicing savior

There are many ways to slice, but all stem from either an out-to-in swing path or an open blade at impact. Some of the more unusual slicing actions are hard to pinpoint, but however obscure yours may be it's essential to find a cure.

Q I'm quite sure that my swing is on plane and path, but I still keep hitting a slice. What could I be doing wrong?

A If your club is on plane, then your blade must be open at impact. One way this happens is if your left wrist is cupped at the top of the backswing. If you have a conventional grip this action naturally opens the blade at the top.

It is very difficult to return the blade square at impact as the tendency is to hold the hands in the same position on the downswing. This means that you lead into impact with the back of your left hand facing well right of target instead of being square. The blade is therefore open and the ball starts straight but curves violently right.

Flat wrist, square blade

If your takeaway is good with just the right amount of wrist and forearm roll, your blade should stay square throughout the backswing. At the top, the back of your left hand and forearm should form a straight line. If your grip is good this makes sure that the blade is square.

From this position it's easy to swing down into impact with the blade still square. At impact the back of your left hand should face the target.

LEFT WRIST CUPPED AT THE TOP

BLADE OPEN

HANDS NOT SQUARE TO TARGET – BLADE OPEN AT IMPACT

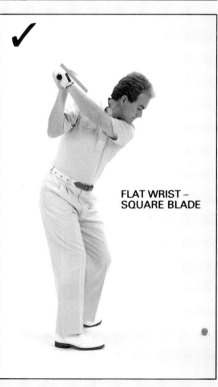

FLAT WRIST – SQUARE BLADE

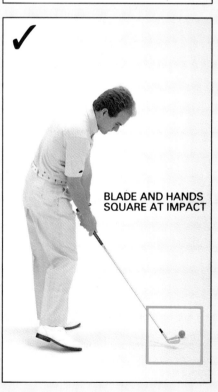

BLADE AND HANDS SQUARE AT IMPACT

INSIDE TAKEAWAY

HANDS AND CLUB LOOP OUTSIDE LINE ON DOWNSWING

OUT-TO-IN ATTACK

Q I've often heard that a slice comes from an out-to-in swing path so I find it hard to understand why I hit a slice when I know I take the club back well on the inside. How could this come about?

A True, a slice usually comes from an out-to-in swing path, and an inside takeaway mostly leads to in-to-out attack and a hook. But it is still possible to take the club back well on the inside and hit a slice.

If you know that you take the club back on the inside, you sometimes try to compensate for this by looping it on the downswing in an attempt to find the correct plane. You loop the club so much that it attacks the ball from outside the line – hence the slice.

ON LINE TAKEAWAY

DOWNSWING ON PLANE

CORRECT IN-TO-IN ATTACK

Perfect plane

To avoid any hint of an out-to-in downswing path, the club must be on plane throughout the swing. At the full extent of your takeaway the club should be on line with your feet and parallel to the ground.

This automatically leads you into a good top of backswing position from where it should be easy to swing down on the correct plane with no hint of loop. With an on plane downswing you move naturally into and through the ball on the correct, slightly in-to-in path.

Tormenting shank

Shanking is the most destructive and mentally damaging of all golfing afflictions. After making a seemingly decent swing you shoot the ball violently right. But you can take away the fear of the shot with careful preparation and a controlled swing.

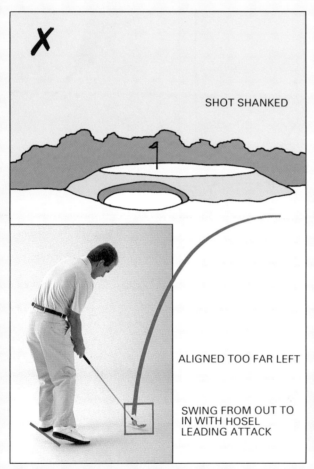

X

SHOT SHANKED

ALIGNED TOO FAR LEFT

SWING FROM OUT TO IN WITH HOSEL LEADING ATTACK

Q When I try to hit a high lob shot over trouble, I often shank. Why?

A Even though you understand the technique needed to play the cut-up shot, you overdo the set-up. You feel that you need to create as much loft on the clubface as possible and so align way left of the target while keeping the blade square.

Because you swing along the line of your feet, the clubhead path is severely out to in. This means that you lead into impact with the hosel of the club. If you're lucky you strike the ball with the face, but you are more likely to catch it with the neck of the club first – hence the shank.

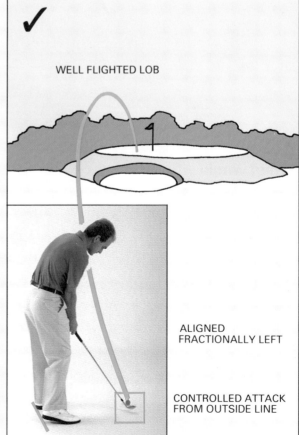

✓

WELL FLIGHTED LOB

ALIGNED FRACTIONALLY LEFT

CONTROLLED ATTACK FROM OUTSIDE LINE

Subtle set-up

For the cut-up shot to come off you do need to set up aligning left of target with your blade square, but the change should not be too drastic. The sand wedge is naturally designed to loft the ball high, so you only need to open your stance a little.

When you square the blade, make sure that you can swing into impact from an outside line without the hosel leading the attack. A few small practice swings should give you a good idea whether the clubface can contact the ball first. Then swing smoothly and be confident that the blade will do its work – thinking you might shank never helps.

Q Now and again a shank appears from nowhere – especially with my short irons. I have no idea why, because normally I strike all my clubs well. Can you help?

A Forced irons are a major cause of shanking. If your tempo quickens and you try to squeeze extra distance out of a club your co-ordination goes awry. Thrashing a wedge hard often leads you to get ahead of the ball at impact.

Your lower body tends to drive too far forward coming into impact and it is difficult for the clubhead to catch up with your hands. And because you are swinging at speed, the clubhead tends to swing on a slightly wider path than normal.

This combination means that the blade attacks the ball with the hosel leading the way, and you have no chance of making contact with the middle of the clubface. At best, a push is the result; at worst, you hit the shank.

Swing within yourself

The sure way to avoid a shank with the short irons is to swing easily. A smooth, controlled action dramatically increases the chances of the blade returning square and on the correct in-to-in path.

Instead of trying to hit a wedge a distance on the edge of your limit, go down a club and hit an easy 9 iron. You are much more likely to keep your arms and body working in unison, so that the clubhead strikes the ball with the middle of the face and not the hosel.

FORCED DOWNSWING

HANDS AND BODY AHEAD OF BALL AND CLUBHEAD

HOSEL STRIKES BALL – SHOT SQUIRTS SHARPLY RIGHT

CONTROLLED ATTACK FROM INSIDE WITH SQUARE BLADE

CORRECT THROUGHSWING BACK ON INSIDE – BALL FLIES TRUE

Topping terrors

**A puzzled expression usually appears on the face of a player
who has just topped a shot, as he wonders
why a swing that felt good produced a scuttling stroke. But
careful preparation of the shot and a
simple swing should see the affliction die away.**

Q I'm quite sure that my swing is on plane and there is little wrong with my body action, but I still occasionally hit a top with my driver. Please tell me why?

A If you feel that your swing is good, your set-up must be wrong. Ball position is critical to driver success.

It is important to strike the ball slightly on the up but not violently so. The bottom of your swing arc is around a point opposite the inside of your left heel. Pushing the ball too far forward of this point means that your club is swinging too much on the up as it makes contact. The bottom edge of your driver strikes the top half of the ball, and from a seemingly good swing you produce a top.

Perfect placing

Because the driver has the widest swing arc of all clubs, you must place the ball in exactly the right spot to have any chance of timing the stroke well. As the bottom of your arc is inside of your left heel, you need to place the ball just forward of this point to make sure you strike the ball slightly on the up.

Although the exact placement varies from person to person, it should not be outside the range of an inch (2.5cm) either side of the point opposite the inside of the left heel. This means that the club can strike the ball squarely on a slight upward path.

✗ BALL TOO FAR FORWARD IN STANCE

✗ CLUB ATTACKS BALL ON THE UPSWING

SOLE STRIKES TOP OF BALL – SHOT TOPPED

✓ CORRECT ADDRESS FOR DRIVER – OPPOSITE INSIDE LEFT HEEL

✓ ATTACK ON SLIGHT UPWARD PATH – CLUB CATCHES BALL SQUARELY

Q I have a habit of topping my long irons, and I don't understand why. Can you help?

A All tops come from the club striking the upper half of the ball. The reason this happens with your long irons is mainly psychological. Because these clubs have a reputation for being hard to hit and look – to some – frighteningly straight-faced, the tendency is to try and lift the ball off the turf. You have no confidence in the iron alone getting the ball airborne.

Your body tends to lean back coming into impact with all your weight on the right side. The blade attacks the ball on a slight upward path. And through impact your body rises up and out of position, all helping to promote the poor swing path.

If the blade catches the ball anywhere above center you hit the top.

Make the club do the work

Long irons are designed to launch a low penetrating flight and do not need any help to get the ball airborne – their natural loft does the work.

You must swing into impact on a downward path and keep your body balanced. Your weight should be shifting on to the left side but you must still stay behind the ball at impact. Make your extension through the ball full and wide, and remember to release properly. There should be no sign of the body rising up out of the shot by this point.

If your attack has been from a slightly downward path and your body position good, the natural loft of the clubface is enough to send the ball away on the correct flight.

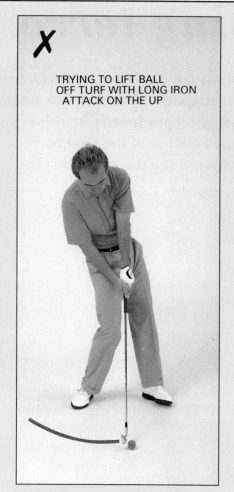

X

TRYING TO LIFT BALL
OFF TURF WITH LONG IRON
ATTACK ON THE UP

X

BODY MOVES UP
OUT OF POSITION

BLADE STRIKES
TOP HALF OF BALL

✓

CRISP DOWNWARD BLOW
TO LET NATURAL LOFT
OF IRON DO THE WORK

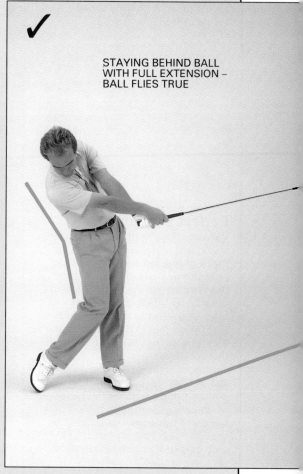

✓

STAYING BEHIND BALL
WITH FULL EXTENSION –
BALL FLIES TRUE

Thinning traumas

**Just when you need a decent strike to be sure of hitting a par 3
or firing a chip in close, poor technique lets you down.
A thin is one of the more common results of a bad swing, but you
can avoid it by making a few simple changes in your style.**

Q **I thin my irons off a tee peg.
Please can you tell me why?**

A Your problem could well be that you tee the ball up too high. When a ball teeters on top of a peg about an inch (2.5cm) above ground level, you are forced into striking it on the upswing.

Seeing a ball sitting up high on a tee naturally makes your body move in the wrong positions. Your left shoulder tends to rise up too quickly in your attempt to swing the clubhead up and into the back of the ball.

If you're lucky, the face catches the ball squarely and you strike it well but on a higher trajectory than you want. But the bottom of the blade is equally likely to strike the middle or just below the center of the ball – hence the thin. It doesn't have to be a very badly bladed shot for the ball to shoot through the green – even a mild thin can do that.

Peg it down
A sure cure is to tee the ball much lower. You should use a tee peg to give you a better lie than you would get on the ground. This means raising the ball off the turf only a fraction – not propping it up way off the deck.

Playing from a pushed in tee peg – so only the head is visible – makes the ball sit invitingly without being too high off the ground. What's more important is that this teeing method makes your swing naturally better.

To strike your irons and flight the ball well, you need to swing into impact on a downward path. Teeing the ball down promotes this correct swing and helps you extend fully through the ball.

X BALL TEED HIGH

CLUB STRIKES ON UPSWING

X NO EXTENSION – CLUB SWINGS UP SHARPLY

SHOT THINNED

✓ BALL TEED LOW

CLUB ATTACKS ON DOWNWARD PATH

✓

CRISP STRIKE, FULL EXTENSION – ABLE TO FLIGHT SHOT PROPERLY

✗ TOO WRISTY ON BACKSWING

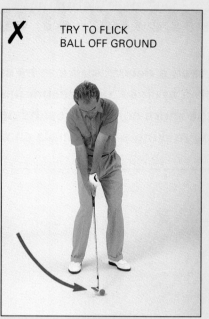

✗ TRY TO FLICK BALL OFF GROUND

✗ SHOT THINNED

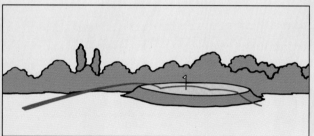

A The strike off hard pan needs to be very precise if you're to avoid the thin. If you don't use the correct technique your chances of hitting an accurate chip are remote. The most common fault is a too wristy swing.

A steep, wristy backswing automatically promotes a steep, wristy downswing. This action makes it hard to time the shot properly. You tend also to try and flick the ball into the air off the hard ground rather that let the natural loft of the clubface do the work. The blade either bounces into the back of the ball or hits it slightly on the up.

Q I often thin my wedges way past the flag when I have to play a chip off bare and hard ground. Why?

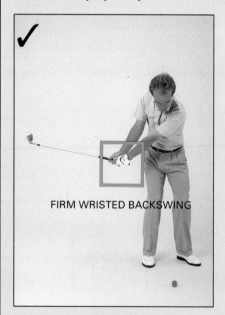

✓ FIRM WRISTED BACKSWING

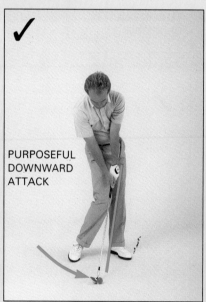

✓ PURPOSEFUL DOWNWARD ATTACK

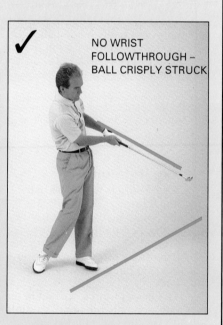

✓ NO WRIST FOLLOWTHROUGH – BALL CRISPLY STRUCK

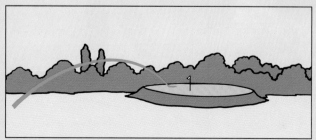

Hit down from hard pan

To ensure a good strike you must make contact with the ball before the ground. Swinging with a firm-wristed action makes timing the shot a lot easier. Place the ball between your right heel and center of stance, and push your hands forward. Swing back with no hint of wrist cock. Hit down on the ball keeping your wrists firm and don't quit. The shot should be well struck with a good deal of checkspin.

Pushing frustrations

**A push to the right of target is a common and irritating yet
slight problem. Most pushes are well
struck – which makes the fault even more upsetting – and come
from tiny flaws in your technique.
Concentration and confidence should wipe out your frustrations.**

NERVOUS, STIFF
ACTION – BALL
GUIDED TO RIGHT

BLADE SLIGHTLY
OPEN AT IMPACT

FULL AND POWERFUL
RELEASE – BALL
FLIES TRUE

BLADE SQUARE AT IMPACT

Q Every so often I push my tee shots and I don't
know why. I seem to suffer a little more from
this problem when the pressure is on. What could I
be doing wrong?

A Nerves can play havoc with even the best
golfers' swings. Coming down the final stretch
in a tight match or with a good score going it is
natural for the golfing muscles to become a little
tight.

Even if your set-up is perfect your swing becomes
stiff and tentative. Your hands don't work as they
should coming into impact and the blade tends to
strike the ball with a fractionally open clubface.

Your action continues to be hesitant through the
ball and your hands remain fairly passive. This
guiding movement holds the blade slightly open just
after impact and you push the shot right.

Flowing release

To be sure of eradicating the push under pressure
from your list of shots, your swing must be flowing.
You must strive to use your hands throughout the
swing particularly into and through impact.

If you concentrate on releasing fully through the
ball your whole action should become more fluid.
Your brain tells you to work your hands and wrists
into impact so that the clubhead strikes the ball with
a square blade. And the full release ensures you
don't hold the clubface square for too long – which
would produce a guided shot a fraction to the right of
target.

Q I play the low punch shot into wind quite well, but struggle slightly when the breeze comes in from the right. I aim right of target but tend to leave my shots out to that side. Why?

A The push comes from poor swing thoughts, and slightly incorrect body positions. If you don't concentrate on the proper punch technique and only worry about whether the wind will bring the ball back to the target, your action naturally changes.

Your brain tells your body that the ball needs to be hit right of the target to counter the effect of the wind – you may be worried about pulling the shot.

Forgetting that you are already aligning and aiming a fraction right of target your body shapes for a push. The blade is open at impact and your swing through the ball guides the shot even further right, and it holds up on the wind.

ATTEMPT TO HOLD BALL IN WIND – BLADE SLIGHTLY OPEN AT IMPACT

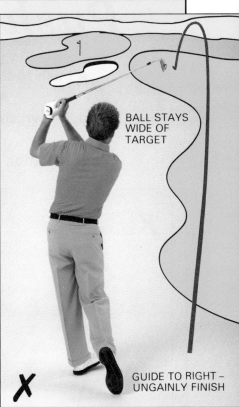

BALL STAYS WIDE OF TARGET

GUIDE TO RIGHT – UNGAINLY FINISH

Work with the wind

To play the punch shot effectively in a right-to-left wind, you must take care to align and aim correctly and use your normal technique. Be confident that the wind will drift the ball back to the target.

Once you have aligned and aimed slightly right of the target, forget about the wind. Concentrate solely on playing your usual straight punch shot. Release through the ball into a controlled finish, making sure the club has swung on the correct in-to-in path. Your shot should fire straight at a point to the right of the target and then be brought back on the crosswind.

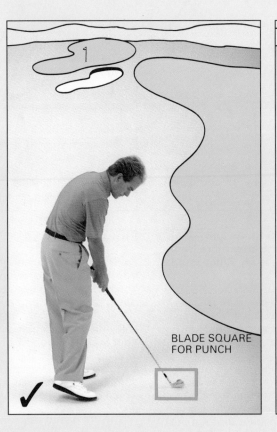

BLADE SQUARE FOR PUNCH

HANDS RELEASED – BALL HIT STRAIGHT THEN MOVED BACK TO TARGET BY WIND

Pulling predicament

**The yank to the left of the target is unwelcome as well as baffling.
As soon as you strike the ball you can feel yourself
pulling the shot and it is often hard to work out why. However,
setting up correctly sorts out most pulling problems.**

Q Whenever the ball is perched up on a tuft of grass, I have a tendency to pull hook the ball. Why?

A This probably happens because you allow your swing plane to become flatter. This is often the natural reaction to standing with the ball above the level of your feet, but it does tend to make the ball fly left.

When your arms swing more around the body, you tend to roll your hands through impact and turn the clubface over too soon. The shot itself is dangerous because the ball flies quite low and hooks violently – this makes it almost impossible for you to stay in control.

X

SWING BECOMES
FLATTER THAN NORMAL

BALL PERCHED UP
IN ROUGH

X

BALL PULL HOOKED

DOWNSWING TOO MUCH
FROM INSIDE – EASY
TO TURN HANDS OVER
THROUGH IMPACT

Plane sailing

Treat this shot as if you were playing from a sloping lie – this means keeping your swing plane as normal as possible to keep the ball on a straight flight path.

Grip down slightly. This allows you to stand normally at address, while keeping the clubhead at the same level as the ball – important when it comes to striking correctly.

Make sure the back of your left hand, and therefore the clubhead, faces the target through impact – almost as if you were delaying the release slightly. This minor alteration guards against the tendency for the clubface to turn over.

✓

SWING ON NORMAL
PLANE – HANDS KEPT HIGH

✓

BALL FLIES TRUE

CORRECT IN-TO-IN ATTACK
– RELEASE NOT TOO EARLY

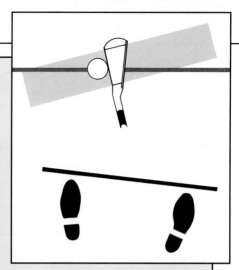

X

TARGET LOOKS TO BE OVER LEFT SHOULDER

ALIGNED RIGHT

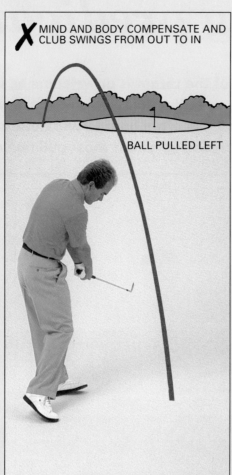

X MIND AND BODY COMPENSATE AND CLUB SWINGS FROM OUT TO IN

BALL PULLED LEFT

Q Every part of my set-up and swing feels good and I'm striking the ball well. So why do I pull?

A Even though you may feel as if you are setting up perfectly square to the target, your alignment is probably wrong. Standing slightly closed – so your feet, hips and shoulders all align right of the target – is a major cause of the pull.

As you glance up at the target you sense the flag is over your left shoulder. Your brain tells your body to swing the club at the target and so you create a looping effect. Even if you swing on plane to the top, your body compensates for your alignment and attacks the ball from the outside. Since your blade is likely to be slightly shut you hit the pull.

Parallel lines

It is critical to set up square to avoid the pull. If you're aligned parallel to the target line, you should naturally sense the flag to be in the correct spot as you look up at address. It then becomes easy to swing the club straight at the target on the correct path. There is no need for your body to compensate for your alignment by attacking the ball on the wrong path in an attempt to swing at the target.

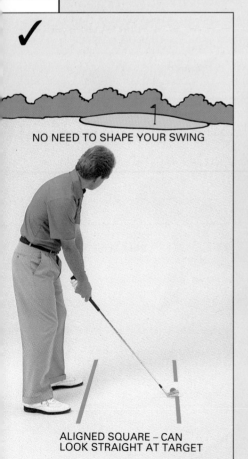

✓

NO NEED TO SHAPE YOUR SWING

ALIGNED SQUARE – CAN LOOK STRAIGHT AT TARGET

✓

CLUB NATURALLY SWINGS AT TARGET

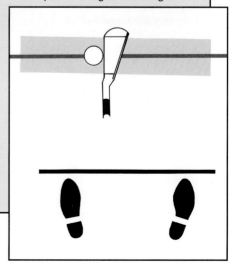

Avoid the sclaff

Hitting the ground behind the ball just before impact – known as "sclaffing" when the problem is extreme – loses you distance and control.

It's a frustrating feeling because often you don't know what's gone wrong during the swing. Usually the sclaff is caused by bad timing, when one part of your body moves out of the correct sequence. Tension is often the culprit.

You may find that you hit the ground before the ball with one particular club. As you're not confident with the club – many players suffer the problem with the long irons – anxiety builds up and you lunge at the ball.

MOVING AHEAD

One of the most common ways of sclaffing or hitting the ball "fat" – a less violent sclaff – is when your right shoulder moves ahead of the clubhead during the downswing. This causes you to drag the club through, making it arrive too late. Your body pushes through before the club, and the clubhead hits the ground.

Train your arms and hands to swing the clubhead through ahead of your right shoulder. Stand with your feet close together. Then hit some balls, using

HOW A SCLAFF HAPPENS
One part of your body moving out of sequence often causes your right shoulder to move ahead of the clubhead. This inevitably makes you stab the club into the ground before impact – often known as a sclaff.

Hitting the ball fat
Striking only just in front of the ball – hitting it fat – means that you still make contact, although you're certain to lose distance and control. How much you lose depends on how fat you strike. For instance, if you hit fractionally before the ball the reduction in distance is small.

With a violent sclaff, the club jars into the ground well before the ball, so that you don't touch it at all.

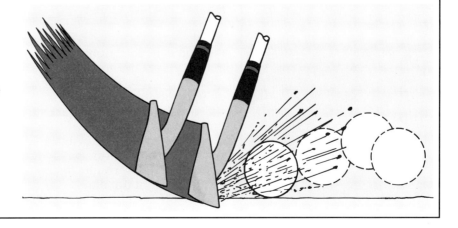

MOVING AHEAD OF THE CLUBHEAD

TENSE BACKSWING
Even when you make a smooth, correct backswing –
with your weight transferring fluently to your right side
– tension can make you move ahead.

SHOULDER PUSHES AHEAD
As the downswing begins, your right shoulder starts to
push round, making it impossible for your arms and
hands to swing the clubhead ahead of your shoulder.

Sclaffing from bad lies
A sclaff is likely from a tricky lie –
lack of confidence makes you
tighten up and your timing
suffers. And grass may come
between ball and clubface,
increasing the risk of a sclaff.

Open your stance for a slightly
out-to-in swing path. This helps
create a cleaner hit.

a smooth, unhurried half swing.

This helps you develop good
timing – vital if you're to strike
cleanly. When your timing is fine
tuned, good distance and accuracy
follow in its wake. Practicing this
exercise teaches you that timing,
not strength, sends a ball long distances
down a fairway.

RIGHT HAND ONLY

Another good exercise is to swing
the club with your right hand and
arm only. Take the normal address
position and place your left hand
on your left thigh.

Swing the club halfway back and
through. Grip lightly with your
right hand and let the club swing
easily. Club momentum pulls your
right shoulder through, helping
smooth weight transfer.

Start off by hitting short distances
– 20yd (18m) or so. As you

sharpen your striking, increase
these distances. Notice how your
clubhead feel – vital for all golfers
– becomes more acute.

BODY TURN AND WEIGHT

Incorrect weight transfer also
causes the club to crash into the
ground. It happens when the
weight does not transfer to the
right foot on the backswing.

Only when the downswing begins
does the weight move to the
right – by this time it should be
easing from right to left – giving
the club no chance of hitting the
ball correctly.

To rid your game of this fault,
practice your body turn. Correct
rotation helps your weight be in
the proper place at the top of the
backswing. Turning your body
smoothly back and through invites
your weight to do the same.

DRAGGING THE CLUB
The early movement of your right shoulder causes you to drag, rather than swing, the club through. Even if you manage to hit the ball, you catch it fat.

LOSS OF DISTANCE
If you've hit the ball, you're certain to lose distance and accuracy. Confidence and good timing are the keys to clean striking.

SWING WITH RIGHT ARM ONLY

① BACKSWING
This exercise increases your feel for the clubhead. Placing your left hand next to your thigh, smoothly swing back halfway.

② DOWNSWING AND IMPACT
Keep your right wrist loose so that the club can swing through easily. The club's momentum pulls your right shoulder round.

③ THROUGHSWING
Swing through to halfway. Start off by hitting short distances – 20yd (18m) or so. As your strike and confidence improve, hit further.

SHARPEN YOUR TIMING

FEET CLOSER TOGETHER
If you feel that you're pushing your body ahead of the club, you must train your arms and hands to swing the clubhead ahead of your shoulder. Set up with feet close together.

HALF SWING
Make an unhurried swing – preferably halfway back, certainly no more than three-quarters. The exercise improves clubhead feel as well as helping your hand and arm movement.

KEEP IT STEADY
Swing through smoothly at the same even tempo. Don't try to apply power – too much force is likely to push your right side ahead of the club, making a sclaff very possible.

STAY BALANCED
Swing through to halfway or no more than three-quarters. Let clubhead momentum pull your right side through – if you lose any balance, you've used too much force. Repeat the exercise until your strike improves.

Why do you slice?

When you slice a shot the ball starts slightly left of target and curves dramatically to the right in the air. The slice is a fault that has a frustrating habit of reappearing in your game – just when you thought you'd cured it. If a slice continues to ruin your scores, analyze your technique.

The typical slicer's swing is on an out-to-in path. The clubhead strikes the ball with a glancing blow which gives lots of sidespin and loses you distance on the shot.

More often than not if you hit a slice you're punished severely.

A PERSISTENT FAULT

Far more golfers slice than hook and this is particularly true of beginners. Seldom does a high handicap player consistently hook or draw the ball.

If you slice frequently you probably find a few of your shots are pulled. The clubhead travels on the same path as a slice but for a pull your hands are more active through impact. The result is a shot that starts left and stays there. The two shots are closely related and can be eliminated by correcting the same errors.

GOOD SET-UP

To correct a persistent fault in golf it's important you reinforce the right moves.

Align parallel to the target line to hit a straight shot. The first reaction to slicing the ball is usually to aim further left but this makes the problem worse. It causes you to swing more out to in than you were before and your slice soon becomes totally out of control.

Check your posture if you're trying to avoid a slice. Your weight should be evenly balanced at address. Too much weight on your left side restricts shoulder turn and encourages you to pick the club up outside the line on the backswing.

A correct backswing increases your chances of hitting a good shot. Take the club back on a line parallel with the ball-to-target line for 12in (30cm). This encourages a long wide backswing and a full shoulder turn.

Ask a friend or professional to check that the club points down the target line at the top of the backswing. It should never travel past the horizontal.

On the downswing pull the club down with your left hand. This helps you apply the clubhead to the ball from inside the line.

When you start the game it's easier to let the bigger muscles – such as the shoulders – dominate the downswing. If you start the downswing with your shoulders

SET-UP CHECK
If you often slice, check you're aligned correctly before you start looking for faults in your swing. Most problems in golf can be traced back to a poor set-up position. Ask someone to place a club between your elbows at address. If your shoulders are aligned correctly the club should point parallel to the target line.

CORRECTING SLICE FAULTS

1) ADDRESS POSITION
It's important to give yourself a good base to work from. Align your feet, hips and shoulders parallel to the target. Aligning left encourages you to take the club back outside the line which causes a slice. If you start the backswing badly it's difficult to put right later in the swing.

3) APPROACHING IMPACT
The correct moves help you lead the clubhead into the ball from the inside – the ideal path for a good shot. Don't allow your shoulders to dominate the downswing. Your hands generate clubhead speed – a lunge at the ball with your upper body doesn't help you hit it further.

(2) SOLID AT THE TOP
A correct backswing encourages a full shoulder turn so that the body is nicely coiled and the club is parallel to the target line at the top. If you take the club back outside the line your shoulder turn is restricted and the club points left of the target at the top. That's the direction your clubhead travels through impact.

(4) IMPACT
Pull the clubhead down into impact with the back of your left hand. Your body is nicely poised behind the ball and the left side provides support in the hitting area. Throwing the clubhead outside the line makes you cut across the ball. Everything points left of target and that's the direction the ball flies, curving right in the air.

you immediately throw the club-head outside the line. From this position there's every risk of slicing the ball.

SLICING YOUR WOODS

If you suffer from slicing the ball you'll know it occurs most when you use your driver. To strike a wood shot correctly the clubhead must approach the ball at a shallow angle of descent.

The clubface hits the ball near its equator. This produces very little backspin at impact, but potentially lots of sidespin. It's the sidespin that makes the ball slice. Long suffering slicers of the ball find the heel of the clubface wears out from the constant battering on that part of the club.

Cast your mind back and try to remember how many sliced 9 iron shots you've hit – probably very few. Hitting down into the bottom of the ball with an iron generates more backspin than sidespin – the ball is less likely to curve either way in the air.

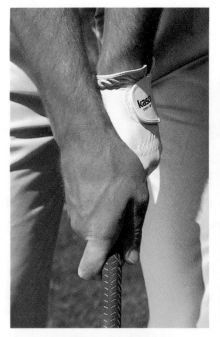

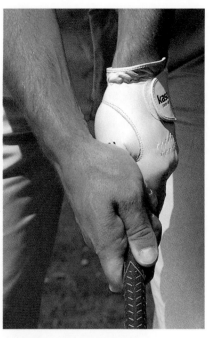

✗ COMMON WEAKNESS
If a golfer has a weak grip the fault is usually to be found in the right hand. A weak right hand makes it difficult for you to return the clubface correctly square to the ball. This is a sure way to start slicing.

✓ BACK TO NEUTRAL
Work hard on building a neutral grip into your game. Look for two knuckles on your right hand when you check your grip in a mirror. The V shape created by your thumb and forefinger should point at your right shoulder.

pro tip

Practice drill
The practice green is the ideal place to cure your slice. Hit shots with your right foot set back from your left – keep your shoulders square to the target line. Don't make an effort to change anything else – just swing normally.

The set-up encourages you to take the club back wide and slightly on the inside. It also helps you to make a full shoulder turn. This practice drill gradually rids your swing of an out-to-in path. You should soon start to hit the ball straight, perhaps even with a touch of draw.

Surviving the slice

If you're stuck out on the course with a slice don't attempt drastic solutions. Trying to stop your slice becoming worse is your main objective.

Avoid aiming further left off the tee thinking your ball will finish on the fairway if you do. You merely succeed in making your slice more severe. Put your driver in your bag and leave it there. The driver is the easiest of all the clubs to slice with. Take a more lofted club off the tee – an iron if it means keeping your ball in play. Tee up on the right side of the teeing area – particularly if there is trouble on the right. You effectively make the fairway easier to hit and increase your margin for error.

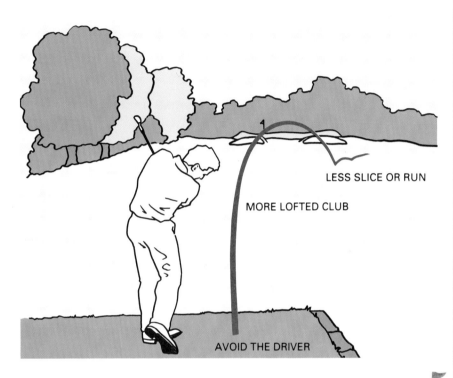

LESS SLICE OR RUN

MORE LOFTED CLUB

AVOID THE DRIVER

Slice Saver

Aiming right

Q I thought I'd eliminated the slice from my game but in a couple of recent matches the shot once again wrecked my card and my confidence. How can this be?

A Having cured the slice, many golfers drift to the other extreme and over compensate. They begin to align right and loop the club outside the line at the top of the backswing. This often feels natural because you think you're correcting the poor alignment. The looping action puts the swing on an out-to-in path which causes the slice.

Don't fall into this trap – place a club along the line of your feet at address to check your alignment is correct.

Clubhead direction

Q I often spend fruitless hours on the practice green finding I'm never any closer to curing my slice. How can I be sure I'm swinging on the correct path?

A It's very simple to check your swing path in practice. Stand in light rough and swing a 5 iron as you would for a full shot – but without the ball. Make sure the clubhead swishes through the rough leaving a path in the grass. Then check the direction the clubhead travels through impact – ideally the path in the grass should be from in to in.

Ball position

Q I've spent a frustrating year slicing off the tee. Recently a friend suggested I move the ball further back in my stance – my scores and my temper immediately improved. Why is ball position so important?

A If the ball is too far forward in your stance your shoulders open up – this makes you cut across the ball from out to in. It works the other way too – if your shoulders are open there's every chance the ball is too far forward.

When you use the driver, gradually move the ball back in your stance until the ball is opposite your left heel. This automatically places your shoulders square to target and encourages you to swing the club back on the correct plane.

Tee peg tip

Use tee pegs as a cheap and effective way of checking your swing path. Place one tee peg 12in (30cm) behind the clubhead on the ball-to-target line. Position another the same distance away but 2in (5cm) inside the first one.

Address the ball, making sure you aim parallel to the target line. Draw the club back low over the first tee you put in the ground. Swing down into the ball, making sure the clubhead travels over the second tee. This encourages you to swing on an in-to-in path. It's an excellent way to stop slicing the ball without making drastic swing changes.

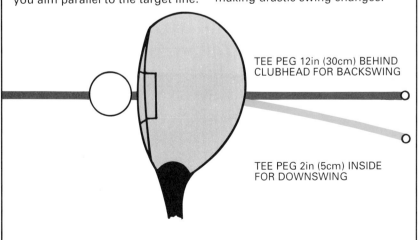

TEE PEG 12in (30cm) BEHIND CLUBHEAD FOR BACKSWING

TEE PEG 2in (5cm) INSIDE FOR DOWNSWING

Work on a flatter plane

A woman's swing plane is often very upright simply because of her bust. An upright swing is very unforgiving and there's every chance you'll suffer from the slice now and then.

Hit shots from a sloping lie with the ball above your feet. This encourages you to turn your shoulders and helps you gradually flatten your swing plane. You'll find it easier to draw the ball and your consistency increases. It's also more difficult to cut across the ball from out to in when you swing the club on a flatter plane.

UPRIGHT SWING PLANE

FLAT SWING PLANE

Why the slice?

Q A slice appears in my game from time to time, but never the hook. Why is this?

A A slice is more common because the correct hand and arm action isn't natural, particularly for beginners. Many golfers swing too stiffly, trying to use sheer force to hit the ball forward. The bigger muscles, such as the shoulders and back, then tend to dominate the swing. But it's the bigger muscles that are least able to generate clubhead speed.

Grip lightly to encourage the hands to play a more active role in the shot. This helps you make a free flowing relaxed swing.

It happens to the best

Pressure can often force you into hitting a slice just when you least want to. Even the best golfers in the world succumb to pressure occasionally, so don't despair if you can't entirely rid your game of this fault.

Greg Norman, playing the 72nd hole of the 1986 US Masters, needed a par to tie Jack Nicklaus who was already in the clubhouse. From the middle of the fairway Norman hit a disastrous slice right of the green and into the crowd. A chip and 2 putts later he had lost to Jack by 1 shot.

Why do you hit right?

If you often experience the frustration of watching your ball finish right of target, you're suffering from either the slice or the push, two very common complaints.

While the end result – usually a trouble spot – is the same, the moves leading up to impact couldn't be more contrasting.

The main cause of a slice is an out-to-in swing path and an open clubface. The shot often flatters to deceive – it heads roughly along the intended line at first, only to veer right on a flight towards disaster. Strangely, the closest relation to the slice is a shot that flies in completely the opposite direction – the pull.

The push flies right as soon as the ball leaves the clubface. The fault happens with an open clubface when the clubhead travels on

RIGHT OF WAY
Hitting the ball right of target is disappointing, but it happens to the best of players every now and then. If lots of your shots fly in that direction it's doubly annoying – your confidence starts to crumble when your ball keeps finding trouble. Examine the basics – once you identify the fault you're well on your way to a cure. A common cause is a severe out-to-in swing path with an open clubface.

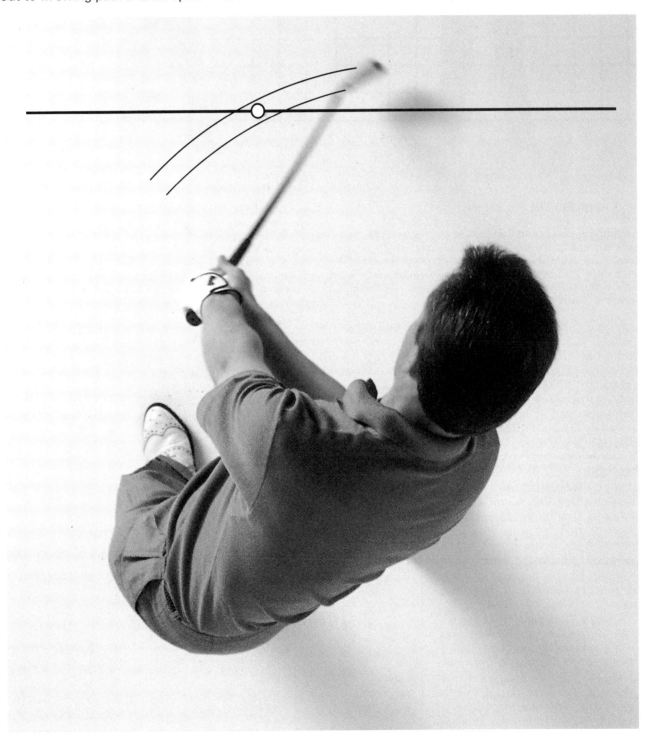

CURE THE SHOT THAT FLIES RIGHT

①ADDRESS THE PROBLEM
As always in golf, if there's a fault that needs correcting you should first look at your stance. Make sure the ball is positioned properly – fractionally further back from opposite your left heel is perfect for a mid iron shot. This encourages you to place your hands in a very orthodox position, with your left arm and the club forming a straight line down to the ball.

②CONTROL AT THE TOP
Sweep the club away from the ball on a wide arc to pull the body into a coiled position so that your upper back faces the target. The shoulders have turned fully and the club is just short of horizontal – a strong yet controlled position at the top. It's extremely difficult to reach this position if you pick the club up too quickly on the backswing and outside the line.

a severe in-to-out swing path.

If you're consistently hitting the same bad shot, go straight back to basics – don't search for a miracle cure. It's likely that one of the golfing fundamentals has temporarily deserted you.

BASIC CHECK

The slice is a poor stroke that every golfer suffers from at some time or other. When you look for the cure, first make sure you are aligned correctly with your feet, hips and shoulders square to the ball-to-target line. It needs only one part of your body to aim left at address for you to invite the slice.

Always keep a watchful eye on your grip on the club. If either hand is in a weak position you need to be a strong player to hit the ball straight. There's every chance you're continually struggling to return the clubface to square at impact – it's all too easy to slice

the ball.

Notice how methodically many top professionals place their hands on the club – by making it a part of their pre-shot routine they ensure they never forget about the grip.

Check the position of the ball in

your stance. It should be opposite your left heel with the driver and long irons, and progressively further back until it's central when you use the most lofted irons.

If the ball is too far forward in your stance, the clubhead is on the correct path well before im-

✗ MOVES TO AVOID

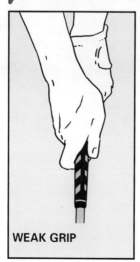

WEAK GRIP

OPEN STANCE

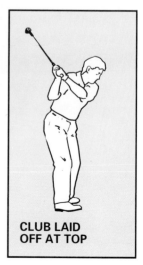

CLUB LAID OFF AT TOP

③ RELEASE THROUGH IMPACT
A smooth transfer of weight towards the target helps you strike down and through the ball. Note how the head has moved very little from its position at the top of the backswing – this stops you getting ahead of the ball which is a major cause of the push. The swing is free from tension, allowing the hands to deliver the clubhead square to the ball and release through impact.

④ BALANCED LOOK
A classic followthrough position looks effortless and natural, but it's achieved only by swinging the club correctly from the start. The pull of your arms through impact brings you up into a rounded followthrough position. The telltale sign of the push or slice would look quite different, with the hands held much higher and the clubhead closer to the body.

pact. When it finally comes into contact with the ball it's cutting across from out to in.

Have someone take a close look at your backswing. Is the club sweeping correctly back along – or slightly inside – the ball-to-target line? You may think there's

nothing wrong with this part of your swing, but it's often hard to judge – particularly if you've unwittingly slipped into bad habits.

If **the push** is an-all-too common feature of your game, look at the same elements of your swing as you would for the slice. But take

heart – a push is far from serious. For a good shot you must attack the ball from the inside – a push is simply an exaggeration of this move.

If you align right of target it's easy to swing along the line of your body. This naturally produces a severe in-to-out path, with little hope of the clubhead returning to square at impact. Positioning the ball too far back in your stance causes the same problem. An open clubface sends the ball right and it usually stays there.

Correct weight transfer is essential to strike the ball well, but be careful not to overdo it. Your head should never move in front of the ball on the way down. If you shift your weight too far forward on the downswing – known as getting ahead of the ball – you risk delivering the clubhead in an open position at impact.

One practice drill can help you cure both the slice and push. Hitting practice shots with a very light grip on the club encourages your

REVERSE PIVOT

CLUB THROWN OUTSIDE LINE

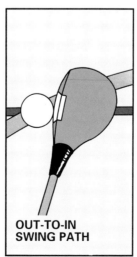
OUT-TO-IN SWING PATH

hands to play a more active role in the swing. Start with half shots and gradually work up to your normal full swing as you grow in confidence. This exercise promotes a fluid and powerful strike.

If your swing is too stiff wristed it's extremely difficult to generate clubhead speed and release your hands through impact. The clubface fails to return to square at impact and blocks the ball out to the right.

By gripping the club lightly you release tension in your arms and shoulders – a vital feature of every good swing.

pro tip

Exercise the muscles

If your game is plagued by the shot that flies right, the 1st tee is bound to cause problems. Slight stiffness and pre-round nerves often come together to produce a push or slice.

Instead of resigning yourself to being a slow starter, make an effort to eliminate stiffness from your game with a warm up routine. Some friends may scoff at what they take as over keen behavior, but be resolute – you're the one who benefits when you step on to the tee.

Pick two clubs of similar length from your bag and take 20 slow, rhythmical practice swings. This action gets the correct golfing muscles working. The heavier weight in your hands loosens up the bigger muscles – such as the lower back and shoulders – which are especially prone to stiffness. When you warm up you increase your chances of starting with a good shot.

Supple skills

Most young players have a relaxed, easy movement, while many adults inhibit their progress by swinging too stiffly – this type of action is always prone to the push or slice.

Learning to play golf at an early age has several benefits – not least of which is the freedom juniors have to swing the club. A supple body goes some way to making up for the natural weakness of young golfers.

A junior also tends to have a carefree attitude to the game – thoughts are often simply focused on striking the ball. This leads to a free flowing swing which allows the hands to release through impact. With good guidance the correct swing path can be built into the young golfer's game – it often stays with the player for many years.

Every golfer – regardless of age – can learn a valuable lesson from juniors and develop a relaxed swing. A useful exercise is to hold a club straight out in front of you – similar to the way a baseball bat is held. Swing your arms freely back and through on a flat plane to encourage a flowing movement. Your one concern should be that your body is free from tension – forget about technique for this drill.

Why do you hit left?

The results of continually hitting the ball left of target are depressingly plain to see. But identifying the cause is often less obvious.

There are two main shots that send your ball flying to the left – the pull and the hook. While the end result is roughly the same, the moves leading up to each one are very different.

A **hook** is the lesser of the two

evils and is caused by a combination of an in-to-out swing path and a closed clubface. It's often known as the good player's bad shot, so don't be too disheartened if you regularly suffer from this problem.

A **pull** is the result of an out-to-in swing path and a closed clubface. The clubhead is on the wrong line, but you can take some comfort from the fact that the clubface is shut at impact. It's not

FAULTY AIM
There are many causes of hitting the ball left. Strangely, aiming right off target is a classic example. This faulty set-up prompts you to swing back too far inside the line so that the club points right at the top. This makes it extremely hard to deliver the clubhead to the ball on the correct path. More often than not you generate a severe in-to-out path – a major cause of the hook.

STRAIGHTEN OUT YOUR GAME

① SOUND ADDRESS
Align square with your feet, hips and shoulders parallel to the ball-to-target line. Note how the knees are comfortably flexed and the back straight – this allows your arms to hand down naturally. There's not a single technical flaw in this address position and it's completely free from tension.

② DOWN THE LINE
At this stage of the takeaway the shaft of the club should point along the line of your feet – parallel to the ball-to-target line. The clubhead points straight up. This is an excellent point to remember when you're on the practice ground. When you're on the course never look at the clubhead once the swing is in motion.

③ POISED TO ATTACK
The good moves earlier in the backswing lead to a perfect position at the top. The left knee points in towards the ball as your weight transfers on to the right side. Your hips should turn 45° and the shoulders 90° – this coils the body behind the ball and places you in a strong position to begin the downswing.

④ PERFECT PATH
Pull down with your left hand as you gradually transfer your weight on to your left side. These moves help deliver the clubhead to the ball on a path slightly inside the line – the ideal angle of attack to eliminate the shot that flies left. The back of your left hand should face the target at impact to guard against the clubface turning over too early.

ideal but at least your hands are active during the swing.

SECURE SET-UP

Most faults can usually be traced back to your address position – curing the hook is no exception. First make sure your **alignment** is square to the ball-to-target line. This encourages you to swing the club back along the correct path.

One of the most important check points is to make sure the **clubface is square**. It's much easier to analyze clubface alignment from behind the ball, so ideally ask a friend to take a look for you. Alternatively, adopt your address position and then step away, being very careful not to move the club.

If you address the ball with a closed clubface you're always fighting the hook. To neglect this aspect of the address position is frustrating as well as potentially disastrous. You can make a perfect swing, but if the clubface is either shut or open, there's no hope of the ball traveling in the direction you want.

Take a close look at your **grip** – ideally you should see two knuckles on each hand. If either hand is in a strong position your swing is bound to be prone to the hook.

BALL PLACEMENT

The grip is a part of your game that needs constant attention. But never attempt to change it when you're on the course – even the slightest alteration feels extremely awkward. Cope as well as you can and then set out to correct it when you're next on the practice green.

Check the **ball position** in your stance. There are many permutations but two faults in particular relate to your ball going left.

If you stand with the ball too near your back foot, a good swing usually sends the clubhead into the ball on an in-to-out path. A square or closed clubface generates sidespin and the result is a hook.

When the ball is too far forward in your stance, the clubhead is beyond the ideal path at impact and traveling out to in. If the clubface is either square or closed

Drive through impact
One of the fundamentals to hitting the ball straight is keeping the clubface square through impact. One drill in particular can help you eliminate the shot that flies left.

A mid iron is the ideal club to begin with – the practice green the perfect location. Place a tee peg in the ground about 12in (30cm) directly in front of your ball and in line with the target.

As you swing down, feel the clubhead traveling over the tee peg through impact. Concentrate on driving the back of your left hand through to the target – this prevents the clubface turning over as it meets the ball.

5 CONTROL THROUGH THE BALL
As your hands release through impact the movement in your swing should feel free flowing – don't thrash at the ball. The position of your right foot shows clearly the weight distribution during the swing – almost all of it should now be supported on the left foot.

6 STRAIGHT AS AN ARROW
The body unwinds fully as you complete the swing. Your reward for maintaining control throughout the swing is a perfectly balanced followthrough. The ball flies precisely where you're aiming and straight as an arrow.

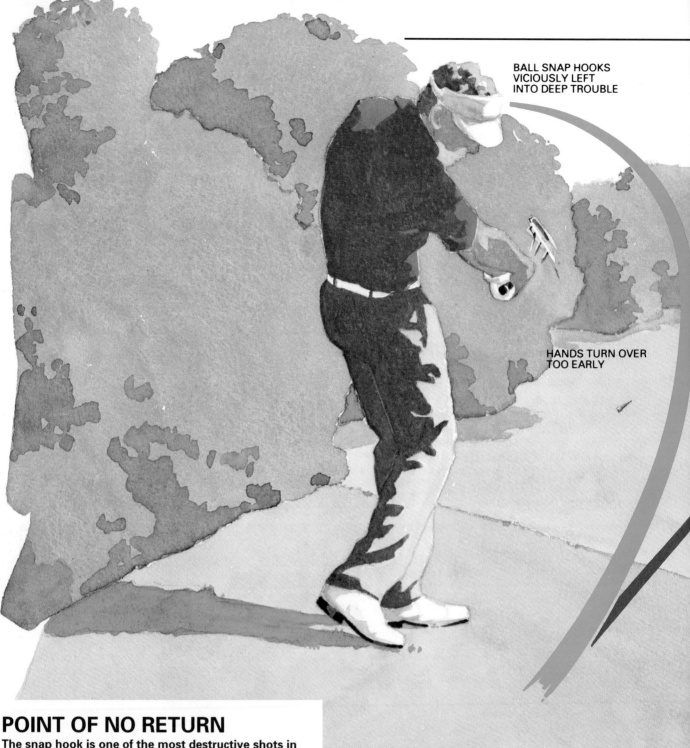

BALL SNAP HOOKS
VICIOUSLY LEFT
INTO DEEP TROUBLE

HANDS TURN OVER
TOO EARLY

POINT OF NO RETURN

The snap hook is one of the most destructive shots in golf – it usually happens with the driver or your long irons. The ball dives sharply left almost as soon as it leaves the clubface. The shot is bad news even if you're lucky enough to have no hazards to the left. But when trees and bushes line the fairway, you're in serious trouble. It's important to understand the cause of the snap hook so you can avoid it at all costs.

For such an awful shot the moves are not as terrible as you might think. The clubhead usually travels along the correct in-to-in path, but a severely closed clubface at impact causes all the damage. This is the result of releasing the hands too early in the swing. When there's trouble on the right, it's easy to let anxiety in the mind bring your right hand into the action to stop the ball flying to the right.

Concentrate on rhythm and tempo and drive the back of your left hand through towards the target. This should prevent the clubface turning over at impact – the key to eliminating the snap hook from your game.

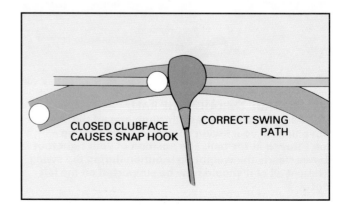

CLOSED CLUBFACE
CAUSES SNAP HOOK

CORRECT SWING
PATH

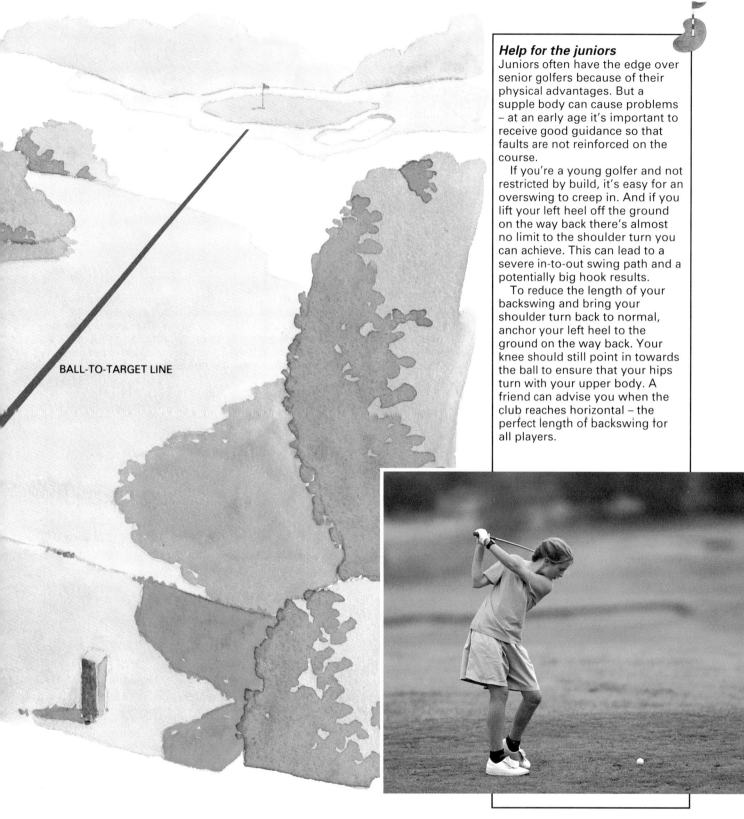

BALL-TO-TARGET LINE

Help for the juniors

Juniors often have the edge over senior golfers because of their physical advantages. But a supple body can cause problems – at an early age it's important to receive good guidance so that faults are not reinforced on the course.

If you're a young golfer and not restricted by build, it's easy for an overswing to creep in. And if you lift your left heel off the ground on the way back there's almost no limit to the shoulder turn you can achieve. This can lead to a severe in-to-out swing path and a potentially big hook results.

To reduce the length of your backswing and bring your shoulder turn back to normal, anchor your left heel to the ground on the way back. Your knee should still point in towards the ball to ensure that your hips turn with your upper body. A friend can advise you when the club reaches horizontal – the perfect length of backswing for all players.

you hit a pull hook – this is one of the most disastrous shots in golf because the balls flies violently left.

WORKING ON THE CURE

Once you lay the foundations of a good swing you immediately increase your success rate. You're already more than halfway towards turning your uncontrolla-ble hook into a penetrating draw.

Concentrate on pulling the club down with your left hand to set the club on the inside. Once you start the downswing on the correct path, there's every chance it's correct at impact.

The pull is caused by throwing the club outside the line from the top. You should never let the first part of your downswing be domi-nated by the shoulders. This action can easily set the club outside the line as soon as the downswing begins.

Hitting the ball left doesn't happen only on the full shots – it can creep into your short game just as easily and is often more costly. Fortunately, the causes of hitting a short shot left are easier to spot than those of a wayward drive.

✓ SEARCH FOR THE CURE

1 **PARALLEL DOWN THE LINE**
If you can achieve a good position at the top you go a long way to eliminating the hook and pull from your game. The club should be parallel to the ball-to-target line. The shoulder turn is perfect – 90° with the upper back facing the target. Note how the left knee points directly at the ball to allow the hips to turn.

2 **ALL SQUARE AT IMPACT**
The position achieved at the top means you can square the clubface at impact, without needing to make adjustments on the way down. The back of your left hand clearly faces the target to stop the clubface closing. The correct swing path and a square clubface add up to one shot – dead straight drive.

✗ THE HOOKER'S SWING

1 **POINTS RIGHT AT THE TOP**
If the swing goes wrong from the start you're flirting with danger – it's extremely hard to correct. The club is taken back too far on the inside, the shoulders turn beyond 90 and the club points way right of target.

2 **CLOSED AT IMPACT**
A poor backswing causes major problems at impact because the clubhead meets the ball on a severe in-to-out path. To make matters worse, the clubface is shut at impact which generates lots of sidespin. Note how the back of the left hand is almost completely obscured – a sign that the right hand has taken over too early. This leads to a violent hook.

Your left hand is the dominant force on any chip shot. The hands are ahead of the ball at address and remain that way until long after impact.

One of the major causes of poor chipping is letting the right hand dominate the downswing. The clubface closes just before impact and the ball flies left, usually traveling much too fast to stop anywhere near the hole.

Putts can easily wander to the left as well if you're not careful. Concentrate on maintaining a constant grip pressure from the moment you adopt your address position until the ball is on its way.

Feel the putter head swinging through towards the hole. The back of the left hand is the key – it should face the target as you strike the ball and on the followthrough. Hitting your putts left is usually caused by the right hand playing too forceful a role in the stroke –

this closes the face of the putter and the ball rolls to the left.

Many golfers don't pay enough attention to the angle of the putter face at address. If it's not square you make it very difficult to hit the ball along the intended line that you've carefully selected.

If you take the putter head back outside the line – even slightly – you risk dragging your putts to the left of the target on a regular basis.

Why do you hit short?

There are many causes of hitting your ball short of the target – most tend to be pretty unpleasant experiences. The stone cold top, where the ball scuttles along the ground, and the heavy, where you hit ground before the ball, are typical examples.

These shots can happen to any golfer – good or bad – so try to accept them as a fact of life. You need only start worrying if you continually hit the same bad shot and can't find the cure.

OVER THE TOP

The topped shot is often caused by trying to hit the ball too hard. Try to stay in control of your swing and you stand a greater chance of controlling the ball.

A frantic flurry of movement causes the legs and hips to act too fast in the swing, which leaves your hands lagging too far behind. This makes it extremely difficult to deliver the clubhead square to the back of the ball. Instead, contact is made above the equator of the ball.

Another cause of a topped shot is swaying too far away from the ball on the backswing. If you fail to transfer your weight back towards the target, you drastically alter the arc of your swing.

The clubhead reaches its lowest point before impact. When it finally meets the ball it's on the way up. At best you hit a top and

DESTRUCTIVE DIVOT
A heavy shot is a common cause of loss in distance. It's often a result of chopping down too steeply into impact. The clubhead rips through the turf, destroying clubhead speed and making poor contact with the ball. To help cure this fault, sweep the club away on a wide arc and stay behind the ball on the downswing.

✓ LESSON IN DISTANCE

①SOLID FOUNDATION
When you set up to hit a wood shot, position the ball opposite your left heel. This encourages you to place your hands in perfect position, with your left arm and the shaft of the club forming a straight line down to the ball. This position should be mirrored at impact to ensure the face returns square.

②COMFORTABLE LEFT ARM
A wide takeaway helps shift your weight on to the right side. Note the position of the left arm – slightly flexed and disproving the myth that it must be straight at the top. Some players are supple enough to achieve this, but above all your left arm should feel comfortable.

③POURING ON THE POWER
The left side totally dominates at this stage of the swing. The back of the left hand pulls the club down into the ball and the left side clears to allow the body to fully unwind through impact. This combination of correct moves generates clubhead speed – it's never achieved through brute force.

✗ LACKING IN LENGTH

①WRONG FROM THE START
There are all sorts of problems at address. The shoulders are hunched over and the hands are in a weak position cupped behind the ball. This is not a good position to start from.

②STEEP BACKSWING
A crouched address position prompts you to pick the club up too steeply – as soon as you reduce the width of your swing arc you're bound to struggle for length. The left arm is bent too severely which makes it impossible to maintain any degree of control over the clubhead – an overswing is the direct result.

③WEIGHT CENTRAL
Halfway through the downswing there is very little sign of the necessary weight transfer on to the left side – it all looks rather flat footed. The clubhead is already on a steep path down which makes it hard to deliver the clubhead squarely to the back of the ball.

④ TEXTBOOK STUFF
This is a perfect example of a "firm left side." The left arm is fully extended with the back of your left hand facing the target. Almost all your body weight is supported by the left leg. The head is in exactly the same position as at address – no dipping or lifting which might cause you to top the ball or catch it heavy.

⑤ FLUID FOLLOW-THROUGH
A sound technique enables you to strike the ball cleanly and achieve the distance you're looking for. The benefits of avoiding tension are clearly visible and a free flowing movement through impact results in a perfect follow-through position.

④ HEAVY CONTACT
Through impact your weight transfer is away from the target, toppling back on to the right side. This limits power and means the clubhead is on an upward path as it makes contact with the ball. The chances of striking the ball cleanly are extremely slim – in this case you hit the shot heavy.

⑤ POOR FINISH
An ungainly follow-through is a sure sign that something has gone wrong during the swing. The poor weight transfer means that you're fighting to stop yourself falling backwards. This sort of swing also puts a dangerous strain on your lower back – an extra reason for curing the fault as soon as possible.

at worst you hit a fat – the end result is the same.

A sure way to correct a severe sway is to hit practice shots standing with your feet close together. Take only a half swing and maintain your normal rhythm – you should still be able to transfer your weight correctly. It's impossible to sway – unless you intend falling over.

HEAD MOVEMENT

A heavy shot is bound to result in the ball coming up short – the clubhead digging in behind the ball causes the damage. If the ground is wet and soggy you get a mouthful of mud for your troubles too.

The main cause of hitting ground before the ball is lowering your head on the downswing. If your head moves so does the arc of your swing and a heavy shot is inevitable.

Sideways movement of the head during the swing is fine – the important point is that your head remains on the same level. This aspect of the swing can be hard to monitor unless you have a mirror, so ask a friend to take a close look for you.

You needn't make a terrible swing to hit a shot heavy. Pay close attention to your ball position at address. If it's too far forward in your stance, the clubhead reaches the bottom of its arc before making contact with the ball. This can in fact cause a top as well as a heavy – neither shot does wonders for your score!

SHORT RANGE DISASTER

Quitting on a shot is usually the result of anxiety – halfway through your swing the mind plays havoc with your technique.

This complaint most commonly occurs on pitch shots into the green. The clubhead slows down into impact and digs in behind the ball. Always be firm in the hitting area, whatever distance you're playing from.

The length of your backswing is one of the keys to achieving this – it must be just long enough to let you accelerate smoothly down into the ball. Any longer and deceleration is hard to avoid – any shorter and the downswing becomes a frantic jerk as you try to

ZONE FOUR

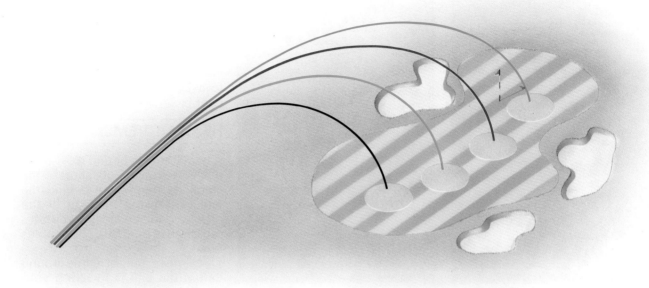

Leaving an approach shot short is often the result of failing to take into account the position of the flag – terrible shots are by no means the sole culprits. On a large putting surface there can be as much as four clubs difference between the front and back of the green. Make sure you're aware of this before you decide on the shot to hit. A superb 7 iron approach is no use if you need a 4 iron to pitch all the way to the flag – the front edge on a green this size is serious three putt range.

On a course you play regularly there's no excuse for ignoring pin position – you should be able to tell at a glance where on the green the flag is situated. But on an unfamiliar course you may have to rely on a yardage chart to confirm what you see with the naked eye.

Consider also the condition of the greens – are they holding or is the surface firm and unreceptive? This has an effect on your club selection and determines where you should aim to pitch your ball. If you're always mindful of conditions, more shots finish close.

generate clubhead speed from a position that makes the game extremely difficult.

UNDERCLUBBING

Hitting the ball short can happen with any one of the 14 clubs in your bag but, surprisingly, it's not always the result of a terrible shot.

One of the most common faults among club golfers is not hitting enough club, particularly when playing into a green.

It's extremely frustrating because you can strike the shot well and enjoy a perfect flight through the air, only to see your ball fall short of the mark. This sort of experience – if it happens too often – can really undermine your confidence.

When faced with a shot into a green, select a club that allows you to swing easily and yet still finish pin high. Only if you're in complete control can you hope to judge distance accurately.

Never force shots, no matter how far you are from the target. Trying to hit the ball too hard

causes miss-hits and even if you strike the ball out of the middle of the club, the distance of the shot is unlikely to reflect the effort you put into the swing.

It's not just full shots that are left short – chips and putts can also suffer a similar fate. The major fault is the same for both – deceleration of the clubhead into impact. The cure is identical too.

Your backswing and follow-through should be the same length for every putt – irrespective of the distance you are from the hole. This encourages a smooth stroke and, more importantly, a gradual

acceleration of the clubhead into the back of the ball.

When you chip from close range, your hands must be ahead of the ball at address and must return to this position at impact. This helps to make sure you strike the ball first and not the ground.

Your backswing can make or break any chip and it's a part of the swing that determines the distance you want on the shot. Keep the stroke short and crisp, accelerating the club into impact. This reduces the risk of a miss-hit and increases the chance of getting the ball up to the hole.

Last resort
The search for extra distance off the tee is an experience every golfer goes through at one time or another. But it's worth remembering, accuracy is usually more valuable than distance.

Be careful not to go to desperate lengths to add yards to

your drives. While there's plenty of equipment on the market to help you achieve this, make sure it suits your game before you part with your money. What adds distance to one golfer's game may send your ball flying into the trees with alarming regularity.

Why do you overshoot?

Watching your ball sail over or through the green is generally less common than the shot that falls short, but it's no less frustrating.

On some courses – particularly on heathland where the holes often weave a path through avenues of trees – danger lurks behind many greens. You only need to overshoot once or twice on a course like this to make a complete mess of your scorecard.

As with most shots in golf there are several causes of hitting the ball too far – some are serious faults and others are simply down to poor judgment. Whichever you suffer from most, take heart – they're all curable.

PUMPED UP PLAY

Adrenalin is a natural hormone present in everyone which plays a major part in competitive sport – golf is no exception. Being "pumped up" can cause you to overshoot, but if you understand the influence adrenalin has on your game you can make it work to your advantage.

FORGET THE FORCEFUL APPROACH
Throwing yourself at the ball with all the force you can muster is the worst possible way to swing the club – particularly when it's just a pitching wedge. You reduce your chances of striking the ball correctly. You either catch it heavy or – as shown – hit a thin. The arms flail away out of control – the ball shoots along the ground and through the green. This sort of shot should be played with control and feel – that is the best way to find the correct distance consistently.

ACCURATE APPROACH PLAY

(1) CONTROLLING INTEREST
The most effective way to find the correct distance is to play within yourself. A controlled swing with a 9 iron gives you far more consistent results than a bash with a pitching wedge. Stand with your feet about shoulder width apart and square to the line.

(2) WIDE ANGLE
Even though you're hitting only a lofted iron you still need to set the club on a wide arc away from the ball. The left arm should be in control of the club, pulling your shoulders under your chin, and the upper body and hips into a coiled position.

(3) CLUBHEAD CONSCIOUSNESS
Stop the club short of horizontal. This helps promote a feeling of control at the top of the backswing – any further and you risk losing an awareness of the exact position of the clubhead. Make a full shoulder turn.

(4) BALL POINTER
Your first move from the top should be to pull down hard with your left hand. Imagine the butt of the club pointing straight down at the ball as you start the downswing – this helps set the clubhead on the correct path towards impact.

It happens at various stages in a round. If you're on a good score in a medal, it's natural to feel a little excited. The same is true if you're on the 1st tee in an important competition and there are a group of people watching.

You need to take adrenalin into account with your club selection because it can literally add yards to your shots. Learn to know when it affects you – what would normally be a 5 iron into the green might be one club less when the adrenalin is flowing.

BLOWN OVER

Weather can also make you overshoot the target. A sudden change in wind conditions can carry an otherwise good shot into trouble. You need to be ever mindful of this to make sure your ball doesn't fly too far.

On a links course it's easy to forecast wind speed and direction, partly because there is sometimes a near gale blowing. But on a tree lined course the wind can often swirl around more unpredictably though not as strongly – your club selection may vary as a result.

When you play a shot downwind always allow for a little more run on the ball – this is particularly important when you're firing into a green. It's difficult to generate much backspin and very easy to finish through the back.

The shape of your shots also affects the distance the ball carries through the air. In a right to left wind, a draw flies much further than a fade. Bear this in mind when you visualize the stroke you want to play.

The shot that curves in the opposite direction to the wind is a good shot to have in your repertoire – particularly when trouble lurks through the back of the green.

For example, a fade in a right to left wind should fly straight and stop more quickly than other shots under similar conditions. But it's quite a tricky stroke to pull off, so you need to be striking the ball well to play the shot in a confident frame of mind.

FAULT FINDER

Thinning the ball is the worst of all the shots that finish beyond the intended target and occurs mostly from close range. It usually results in the ball hurtling through the green – an extremely depressing sight even at the best of times.

There are several causes of the

Ball check
Something as straightforward as the type of ball you play can cause you to overshoot the target from time to time.

It's difficult to generate backspin if you use a solid ball and therefore difficult to stop shots on all but the softest of greens. You may find even your good shots land in trouble.

A balata covered wound ball spins more and can enhance your control over the ball to help you stop it on the greens. However, you must be a consistent striker if you're to reap the full benefits of a balata ball.

(5) LEFT SIDE DOMINATES
This is a good example of hitting against a firm left side – note how the left leg supports the body weight and the head is behind the point of impact ensuring there's no lunge at the ball. The left wrist is firm as you strike down into the bottom of the ball.

(6) CONSISTENT LENGTH
The signs are good on the follow-through. Balance is perfect, weight is on the left side and the upper body faces the target. This controlled swing produces shots of a consistent length – if you try to force the shot the distance the ball carries is likely to vary.

pro tip

Keep it square
If you hood (close) the blade of an iron at address you risk hitting the ball further with that club than normal. The ball is too far back in the stance and the hands are pressed too far forward – a combination of both is effectively

making the club stronger than it should be (left picture).

If the clubhead returns to the same position at impact, the trajectory of the ball is lower and the flight more penetrating – a solid strike is likely to send the ball too far.

Carry out a basic address check to make sure you're not hooding the blade. Position the ball fairly central in your stance with the blade square to the target line. This enables you to make use of the correct degree of loft on the club (right picture).

thin – probably the most common is scooping at the ball in an effort to get it airborne. Remember, you need to hit down on the ball to gain height on an iron shot.

Hitting too much club tends to be rarer than underclubbing, but it can easily happen – particularly on a course you're not familiar with.

The fault is largely down to poor judgement. A yardage chart helps eliminate the problem. Also try looking at the size of the people putting out on the green ahead – you can gain a feel for distance by gauging how big or small they appear.

While finishing through the back having hit a good shot can make you feel a little hard done by, try to remember that it happens to every golfer. There's no simple cure – it's just a case of trying to learn from past experience and drawing on it in the future.

Flying start
It's easy to get a flyer when you play a shot from light rough, particularly if the grass is a little wet. The result is usually a shot that travels further through the air than normal, so it's important to know when to expect a flyer and why.

It happens when grass comes between the clubface and the ball. This eliminates most of the spin and makes it difficult to shape the ball through the air or stop it on the greens.

If the ball is lying fairly well in light rough, make allowances by altering your club selection. You don't need to change your swing – the strike alone adds the extra distance.

TROUBLE-SHOOTING

Bad weather, bad lies, bad luck – these can all lead to situations where you need to call on some creative shot-making skills to get you out of trouble. Whether the problem comes in the form of a poor lie, an uneven stance or merely an obstacle blocking the route you want to take to the hole, the keys to a successful outcome are improvisation and imagination – two characteristics that have formed the cornerstones of Seve Ballesteros's wonderful career. He is the ultimate improvisor, the Houdini of the golf course. You, too, can learn how to play your way out of trouble. First, though, you need the knowledge, and that's what this chapter is all about.

Wet weather hitches

The bane of many a golfer is rain. Wet weather disturbs you mentally and can also affect your technique. Both the damp ground and your clothing are often to blame for poor shots.

Q When I'm playing in the rain my shots often carve away to the right. What could I be doing wrong?

A The main reason for hitting a slice – in any weather – is an out-to-in attack. This slicing swing path is a product of poor turn in the backswing. In the rain you often feel restricted – especially in your waterproofs – and it is all too easy to swing with just your arms.

Picking up your arms quickly feels stable but results in a no turn backswing. The club is laid off at the top, and from this position the natural downswing path is outside the line. Your club cuts across the ball and the shot starts left then swerves away to the right.

Swinging in the rain

To keep on hitting the ball consistently well after it's started raining, you must strive to make a full turn. It's especially important when you have donned your rainsuit, which can be restrictive.

Make your primary swing thought a full turn with a smooth rhythm. This gives you the best chance of swinging down on the correct plane and attacking the ball on the correct in-to-in path.

RESTRICTED IN BACKSWING – ALL ARMS AND POOR TURN

✗

CLUB ATTACKS BALL FROM OUTSIDE THE LINE

✗

TOP OF BACKSWING ON LINE

FULL SHOULDER TURN

✓

ATTACKS BALL ON CORRECT PATH

✓

Q I find it very annoying that I tend to hit the ball fat in wet weather, and the shot flies nowhere. Why is my striking poor?

A To ensure crisp hitting on slightly mushy ground, it's critical to strike the ball first before the ground. If you have the ball positioned in your normal spot or slightly forward of it, the chances of hitting a fat are quite high.

A tiny misjudgment can easily make you catch the ground first, and hitting only a fraction behind the ball leads to a heavy, squidgy strike. The club stubs in the ground and your follow-through is weak and stunted.

NORMAL BALL PLACEMENT ON WET GROUND

EASY TO HIT SLIGHTLY BEHIND BALL – FAT STRIKE AND STUNTED FOLLOWTHROUGH

Damp proof placement

To ensure crisp striking in damp conditions move the ball back in your stance a fraction. This lessens the chance of catching the ground before the ball.

Because you now attack the ball with a more downward blow than normal, the clubface is slightly delofted. So you must choose your club carefully if you're still to play accurately.

Keeping control in the rain is also helped by swinging with a shorter backswing, but you must turn fully and release properly for a crisp straight hit.

BALL MOVED BACK IN STANCE

CRISP DOWNWARD BLOW AND PROPER RELEASE

Wind cheater

When the wind blows some golfers do rock, and unfortunately their shots also waver in the breeze.
Understanding the techniques you need to combat the wind can take the hardship out of playing in rough weather.

Q Why do I often hit wayward shots into wind – especially ones that fall short of my target – even though I take more club than normal?

A Inaccurate shots stem from poor thinking and a misunderstanding of how to tackle a headwind. Too often a golfer feels he must hit the ball harder to counter the effect of the wind. This is the worst possible approach if you want to keep the ball under control.

Trying to hit the ball hard with a full and forceful swing means you strike down firmly which creates a lot of backspin. The ball rises quickly, and the effect of the headwind makes the ball climb higher and balloon. The shot is held on the air and falls short of the target. Because the ball flies high, it can also be easily blown off line in a slight crosswind.

Low under the breeze

To hit accurate shots in a headwind, it's essential to swing with a smooth, easy and controlled action. The key to command into wind is keeping the ball low and on a penetrative trajectory.

To hit the wind cheater, play the ball from slightly further back in your stance and choose more club than usual. The secret to hitting this shot correctly is to keep the backswing shorter than normal and to swing down with slightly less wrist action. This naturally creates a sweeping arc rather than a steep downward attack.

The combination of the club, ball position and the smooth, slow, sweeping swing keeps the ball low. To gain extra control it helps to choke down a little on the club – which also naturally reduces wrist action.

FULL OUT ATTACK MAKES SHOT BALLOON INTO WIND

HARD HITTING PRODUCES HIGH FLOATING SHOT THAT LANDS SHORT OF TARGET

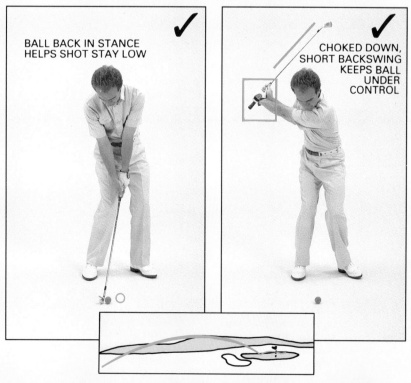

BALL BACK IN STANCE HELPS SHOT STAY LOW

CHOKED DOWN, SHORT BACKSWING KEEPS BALL UNDER CONTROL

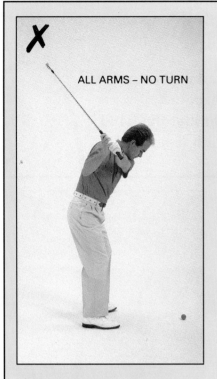

✗

ALL ARMS – NO TURN

✗

DOWNSWING
SLIGHTLY OUT-TO-IN
RELEASED TOO EARLY

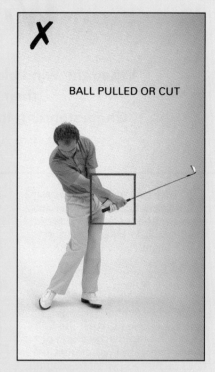

✗

BALL PULLED OR CUT

Q I know what type of shot to hit into a wind – a low, boring shot – but when I try to play it I tend to either pull the ball or hit a cut. Why?

A Even if your set-up and club selection are good, using your hands and arms incorrectly

leads to a wayward stroke. The pull and cut are common faults when trying to hit the low shot. Both stem from an action which uses all hands and arms.

So intent are some golfers on keeping control with the arms that they fail to turn or use the legs properly. A short, stiff backswing with little turn leads to

an attack from slightly outside the line. Most players with this backswing make up for their stiff action by releasing through the ball in an attempt to gain power.

This movement combined with the slight out-to-in attack produces the pull or the cut, depending on whether the blade is closed (pull) or square (cut).

✓

BACKSWING SHORT
BUT TURN IS FULL

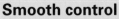

✓

SMOOTH ATTACK WITH
LITTLE WRIST ACTION

✓

BLADE HELD SQUARE TO
TARGET FOR LONGER

Smooth control

For the low shot to come off, you must combine a full turn – even though the backswing is shorter than normal – with a controlled throughswing. Swing down

smoothly and resist flicking at the ball with the wrists.

Be firm at impact and don't release the hands through the ball – hold the blade square to the target for longer than usual.

Your finish position should also be shorter than normal. This short, less wristy, firm throughswing action ensures the ball drills straight at the target.

Sidehill troubles

Few golf courses are totally flat. Most have slopes that can
test your skill to the limit if
you land on one. But crisp controlled striking is easy to
achieve if you understand the technique.

Q When the ball is above my feet I often hit it fat and it turns quickly to the left. Why?

A This is because you fail to alter your technique to allow for the slope. You cannot treat these shots like any other – you have to make changes.

When the ball is above your feet your swing plane becomes flatter than normal – at best this produces a draw, but because of the severity of the slope the shot can easily turn into a hook. This is where your shot that flies left comes in.

Catching the shot fat could be caused by one of several errors. Gripping at the top of the club is ideal on a flat lie, but when the ball is above your feet it's potentially disastrous. You effectively make the club much longer than it really is and this can often cause you to hit ground before the ball.

You must also resist the temptation to dip down into your normal position on the downswing. This is certain to cause a heavy shot with the clubhead thudding into the ground behind the ball.

Stand up to the problem
A few simple changes in technique can help you strike shots properly when the ball is above the level of your feet.
○ Stand slightly more upright at address. Maintain your height throughout the swing to help ensure you make clean contact with the ball. At impact your head should be at exactly the same level as at address.
○ Grip a little further down the club than usual – this puts you in a more normal posture and serves as an added precaution against catching the shot heavy.
○ Remember, when you have an uneven stance the ball tends to naturally fly in the direction the slope falls – in this case to the left. Make allowances for this by aligning and aiming right.

X STANCE MORE UPRIGHT THAN USUAL

BALL ABOVE FEET

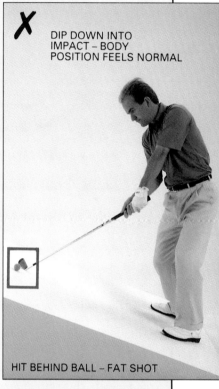

X DIP DOWN INTO IMPACT – BODY POSITION FEELS NORMAL

HIT BEHIND BALL – FAT SHOT

✓ KEEP BODY POSITION STEADY THROUGHOUT SWING

✓ BODY POSITION THROUGH IMPACT SAME AS ADDRESS BALL STRUCK CRISPLY

X BALL BELOW FEET – MORE BENT OVER THAN NORMAL

X STRAIGHTENS UP THROUGH IMPACT – BALL THINNED RIGHT

Q I find it hard to strike the ball well when it's below my feet. My shots often fly low and right. What am I doing wrong?

A Bad shots usually stem from an incorrect position at address and this is probably where your problems begin. You must bend more at the waist and at the knees when the ball is below the level of your feet.

Stand slightly closer to the ball so that you don't have to reach too far away from your body – don't forget the ball is already further from you than normal. Also position your weight more on the heels than usual – this should prevent you from losing your

balance and toppling forward.

The lie of the ground naturally makes your swing plane a little more upright. To compensate, align and aim left of target and allow for the ball to fade back on line.

A common fault occurs at the start of the downswing. If you straighten up into your normal impact position, you can guarantee on hitting a thin out to the right every time. Make sure you keep your head at the same level through impact as at address to ensure you don't catch the shot thin.

✓ HOLD ADDRESS BODY POSITION THROUGHOUT SWING

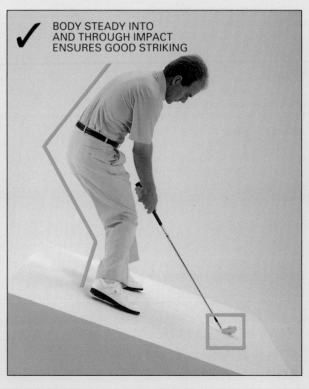

✓ BODY STEADY INTO AND THROUGH IMPACT ENSURES GOOD STRIKING

Rough remedies

After missing a fairway it's crucial to tackle the rough in the correct way if you're to recover profitably.
No drastic steps are needed to cope with thick grass, just a few subtle changes in your technique.

Q Whenever I drive into the rough I find it difficult to flight the ball properly. Often my shots shoot out low and right. Can you tell me why?

A The main cause of badly shaped shots out of rough is trying to hit the ball too hard. Not only do you swing without rhythm, but it destroys any real hope of adopting the correct body positions on the downswing.

Though you need to attack the ball on a slightly steeper path than normal, trying to thrash the ball out often leads you to lunge down from too severe an angle. Your lower body tends to get too far ahead of the ball and the clubhead lags way behind your hands.

The steep attack and your poor body position means that you strike the ball with a delofted and open clubface. The shot is squeezed out of the grass and flies low and right.

Controlled escape

The correct way to tackle a shot from rough is to try and keep your tempo, rhythm and swing as normal as possible. The only real difference between your normal swing and the one needed to escape from rough is the angle of attack. Your downswing path needs to be steeper than usual to ensure as little grass gets between the ball and clubface as possible – the key to good striking.

Keep your downswing smooth and controlled – don't hit from the top. Concentrate on maintaining your rhythm and move into your usual solid impact position – with no hint of your lower body getting ahead of the ball. This near normal action makes sure your shots fly straight and on the correct trajectory.

FORCING SHOT – ATTACK TOO STEEP ✗

BODY TOO FAR AHEAD OF CLUBHEAD AND BALL ✗

BALL CHOPPED OUT LOW AND RIGHT

✓ BALANCE AND RHYTHM HELD ON DOWNSWING – SHOT NOT FORCED

✓ CLUB SWINGS FREELY INTO IMPACT WITHOUT BODY GETTING AHEAD OF BALL

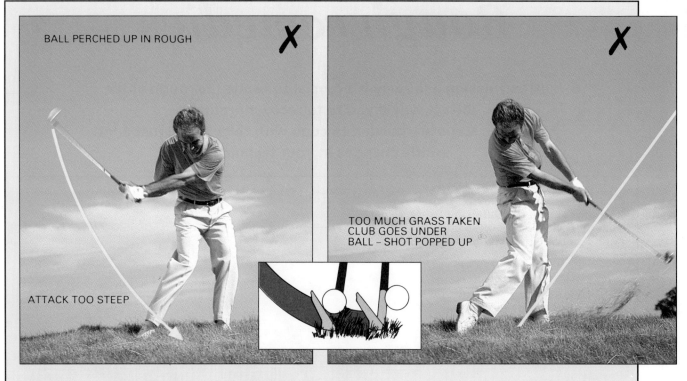

BALL PERCHED UP IN ROUGH ✗

ATTACK TOO STEEP

TOO MUCH GRASS TAKEN
CLUB GOES UNDER
BALL – SHOT POPPED UP ✗

Q When I'm lucky enough to find my ball sitting up in the rough, I often make a mess of the shot. I tend to pop the ball into the air and it lands well short of the target. Why?

A Your problem comes from using the general rough technique. For most shots out of the rough you need to attack the ball from a steeper angle than normal, but when the ball is perched up on the grass your swing must change again.

If you swing down from a steep angle you run the risk of going underneath the ball. You take too much grass and you strike the ball with the top part of your blade, skying the shot.

SWEEPING DOWNSWING ✓

SHALLOW ATTACK CLIPS
BALL OFF GRASS ✓

Sweeping changes

Instead of attacking the ball from a steep angle, you must swing down on a much shallower path. The ideal action is to swing on a wide arc and sweep the ball off the top of the grass. Extending your take-away and moving the club back on a shallow path helps you to swing down and through the ball on the same wide arc.

Keep steady throughout the stroke and extend fully through the ball. Positioning the ball slightly further forward than normal at address also helps you to catch it cleanly and on the up – the secret to long term success.

Uphill and downhill distress

Too many golfers walk into a shot from an uphill or downhill lie with no real idea of the set-up and technique needed to pull it off. The result is wild, uncontrolled hitting. Knowing the correct procedures improves your striking and accuracy.

Q When my ball rests on an upslope I often hit the shot fat and it lands well short of my target. Why?

A The fat shot comes from a poor set-up, with both incorrect posture and ball position. If you try to stand upright as normal, your weight goes fully on to the left side.

This is disastrous, because if you swing from this address position with the ball placed as usual, your attack is too steep. The angle between your downswing path and the slope is too large, and the club strikes down severely on the ball. The shot is stabbed and the club can't swing through fully as it digs into the turf, resulting in a fat.

STANDING UPRIGHT WITH BALL TOO FAR BACK

CLUB ATTACKS FROM TOO STEEP AN ANGLE AND STABS BEHIND BALL

GROUND STOPS CLUB SWINGING THROUGH – FAT HIT SHORT OF TARGET

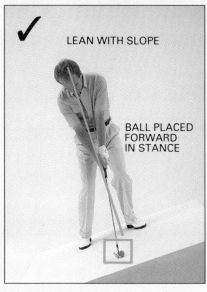

LEAN WITH SLOPE

BALL PLACED FORWARD IN STANCE

BODY POSITION HELD

CLUB SWEEPS BALL AWAY WITH CRISP UPWARD STRIKE

POWERFUL THROUGHSWING – BALL DRIVEN AWAY

Sweeping angle

A good set-up is the key to playing a shot from an upslope. Position the ball further forward in your stance than normal, and lean with the slope. Both these changes encourage a sweeping strike from a shallower angle.

But the different set-up must be coupled with a smooth, balanced swing. Hold your body position until after impact – resist the temptation to move up the slope into the ball on the downswing. By staying steady your club attacks the ball on a shallow angle and clips it off the turf with a sweeping action and no hint of digging into the ground.

Q I lean correctly with a downslope, so that more of my weight is on the left side than normal, but I still regularly hit the ball low, thin and out to the right. What am I doing wrong?

A It is probably down to poor ball position and excessive body movement on the down and throughswing. With the ball placed as normal, the tendency is to try and lift it off the turf to get it airborne.

If you shift your weight on to the right side by leaning backwards on the downswing the club attacks the ball on the up and the blade catches it thin. You end up with all your weight on the right foot. You apply no power or direction to the shot.

Even if the movement backward is only slight it is still impossible to strike down on the ball – especially when it is placed forward. This gives you no opportunity to lift the ball into the air.

✗ BALL TOO FAR FORWARD IN STANCE

✗ TENDENCY TO LEAN BACK INTO IMPACT

✗ COME OFF SHOT – BALL THINNED LOW AND RIGHT

✓ LEANING WITH SLOPE – BALL FURTHER BACK IN STANCE

✓ BODY POSITION HELD INTO IMPACT FOR CRISP STRIKE

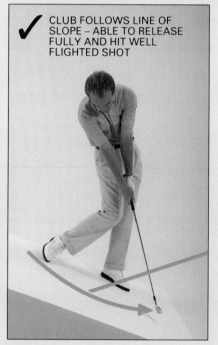

✓ CLUB FOLLOWS LINE OF SLOPE – ABLE TO RELEASE FULLY AND HIT WELL FLIGHTED SHOT

Back and down

The secret to sweet striking on a downslope is to move the ball back in your stance, and hold your body position throughout the stroke. The change in ball placement increases the chances of the blade striking down on the shot, so lessens the risk of you catching it on the up.

But for crisp hitting, altering only your ball placement

is not enough. As you swing back and down, keep as steady and as balanced as possible. Resist shifting your weight on to the right side. This action means that the club can attack the ball on a downward path. Try to swing the clubhead along the line of the slope for as long as comfortable on the follow-through to lessen the chance of you coming off the shot.

Playing from the rough

More than ever, you need a solid technique to play a good shot from the rough. You must also understand the special problems involved to help you turn them to your advantage.

There are small set-up differences between playing a shot from the rough and one from the fairway. But assessing the lie of the ball and choosing the right club are just as important as correct address and a good swing.

Before playing any shot from the rough you must be clear how grass affects club control.

WHEN THE GOING GETS ROUGH
Keep a cool head and select the correct club and you're likely to play a good shot from the rough. When the rough is thick, it's more important to get your ball back on to a good fairway lie than to risk a distance shot.

HOW TO HIT FROM THE ROUGH

1 BREAK WRISTS EARLY
Swing the club back with an early wrist break. This helps create an out-to-in swing path and a sharp angle of attack which prevents you striking grass before the ball.

2 CHOPPING ACTION
Maintain the hinge of your wrists as you swing the club back, so the clubhead can chop the ball from the rough. Keep most weight on your left foot.

Choosing a club

The lie of the ball plays a large part in deciding which club you can use. The thicker the grass and the deeper the ball is buried in the rough, the more lofted a club you need.

IMPACT IN THE ROUGH

In short grass, such as a fairway, the clubhead slides easily over the surface, allowing the clubface to strike the ball correctly. But in long, thick grass, the rough acts as a barrier, slowing down the clubhead. The grass also tangles in the clubhead so that the club turns in your hands and the face closes at impact.

The longer and thicker the grass, the greater the resistance and the more the clubface closes. A closed clubface means you strike with reduced loft – the ball doesn't fly as high as normal – and the ball travels to the left of the target.

Apart from acting as a barrier, rough grass reduces your control over the shot. Blades of grass get trapped between the clubface and the ball and prevent the grooves from giving backspin. This leads to a flyer – the ball rolls further along the ground than normal on landing.

The more grass caught between ball and clubface the less control and backspin you have and the greater run there is.

ASSESSING THE SHOT

When your ball lands in the rough you must first assess the lie. If the grass is fairly short your problem isn't getting the ball out but choosing the correct club for the shot.

For maximum distance use a fairway wood. The clubhead on a wood passes through the grass more easily than an iron. Its rounded, bulky head flattens the grass as it glides through it. With

an iron, there is more resistance.

If you can reach the hole, try to visualize the flight and roll of the ball – you must estimate the flyer effect. Judging the ball's path is the key.

WHICH CLUB?

You need practice to work out how much extra roll each club gives you. As you gain experience, develop a mental conversion chart to deal with the distance shots go from the rough.

You hit an 8 iron from the rough the same distance as a 7 iron from the fairway, because of the flyer effect.

The 8 iron hits the ball higher and shorter than the 7, but the reduced backspin and the extra roll make up the difference. The increased loft also helps you get the

Clean the grooves
Use a tee peg to clean the clubhead grooves before and after hitting from the rough. Clean grooves give you the best chance of control and backspin from the rough. And after the shot, the grooves are likely to be clogged up with grass and mud.

④ FOLLOWTHROUGH
As your club continues through, it moves left because of the out-to-in swing path. When you finish, the back of your left hand should face the sky.

③ IMPACT AND ON
As you swing through, keep your left hand in control and ahead of the clubface for as long as possible. This stops you scooping the ball and hitting grass first.

ball out of the rough.

You may find that you need to move up two clubs – for example a 5 to a 7 iron. Alternatively, it may suit you to take one *less* club and shorten the length of your swing to reduce the ball's distance.

Be flexible to allow for different grass length. You also need to adapt your mental chart when there are hazards or trees between the landing point and the target. If you're faced with a hazard, your choice of club is more difficult.

When you have a small landing area between an obstacle and the hole you have to play safe. Either take a longer club to clear the hazard and accept that your ball will run a long way past the hole or play to the side of the obstacle and finish right or left of the target.

Never gamble. It's better to be long or a little off line than to play your next shot from a bunker, a ditch or behind a tree.

PLAY SAFE IN LONG GRASS

If your ball is in tall, thick grass, use a pitching wedge to hit it out. Don't be over ambitious from a difficult lie. Unless you can reach the green with a wedge, aim simply to get the ball back on the fairway. Accept the bad lie and make sure that your next shot is from a good position.

Many players try to make up for

pro tip

Power wring
Do a simple exercise every day to build up the muscles you use in the rough. Wring an old towel as tightly as you can, repeating the exercise three or four times. This strengthens your hands, wrists and forearms and helps you to keep a firm grip at impact.

lost ground by thrashing far too long a club from thick grass. This usually ends in a poorly struck shot and a worse position than before.

Even if you make a solid strike with a long or medium iron, the ball may not clear the long grass. It becomes entangled in the rough, moving no more than 20-30yd (18-27m). A pitching wedge easily achieves this distance, and gives more height and control.

Leading professionals consider it a risk to use a club with little loft in long grass. The average club golfer shouldn't even compensate it.

CHANGES AT ADDRESS

Once you've chosen the club, address the ball. To compensate for the closed clubface you must make two changes to your normal set-up.

You need to open the clubface slightly at address to offset the amount you expect it to turn at impact. Do this before taking your grip. If you take your grip first, your hands automatically return the clubface to the normal position before you hit the ball. The longer the grass the more open the clubface should be.

Grip the club a little more tightly than usual, and concentrate on keeping a firm hold through impact to stop the club turning in your hands. Align your body parallel to the ball-to-target line and make a normal swing.

Although an effective golf swing depends on correct tempo rather than brute force, this is one time when physical strength can improve your shot. The stronger you are the less the club turns in your hands.

Use a wood in light rough
You're better off using a wood than an iron in light rough when you need distance. The rounded clubhead of a fairway wood glides through the grass, pushing it out of the way as the club travels through. With an iron, grass wraps itself around the hosel and the clubface, closing it at impact – the ball flies left.

WOOD

IRON

Escape from hard sand

For accuracy from sand it's important to distinguish between different textures. Bunker sand becomes hard for several reasons – wet weather is the most common. Wind blows surface sand to the lips of the bunker, leaving the center bare and hard.

Sometimes balls that land in a particular bunker roll down to the same lie. Golfers play out of the same spot and gradually the sand disappears until only a thin layer remains on the base.

To escape successfully from hard sand you need to make

SLOW SWING FOR CLEAN HIT
When your ball is resting on hard sand, swing smoothly and slowly. The sand's firm texture does not let you slide the club under the ball as normal, so you need to nip the ball off the top.

CLIP CLEANLY OFF HARD SAND

(1) HANDS AHEAD OF CLUBHEAD Set up as normal in the sand, with a slightly open stance and your hands ahead of the pitching wedge clubhead – the ball is forward in your stance. Do not let the club touch the sand or you incur a 2 stroke penalty.

pro tip

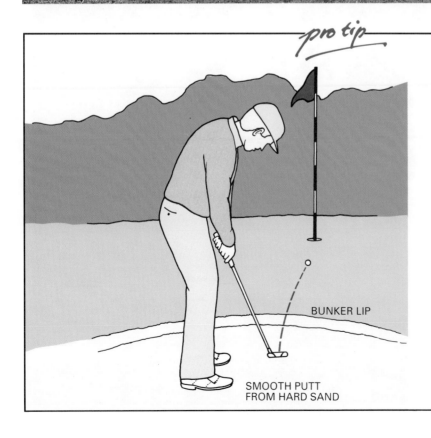

BUNKER LIP

SMOOTH PUTT FROM HARD SAND

Putt out of the sand

Surprisingly, you don't have to take a lofted club to strike your ball out of the sand. In certain circumstances a putter works just as well. The sand must be hard enough to let your ball roll and the bunker lip shallow enough for the ball to clear it with ease.

Ensuring that you don't touch the sand with your putter – making contact incurs a 2 shot penalty – swing slowly and smoothly back and through the ball.

You must judge the shot precisely, taking into account the angle of the bunker lip and how the ball will cross it as well as the distance to the pin. But don't hit so softly that the ball struggles feebly to leave the sand – escaping in one shot is top priority.

② SLOW TAKEAWAY
Start your swing slowly to set the tone for the swing and concentrate on maintaining an even tempo. Keep your head still, with your eyes on the back of the ball.

③ SHORTER BACKSWING
A shorter backswing than usual helps you achieve smooth tempo because it's much easier to maintain your feel for the clubhead.

④ NIP IT OFF THE TOP
You can't take sand so let the leading edge cut into the sand in (1cm) behind the ball – the ball is clipped cleanly off the surface.

⑤ SHORTER THROUGH SWING
Your through swing should be the same shorter length as your backswing for clockwork tempo throughout the shot. Struck cleanly, the ball floats towards the target.

changes to your normal bunker technique. You can't take sand when it's so compressed and compact – the wide soled sand wedge bounces up off the sand into the back of the ball, causing a thinned shot.

SQUARE CLUBFACE

You must still hit slightly behind the ball, but for a successful stroke off wet sand you need the narrower soled pitching wedge instead of a sand wedge. Keep the clubface square to the ball-to-target line and strike about ½in (1cm) behind the ball.

The leading edge must just break the hard, crusty surface of the sand to get under the ball. Nip the ball neatly off the top – you want to take very little sand with the stroke when you play from hard sand. It's not like playing from soft, dry sand when the club passes through without slowing down, and the ball is not touched by the clubhead as it's thrown out of the bunker by a wedge of sand.

Be sure of timing the hard sand stroke well by slowing down your swing and concentrating on an even tempo throughout the stroke. You want to make as clean a strike as possible on the ball – a shorter swing than usual helps you control the clubhead and achieve this smooth, even timing.

Practise playing from different textures of sand – once you have a feel for the various techniques your sand play should show a considerable improvement.

pro tip

Bunker raking
When you rake a bunker make sure that you keep the sand as smooth and flat all over as possible – leave the bunker as you'd wish to find it.

Rake the sand towards the edges to form a basin effect – any balls that fly into the bunker are then likely to roll down to the center. This is preferable to playing from restrictive uphill or downhill lies. But don't leave too little sand in the middle – bare lies develop which are tough to play, especially from deep pot bunkers.

JUDGE THE SAND

BALL LIFTED OUT ON SAND

✓ **Soft sand – sand wedge**
The sole passes through easily, lifting out the ball on a cushion of sand. Clubface and ball do not make contact.

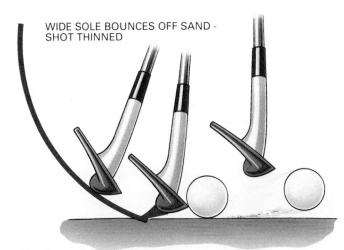

WIDE SOLE BOUNCES OFF SAND - SHOT THINNED

✗ **Hard sand – sand wedge**
Trying to cut through hard sand with a sand wedge is fatal – the wide sole of the club bounces off the sand and sculls into the back of the ball, causing a thinned shot.

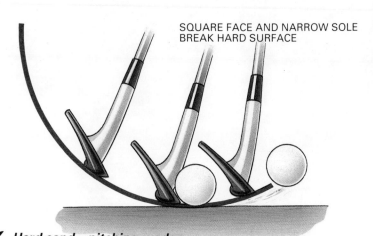

SQUARE FACE AND NARROW SOLE BREAK HARD SURFACE

✓ **Hard sand – pitching wedge**
When the blade is square, the narrower sole of the pitching wedge has a sharper leading edge. This breaks the hard surface of sand, letting the club strike through the bottom of the ball – vital as you can't lift the ball out on sand.

Bunker close-ups: plugged greenside lie

It's easy for your ball to nestle down in a bunker – particularly if the sand is wet. It usually happens when you hit a high approach shot that pitches on the full into a greenside bunker.

Your success rate from a plugged lie depends on understanding the shot. While it's regarded by many handicap players as one of the most daunting prospects in golf, master the technique and you needn't include yourself among the sufferers.

The typical greenside bunker shot rises fast, lands softly and rolls gently to the hole. From a plugged lie you can't hope for such a delicate touch. The combination of square clubface and huge amount of sand between the club and the ball makes backspin impossible to achieve. The result is a lower trajectory shot with plenty of run on landing.

You can put the ball close, though – particularly if there's plenty of green to work with. But your initial thought is to make sure you escape first time – that is the most important step towards avoiding disaster.

SWING SUMMARY

The angle of attack is the big difference between this and any other greenside bunker shot. Swing the club up steeply away from the ball by breaking the wrists early. Your swing path should be slightly out to in, but not as exaggerated as a normal splash bunker shot.

The length of your backswing determines the distance of the shot, so maintain an even tempo on the downswing. Accelerate the clubhead down behind the ball to create a stun effect in the sand. Concentrate on keeping your wrists firm. If the sand texture is thick your followthrough may be slightly cut short.

SKILL AND A GRAIN OF LUCK
All players occasionally face the plugged lie on their way round a golf course. Disaster usually stems from a failure to understand the shot fully. While you need to rely on a little bit of luck , you must know precisely how the ball reacts. Watch the red stripe on the ball through impact in the following sequence – unlike a normal bunker shot, very little spin is applied.

PLUGGED LIE DETAILS

(1) **POISED FOR ACTION**
Avoid touching the sand with the clubhead at address or you break one of the rules of golf. Use the restriction to your advantage rather than regarding it as a problem. Hovering the club helps you sweep it smoothly away from the ball – this sets the pace of your swing and gives you rhythm you can maintain throughout the shot.

KEY POINT
Square clubface to target at address.

(2) **FIRST CUT**
The clubhead of your sand wedge travels down steeply, cutting into the fine sand. The angle created by the hosel of the club and the surface sand is proof that the hands are ahead of the ball at this stage. A wave of sand is displaced yet the ball has barely moved – the red stripe has tilted backwards only a fraction.

Accent on speed
It's always important to accelerate the club through the sand and complete your followthrough – particularly when you have a poor lie.

The biggest cause of poor bunker play is a lack of clubhead speed into impact. This often happens because you have second thoughts during the swing – as your confidence drains you slow down the club. The sand drags the clubhead to a premature halt – the ball is lobbed forward weakly and usually fails to clear the lip of the bunker.

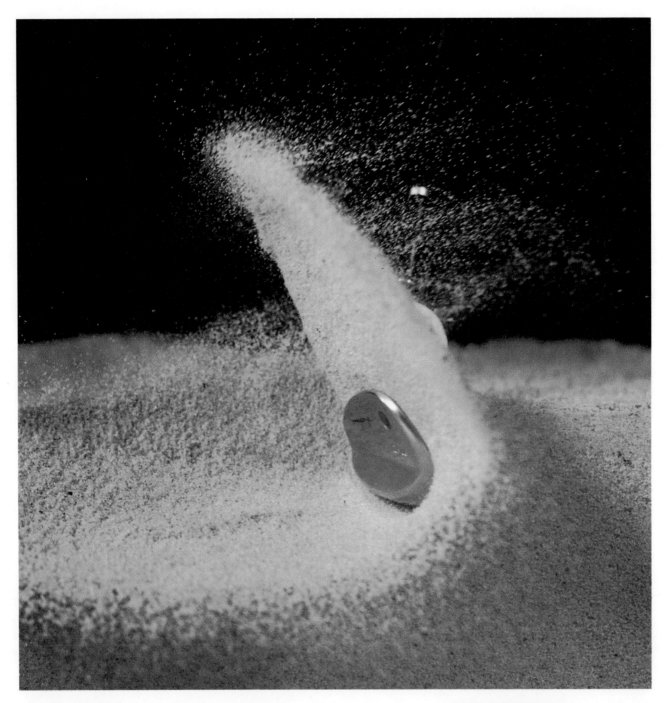

(3) SHARP EDGE
The leading edge of the clubhead continues to cut through the sand like a knife, leaving a well defined trough in its wake. The face remains square to help prevent the clubhead bouncing into the middle of the ball.

KEY POINT
Keep clubface square.

④ **DRIVE DOWN**
Clubhead speed and a steep angle of attack combine to drive the clubhead down and through under the ball. A blanket of sand carries the ball up and forward towards the target. The red line has moved back from the vertical only slightly – proof that you apply almost no backspin from a plugged lie in the sand.

KEY POINT
Clubface and ball must never touch.

(5) **SAFE AND SOUND**
As your ball heads for the safety of the green, a cloud of sand is thrown high into the air. The trajectory of the shot is a little lower than one from a good lie. The slow progress of the red line towards horizontal confirms that the ball carries very little backspin – therefore it must run further on landing than a normal bunker shot.

pro tip

Help is at hand
Think of the positive side to bunker play – the sand wedge is designed to help you as much as possible so let it do just that. Unlike any other club in your bag, the flange (sole) is wide and rounded – this enables the clubhead to slide easily through sand of every texture.

Restricted backswing

You've taken too much club at this par-3 hole,
and your tee shot is now nestling
next to a wall beside the course. You need
to think carefully to limit the damage.

You can't aim straight for the pin
because you have no room for a
backswing.

light rough

The ball is sitting up in fairly thick
rough.

light rough

The ball is lying 32ft (10m) from the
pin. The nearest edge of the green is
3ft (1m) away.

The green is dry and fast in the
warm conditions. There is a slight
wind.

Any shot you play must stay clear of the large
bunker that lurks beside the green.

SAFE SHOT
Chip left

Right-handed players should chip left towards the bunker. Grip slightly lower down than usual and aim to stop the ball quite sharply in the light rough, leaving you short of the bunker.

Left-handed players can play the same shot in the opposite direction, removing any bunker danger.

From the light rough you can putt relatively smoothly from off the green – play a Texas wedge shot.

Although you're likely to score a bogey this way, it's still a sensible strategy to limit the damage – you gain control as you're able to make a proper backswing.

From this tough situation, the direct route to the pin isn't always the best one. If you stab hurriedly at the ball to dig it out, you might fail to move it or miss altogether, leaving you in a worse situation.

First shot
Grip: lower than usual
Stance: normal
Ball position: center of stance
Weight distribution: even
Swing: short but smooth
Swing path: normal
Club: 9 iron

Second shot
Grip: reverse overlap
Stance: normal
Ball position: center of stance
Weight distribution: even
Swing: smooth stroke
Swing path: normal
Club: putter

MATCH WINNER
Bounce shot

The ball is sitting up in the rough, so you can try to leave yourself a single putt for par by bouncing the ball off the wall and on to the green.

Be accurate - you must hit the wall in the right place for a good angle. Make sure that you lift the ball, so that it clears the rough when it bounces back off the wall. Concentrate on the spot you want to hit and make a firm strike to ensure a good rebound to the green.

Beware of the rebounding ball – remember, if the ball hits you at any time during your shot you incur a 2-stroke penalty. In matchplay, you automatically lose the hole.

First shot
Grip: lower than usual
Stance: slightly open
Ball position: center of stance
Weight distribution: mainly on your left side
Swing: half
Swing path: normal
Club: pitching wedge

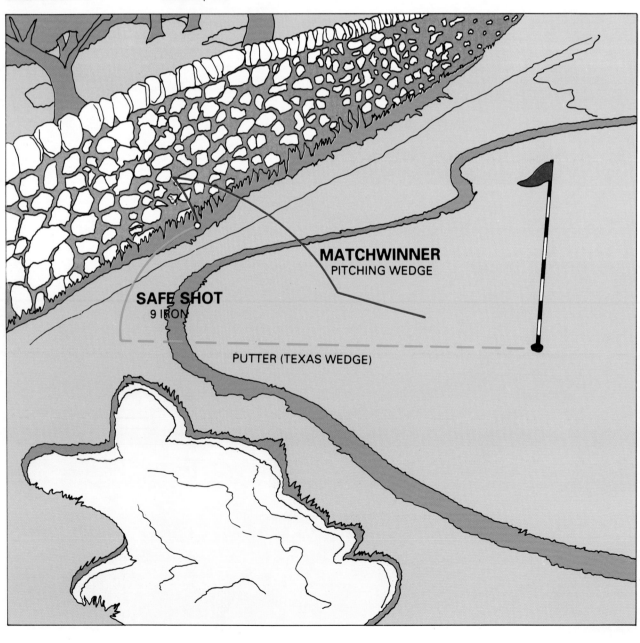

MATCHWINNER
PITCHING WEDGE

SAFE SHOT
9 IRON

PUTTER (TEXAS WEDGE)

Greenside recovery

A hooked tee shot at this par-3 hole has left you in
the rough with a difficult chip to the green.
You have to deal with sloping ground and a large bunker
if you're to recover successfully.

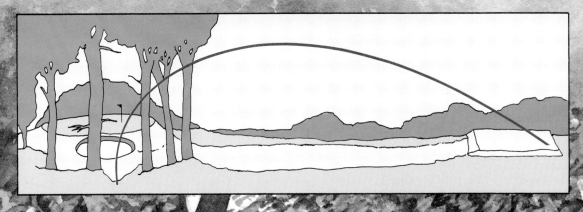

The ground is hard and dry, so your ball is certain to run. A strong breeze blows away from you across the green.

The fairway is quite flat at the bottom of the slope fronting the green.

The ball is entangled in tufts of grass 40ft (12m) from the flag. The gap between the flag and the bunker is 16ft (5m) wide.

Taking a proper stance is tough because of the growth around the tree.

The tree blocks a recovery shot played to the left.

It's risky to go for the flag because the green slopes down towards the back, making it very difficult to stop the ball. There's a steep drop waiting at the far side.

SAFE SHOT
Aim right
Grip down for greater control and play a solid chip. Chip the ball to the right of the bunker – it will roll down to the foot of the slope.

From there you can hit a firm Texas wedge (using a putter) up the slope – send the ball just over the summit to roll it down to the flag.

Don't attempt to pitch the ball over the bunker, because of your awkward stance and difficult lie. You're likely to thin it over the back, or fluff it into the bunker.

First shot
Grip: hands a few inches lower than usual
Stance: slightly open
Ball position: center of stance
Weight distribution: mainly on left side
Swing: half
Swing path: normal
Club: 9 iron

MATCH WINNER
Chip into the bunker
This method needs total confidence – and the ability to get up and down from a bunker in two.

After deciding which area of the bunker will give you the best lie, play firmly into it, taking care not to lose control through impact.

This escape route is not as odd as it first seems – around the green, many pros often prefer to play from sand. After this poor tee shot, it's a relief to escape with a bogey.

First shot
Grip: lower than usual
Stance: normal
Ball position: center of stance
Weight distribution: mainly on left side
Swing: half
Swing path: normal
Club: 9 iron

Second shot
Grip: lower than usual
Stance: open
Ball position: center of stance
Weight distribution: even
Swing: three-quarter
Swing path: out to in
Club: sand wedge

Playing from a path

Play the ball as it lies takes on a whole new meaning when
your tee shot ends up on a path.
This tricky lie on a tough links course involves hitting from
gravel or dropping under penalty.

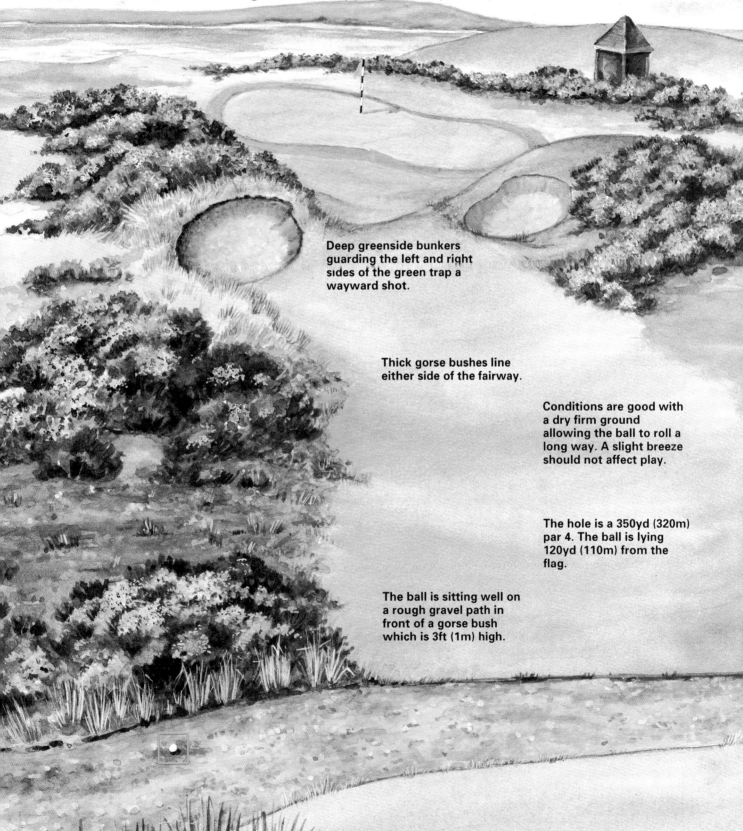

Deep greenside bunkers
guarding the left and right
sides of the green trap a
wayward shot.

Thick gorse bushes line
either side of the fairway.

Conditions are good with
a dry firm ground
allowing the ball to roll a
long way. A slight breeze
should not affect play.

The hole is a 350yd (320m)
par 4. The ball is lying
120yd (110m) from the
flag.

The ball is sitting well on
a rough gravel path in
front of a gorse bush
which is 3ft (1m) high.

SAFE SHOT
Chip to the fairway
A ball on a gravel path is risky for an inexperienced player so be cautious and aim for the fairway.

Take a short iron and aim well right of the gorse to the middle of the fairway. Play a little chip and run. Be careful not to hit too hard – you might damage your club and the dry ground may roll your ball into the rough on the other side.

From the fairway you need a straight pitch of 100yd (91m) to the flag.
First shot
Grip: lower than usual
Stance: slightly open
Ball position: center of stance
Weight distribution: even
Swing: half
Swing path: normal
Club: 8 or 9 iron
Approach shot
Grip: normal
Stance: square
Ball position: center of stance
Weight distribution: even
Swing: full
Swing path: normal
Club: 9 iron

MATCH WINNER
High flier to the green
A crisp 9 iron hit straight to the green flies over the gorse to leave a birdie putt. As you aren't playing from grass it's difficult to get the club under the ball. Pick the ball neatly off the gravel to prevent club damage.

Take care to keep the shot on line to avoid the greenside bunkers. The high flight path makes up for lack of backspin and prevents the ball from running on landing.
Grip: normal
Stance: square
Ball position: center of stance
Weight distribution: even
Swing: full
Swing path: normal
Club: 9 iron

Escape option
If you're inexperienced and you'd rather not risk damaging your club or playing this tricky shot, drop the ball under penalty of 1 shot.

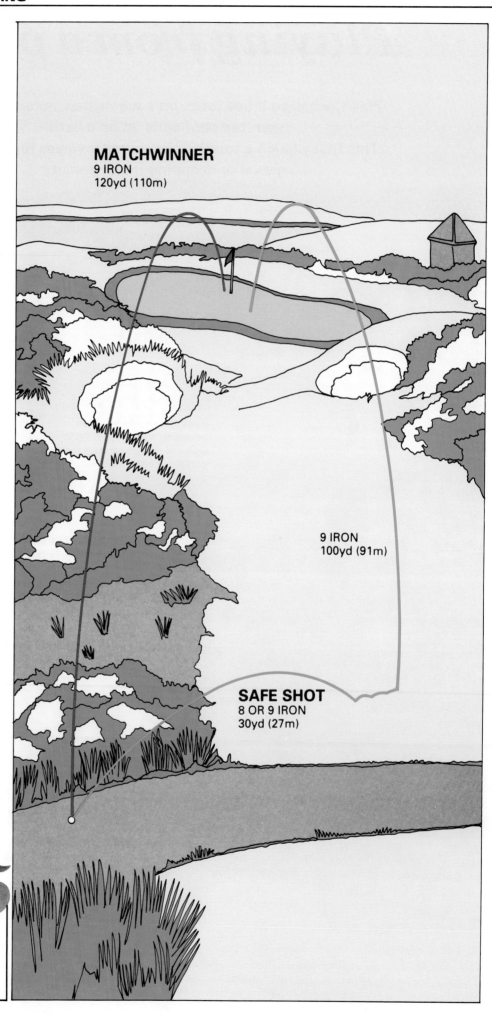

MATCHWINNER
9 IRON
120yd (110m)

9 IRON
100yd (91m)

SAFE SHOT
8 OR 9 IRON
30yd (27m)

Recovery from trees

After a badly pulled second shot you are forced to negotiate trees and bushes to find the green
on this challenging heathland course. You need to play for position to avoid an embarrassing score.

Tall trees with low branches screen your view of the pin.

Conditions are good, with little wind, and the ground is dry. The ball will run on landing.

Although the ball is in rough grass it is lying well about 140yd (128m) from the pin.

The hole is a par 5 of 520yd (475m). Your second shot has landed in the left rough behind trees and low bushes.

SAFE SHOT
Position play

If you're not sure of clearing the trees don't be content with just hacking the ball out of the rough. Choose a club which gets the ball on to the fairway well placed between the two bunkers. Bear in mind that the ball will run slightly on landing.

From this strategic position you have a clear view of the green. A straightforward short iron of about 110yd (101m) gets you to the pin followed by the possibility of a putt for par.

First and second shots
Grip: normal
Stance: normal
Ball position: center of stance
Weight distribution: even
Swing: full
Swing path: normal
Club: 9 iron

MATCH WINNER
High over trees

Ignore the risky option of hitting low under the trees. Instead play a high 7 iron over the treetops and on to the green.

Study the green from the fairway so you know exactly where the pin is. Aim the clubhead at the target with your feet slightly left of the ball-to-target line. Keep the blade a little open at address as rough grass tends to close the face at impact making the ball fly off low and to the left.

A successful approach shot gives you the chance of a birdie putt.

First shot
Grip: normal
Stance: slightly open
Ball position: opposite inside of left heel
Weight distribution: even
Swing: full
Swing path: normal
Club: 7 iron

MATCHWINNER
7 IRON
140yd (128m)

SAFE SHOT
9 IRON
100yd (91m)

9 IRON
110yd (101m)

Recovery from sand

After a badly sliced tee shot your ball has landed in a bunker.
Despite the difficult situation
you still have a good chance of par – or even a birdie -
if you make the correct moves.

The hole is a par 4 of 296yd (271m) on parkland. The green is dry and firm, making the ball roll on landing.

The flag is 42ft (13m) from the fringe of the green.

A greenside bunker is likely to trap any shots that fall short.

The face of the bunker measures 4ft (1m).

After your first shot the ball is lying in a bunker 60yd (55m) from the hole – an awkward distance to play from sand.

SAFE SHOT
Splash shot to fairway
If you aren't comfortable with your bunker shots aim just to get out of the trap. Play to the left to avoid a difficult chip over the greenside bunker.

Your approach shot involves a little chip and run on to the front of the green – the ball should roll up to the hole, leaving you a tap-in putt for par.

First shot
Grip: hands slightly lower than usual
Stance: open
Ball position: opposite left heel
Weight distribution: even
Swing: three-quarters
Swing path: out to in
Club: sand wedge

Approach shot
Grip: hands a little lower than usual
Stance: normal, but feet slightly narrower
Ball position: center of stance
Weight distribution: favoring left side
Swing: quarter
Swing path: normal
Club: 7 or 8 iron

MATCH WINNER
Mid-range bunker shot
A tricky shot, but with skillful judgement you can take a direct line to the pin. The margin of error is narrow – timing must be spot on. Make a clean strike to avoid thinning the ball and meeting the face of the bunker.

Keep away from the trees and land the ball close to the hole – the backspin stops it running on the firm green, leaving you a short putt for a great birdie opportunity.

Approach shot
Grip: normal
Stance: normal
Ball position: midway between center of stance and left heel
Weight distribution: even
Swing: three-quarters
Swing path: slightly out to in
Club: sand or pitching wedge

7 OR 8 IRON
30yd (27m)

SAFE SHOT
SAND WEDGE
40yd (37m)

MATCHWINNER
SAND OR PITCHING WEDGE
60yd (55m)

Ball below feet

A poor second shot has hooked left, leaving the ball in rough
below your feet on this heathland par 4.
Weigh up your strengths and weaknesses when considering a plan
of action for the awkward downhill lie.

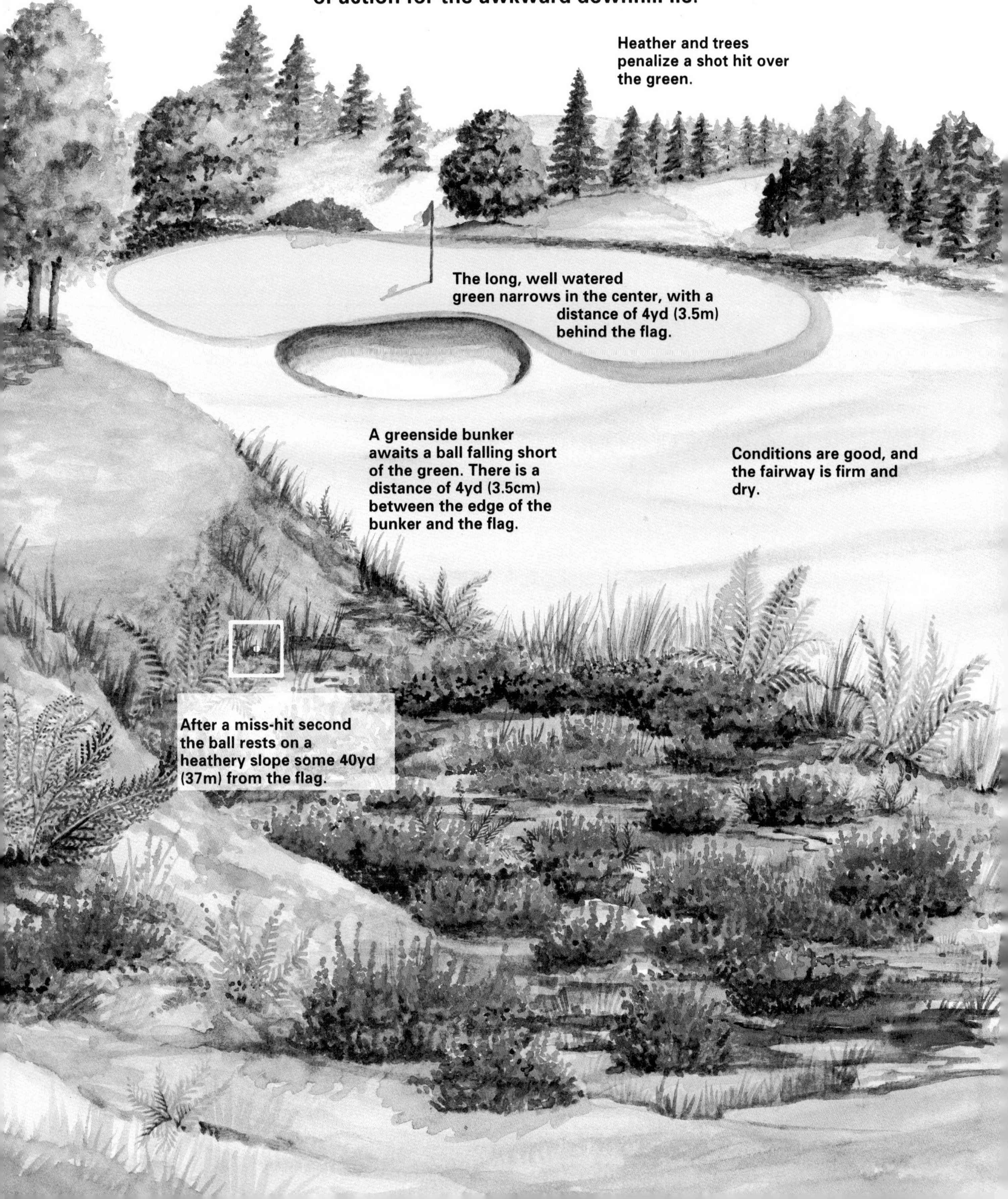

Heather and trees
penalize a shot hit over
the green.

The long, well watered
green narrows in the center, with a
distance of 4yd (3.5m)
behind the flag.

A greenside bunker
awaits a ball falling short
of the green. There is a
distance of 4yd (3.5cm)
between the edge of the
bunker and the flag.

Conditions are good, and
the fairway is firm and
dry.

After a miss-hit second
the ball rests on a
heathery slope some 40yd
(37m) from the flag.

SAFE SHOT
Low risk out of trouble

From this lie it's wise to accept your limitations and avoid the humiliation of a shank or even a complete duff. Reconcile yourself to a dropped shot and play a sand wedge safely to the middle of the fairway. Keep your knees flexed throughout the three-quarter swing. A careful chip and run over the apron has you well placed on the green.

First shot
Grip: a little lower than normal
Stance: slightly open
Ball position: opposite inside left heel
Weight distribution: just favoring left side
Swing: three-quarter
Swing path: slightly out to in
Club: sand wedge

Second shot
Grip: a little lower than normal
Stance: square
Ball position: middle of stance
Weight distribution: favoring left side
Swing: quarter
Swing path: normal
Club: 9 iron

MATCH WINNER
Pitch to the flag

It's a tricky one, but take a chance. Stay well down to keep a good posture through impact – this helps you avoid sculling the shot – and hit a neat pitch to the flag with a sand wedge. Open the blade slightly and give the shot plenty of height – it will stop quickly on the well watered green to give you a chance of par.

Take care, when you open the blade, that you don't change your grip. First lay the blade open and then grip down the club about 1in (2.5cm) lower than normal for extra control.

Grip: a little lower than usual
Stance: slightly open
Ball position: opposite inside left heel
Weight distribution: just favoring the left side
Swing: three-quarter
Swing path: slightly out to in
Club: sand wedge

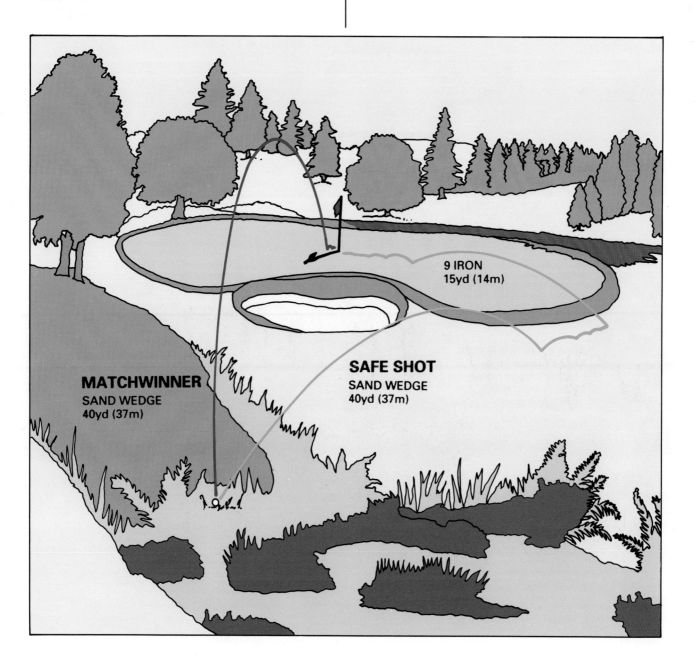

9 IRON
15yd (14m)

MATCHWINNER
SAND WEDGE
40yd (37m)

SAFE SHOT
SAND WEDGE
40yd (37m)

Sidehill tactics

**With trouble all round and the ball lying slightly above
your stance, the green is reachable
– just – but dare you risk tiger tactics? Take care.
A weak response is a card wrecker.**

The fairway slopes down to
a well watered green on
this 480yd (439m) par 5.

Conditions are good and
the fairway is dry. There is
a slight breeze which
shouldn't affect play.

Go too far right on the
fairway and trees and
rough may gather your
ball.

The fairway in front of the
green slopes down to a
lake.

A miss-hit going left is
likely to find the lake or
thick rough.

After your tee shot the
ball sits well on a sidehill
lie some 220yd (201m)
from the flag.

SAFE SHOT
Play short of trouble
This isn't a place to take risks – you need to play well within your limits to avoid a rough or watery grave. But with careful planning you can still manage a par 5.

From the sidehill lie it's easy to find water so play safely short of the pond. A ball above your feet leads to a flatter swing plane – take a short iron and you reduce the chance of a pull.

Careful placement leaves you with a reasonable 9 iron to the pin and the chance of par.

First and second shots
Grip: normal
Stance: normal
Ball position: center of stance
Weight distribution: even
Swing: three-quarter for first, full for second
Swing path: in to square to in
Club: 9 iron

PAR PLAY
Approach with caution
With a club you are confident will keep you on the fairway, place your approach as close as possible to the green. Bear in mind that a ball lying slightly above your stance promotes a draw or hook so aim the club up the middle of the fairway and align your body slightly right of the target line. You're left with a short pitch then a definite par or a single putt for birdie.

First shot
Grip: normal
Stance: slightly right of target
Ball position: opposite inside of left heel
Weight distribution: even
Swing: full
Swing path: slightly in to out
Club: 5 wood

Second shot
Grip: normal
Stance: normal
Ball position: center of stance
Weight distribution: even
Swing: three-quarter
Swing path: in to square to in
Club: pitching wedge

MATCH WINNER
Bold wood to pin
The brave golfer with a sound technique has an exciting chance of an eagle here. The green is soft enough to hold a bold fairway wood. But take care – there is a carry of some 200yd (183m) to the safety of the fringe of the green, which is no mean feat and certainly not a shot for the faint hearted or anyone struggling after distance.

As the ball is slightly above your feet you can expect a draw. Aim the club on the center of the green, align yourself slightly right of center and hit a high draw. This leaves you a putt for an eagle or a certain birdie.

Grip: normal
Stance: slightly right of target
Ball position: opposite inside of left heel
Weight distribution: even
Swing: full
Swing path: slightly in to out
Club: 3 wood

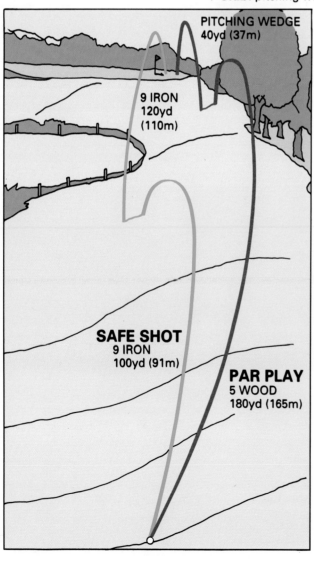

PITCHING WEDGE
40yd (37m)

9 IRON
120yd
(110m)

SAFE SHOT
9 IRON
100yd (91m)

PAR PLAY
5 WOOD
180yd (165m)

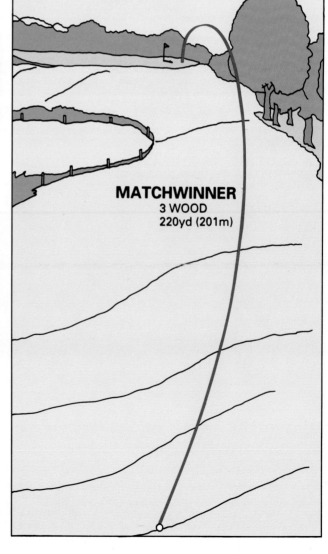

MATCHWINNER
3 WOOD
220yd (201m)

Grass bunker lie

Golf courses change over the years. Sometimes a hole may be lengthened and a bunker taken out of use. With the sand removed and long grass growing in the hollow, a disused bunker is a nasty trap. How do you escape unscathed?

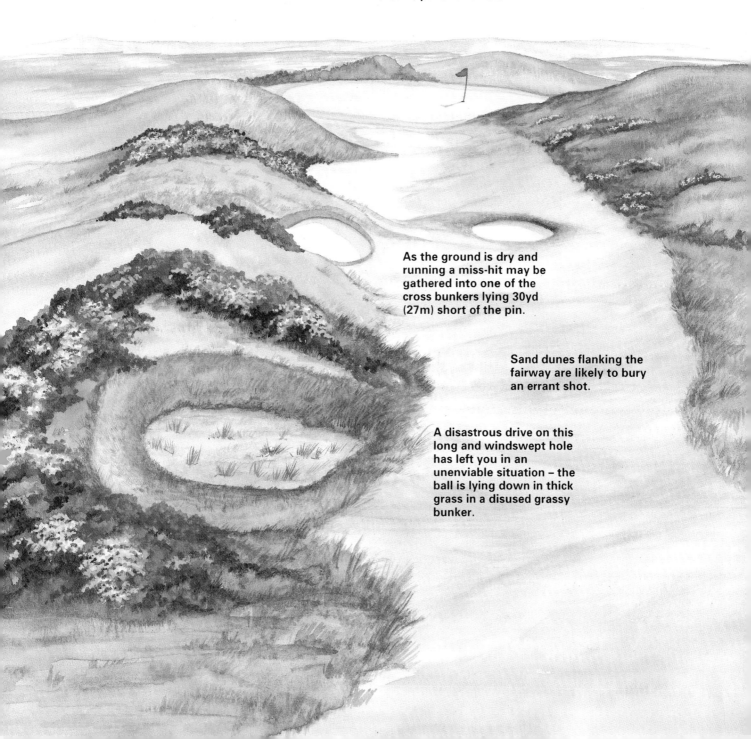

A crosswind blows from the right on this 224yd (205m) par 3 links hole.

As the ground is dry and running a miss-hit may be gathered into one of the cross bunkers lying 30yd (27m) short of the pin.

Sand dunes flanking the fairway are likely to bury an errant shot.

A disastrous drive on this long and windswept hole has left you in an unenviable situation – the ball is lying down in thick grass in a disused grassy bunker.

SAFE SHOT
Ball back into play

Resist the temptation, after your disappointing play from the tee, to go for the pin with your recovery. A lucky shot would reach the green but it's safer to limit the damage and send the ball back into play.

Although the green is only 70yd (64m) away, a weak pitch may hit the face of the old bunker and leave you with the same escape problem. Reach for your sand wedge. With its heavy sole you can cut through the long grass – treat the shot as bunker play and plan to land short of the cross traps. Pick a mid fairway spot that leaves you a clear route to the pin. A little pitch and run gives a chance of a single putt for bogey.

First and second shots
Grip: normal
Stance: normal for first shot, align slightly right of pin for second
Ball position: opposite inside of left heel for first, centre of stance for second
Weight distribution: even
Swing: three-quarter
Swing path: slightly out to in for first, in to in for second
Club: sand wedge followed by pitching wedge

MATCH WINNER
Use the wind

After a poor drive it's important not to let your temper affect the next shot. It's all too easy to allow one bad shot to ruin your card. Accept the drive as a likely dropped shot, and set all thoughts of the disastrous stroke to one side – an even frame of mind may well produce birdie opportunities later in the round.

Play a crisp sand wedge to the pin – take a pitching wedge if you're doubtful about reaching the green. Aim just right of the flag – the wind will work in your favor and bring the ball back to the center of the green. You may still single putt for par. If you take two be grateful you've limited the damage to a bogey.

Grip: normal
Stance: align right of pin
Ball position: opposite inside of left heel
Weight distribution: even
Swing: full
Swing path: in to in
Club: sand wedge

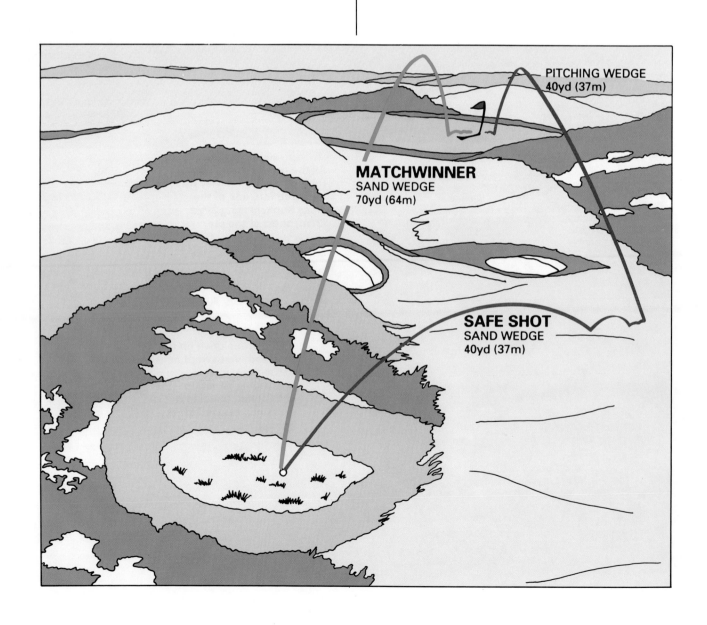

Divot decision

"Golf was never meant to be fair," said Jack Nicklaus –
but one of the most frustrating experiences
is to hit the perfect drive only to find your ball deep in
a divot mark. Here, a simple 130yd (119m)
short iron to the pin becomes very much more complicated.

The rough on the left of the fairway is about 90yd (82m) from the ball.

A shot played too safely left of the pin may roll into the large greenside bunker.

The green is dry and firm though it will hold a well struck shot.

The flag is in a tricky spot, protected by a large bunker guarding the right side of the green.

A direct shot to the green has a perilous carry over a water hazard which dominates the right.

Your ball is sitting down in a divot mark after an exhilarating drive on this 370yd (338m) par 4 parkland course.

Divot relief

 ‚) You play a ball in a divot mark as it lies, but there are exceptions – for example, you can take a free drop if the area is seeded.

 ‚) Take relief from casual water if the divot mark is full of rain – drop the ball on dry ground within one club length but not nearer the hole.

 ‚) Claim relief under winter rules – mark, lift, clean and place the ball within 6in (15cm) of the divot mark but not nearer the hole.

 ‚) A divot can be classed as a loose impediment and removed only if the clod is detached from the ground. Take care your ball doesn't move.

SAFE SHOT

Pitch left of lake

Though it's irksome to find a potentially good score threatened by another player's lack of consideration, your first challenge in this situation is to set aside your frustration after such a fine drive. Accept the rough with the smooth and turn your attention to limiting the damage.

You would be wise to avoid going over water. If panic sets in, many golfers swing too quickly, fail to turn and end up sclaffing the ball straight into the hazard. Instead, take a wedge and pitch safely left of the lake. Another easy wedge and you're close to the flag.

First and second shots
Grip: normal
Stance: normal
Ball position: center of stance
Weight distribution: even
Swing: full
Swing path: in to in
Club: pitching wedge

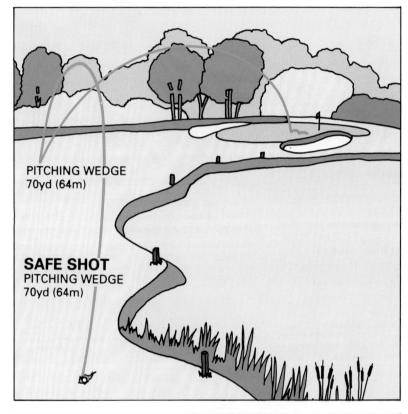

PITCHING WEDGE
70yd (64m)

SAFE SHOT
PITCHING WEDGE
70yd (64m)

MATCH WINNER

Short iron for par

Normally with this length of shot you'd head straight for the hole. But pause a while. From the divot mark there's a risk of a fat or thinned shot – you'll find sand or, worse, dump the ball in water. Exercise caution and settle for a solid shot to the middle of the green.

Keep your hands well ahead at address, with the ball 2in (5cm) further to the right. This helps you strike down on the ball, avoiding the risk of taking turf first. A crisp shot with backspin ensures the ball won't run through the firm green.

Be content with 2 putts for par. As you head for the next tee, recite to yourself Richard Armour's lines:
The divot is a piece of sod
That ought to be replaced and trod.

Grip: normal; hands ahead at address
Stance: normal
Ball position: further right than normal
Weight distribution: even
Swing: full
Swing path: in to in
Club: 8 iron

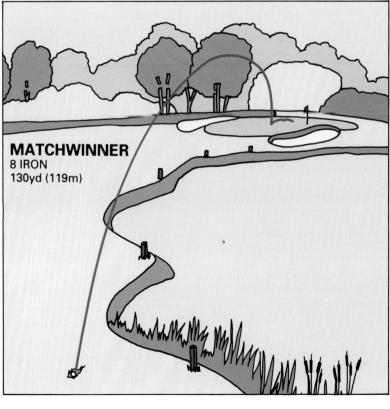

MATCHWINNER
8 IRON
130yd (119m)

Under the tree

After a long but sliced drive, getting away with
a respectable score on this
dog-leg par 4 requires great skill and a
careful choice of strategy.

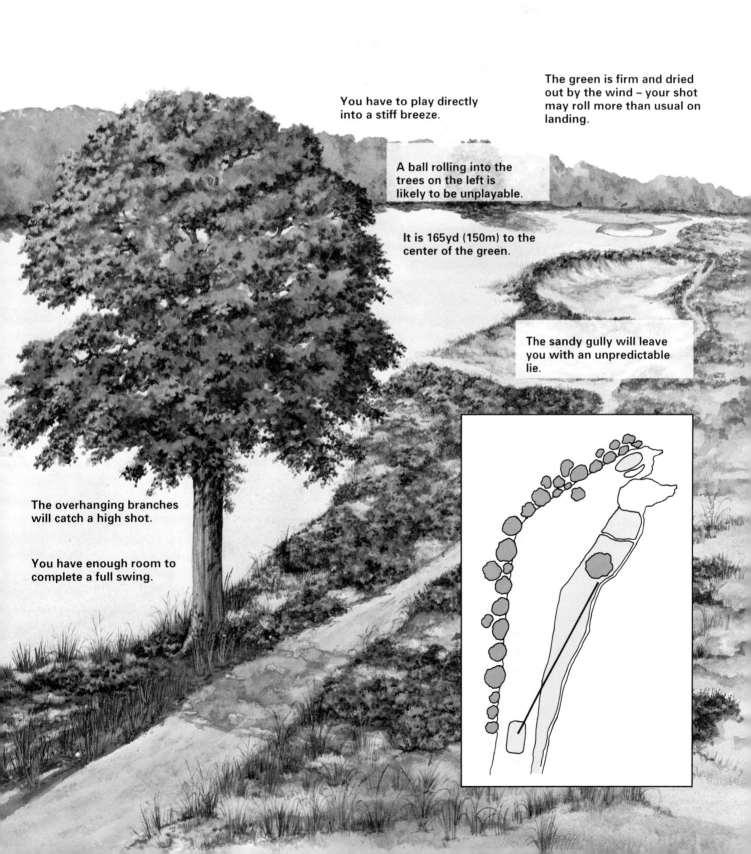

You have to play directly
into a stiff breeze.

The green is firm and dried
out by the wind – your shot
may roll more than usual on
landing.

A ball rolling into the
trees on the left is
likely to be unplayable.

It is 165yd (150m) to the
center of the green.

The sandy gully will leave
you with an unpredictable
lie.

The overhanging branches
will catch a high shot.

You have enough room to
complete a full swing.

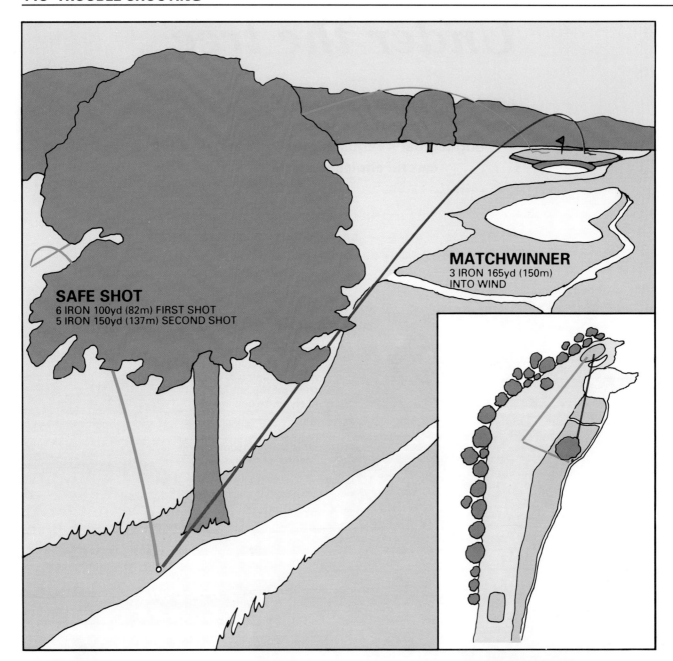

SAFE SHOT
Mid iron escape
Forget any thoughts of pulling off a Ballesteros recovery. It is more likely to result in a lost ball and unnecessary penalty shots.

Take a mid iron, as a wedge might send the ball into the tree. Chip the ball out safely below the branches. Hit firmly but with only a half swing. You don't want to shoot the ball across to the trees on the other side.

From the center of the fairway you should have no more than 150yd (137m) to the flag. Played with an easy 5 iron, you should escape with a bogey 5 or even an outside chance of making par.

First shot
Grip: 2in (5cm) lower than usual
Stance: square
Ball position: centre of stance
Weight distribution: favoring left side
Swing: half
Swing path: normal
Club: 6 iron

Second shot
Grip: normal
Stance: square
Ball position: midway between left heel and center of stance
Weight distribution: even
Swing: full
Swing path: normal
Club: easy 5 iron

MATCH WINNER
Long and low
While laying up is the safe option, it might result in a bogey 5. Take the bold approach and go for the green.

Make a full strike and don't be intimidated by the overhanging tree or you might thin the shot and find a heathery grave in the gully. Allow an extra two clubs for the wind. Select a 3 iron and aim for the pin.

Address the ball 1in (2.5 cm) further back in your stance. This ensures your shot doesn't clip the branches as it flies towards the hole.

Grip: normal
Stance: square
Ball position: midway between left heel and center of stance
Weight distribution: even
Swing: full
Swing path: normal
Club: 3 iron

MANAGING
━━ YOUR ━━
GOLF GAME

Intelligent course management is the invisible secret to low scoring. It may not manifest itself in, the same spectacular way as a 300-yard drive or a 60-foot putt, but it's just as important, if not more so. The strategies you adopt on the course determine whether good ball-striking is converted into a good score, or just an average one. Similarly, clear, sensible thinking can convert an indfifferent ball-striking round into a good score. Jack Nicklaus, the ultimate thinker, is the finest exponent of this art. The Golden Bear would be the first to say that yes, a great swing is an asset, but only if it is combined with a smart brain. This chapter can help you make good decisions on the golf course.

Parkland plights

Each style of course has it's own way of being played. But you
must also be prepared to change the standard
type of shot to suit the conditions. When a parkland course
becomes slightly soggy you must make a few minor changes in
your technique to ensure crisp striking.

Q Now and again I fat
my irons off the
fairway – especially in
damp conditions – and the
ball goes nowhere. Why?

A The nature of
parkland turf is very
unforgiving to anything
but a crisp strike. The soil
is heavy – especially when
it's wet – and if the blade
catches the ground even a
fraction behind the ball
the clubhead snags. Turf
gets between the blade
and the ball, and the shot
is fatted.

On a soggy, muddy
fairway, positioning the
ball as normal – inside the
left heel for a long iron –
increases the chances of
hitting the fat. Just a slight
fault on the downswing
means you can't
guarantee striking the ball
first – critical for crisp
hitting.

Move it back
The simple way to better
your striking and avoid the
fat is to move the ball back
in your stance. The
change needn't be drastic
– just an inch further back.

This naturally lessens
the risk of fatting since it
increases the chances of
striking the ball before the
ground. The club attacks
the ball from a slightly
steeper angle than normal
and the shot is squeezed
off the turf.

NORMAL
FORWARD
BALL POSITION

EASY TO
HIT SLIGHTLY
BEHIND BALL

SOGGY AND MUDDY
GROUND STOPS
CLUBHEAD – SHOT FATTED

BALL FURTHER
BACK IN STANCE

CRISP STRIKE

ABLE TO RELEASE FULLY

SHOT FLIES TRUE

Q Why do I regularly duff short pitches, especially from poor lies?

A Playing the shot with too little force is one of the most common reasons for duffing a short pitch from a claggy parkland lie. If you play the stroke without conviction and a firm, purposeful action, it is easy to quit on the ball, catch the heavy ground and fluff the shot.

Addressing the ball as normal – aligned square to target – doesn't allow you to play as full a shot as you need to ensure a firm and forceful strike. You try to play the shot too delicately and the heavy ground can easily grab the clubhead.

Bunker blast

The way to conquer the duffs is to play your short pitches with a bunker style technique. Align left of the target but keep the blade square. You can then afford to make a fuller swing than normal without the fear of hitting the ball too far. The firmer the swing, the less likely you are to quit on the ball through impact.

Be forceful and take whatever lies behind the ball with the shot – like you do with sand in a bunker. The firm swing prevents the ball from being fatted even if you take a bit of mud and grass with the shot.

PITCHING WITH NORMAL TECHNIQUE FROM POOR LIE – EASY TO QUIT

CLUB CATCHES BALL HEAVY – SHOT FLUFFED

BUNKER TECHNIQUE – FIRM ATTACK FROM OUTSIDE LINE

CLUB TAKES GRASS AND BALL ABLE TO SWING THROUGH FULLY

Hitches on the heath

Heathland courses are thinking golfers' courses. You need to plan and swing to the best of your ability to keep the ball on the fairways, as missing them is very penal. But if you find heather, the recovery shot needn't be traumatic. A simple change in set-up and a little luck should do the trick.

Q When I knock a ball into heather, my recovery usually hooks, sometimes into further trouble. Why?

A Heather is tough stuff and cutting a clear path through it is hard work. If the ball is sitting down, you need to be forceful to have a chance of getting the ball out. But as you strike hard down on the ball the heather tends to wrap itself around your club.

As the shaft tangles with the heather the club turns in your hands and the blade closes. If you set up with the clubface square and swing normally, your blade shuts slightly at impact and the shot is hooked. The amount it moves from right to left depends on the toughness of the undergrowth and which club you have hit.

Open and shut blade

You must alter your normal set-up to counter the effect of the blade closing through impact. Address the ball with the clubface slightly open – aiming a fraction right of the target line. Align square as normal and then make your usual swing.

Just before impact the blade is still open, but as soon as the club comes into contact with the heather it begins to shut. At the point of impact the blade should be square and the shot flies true.

There is a little luck involved, but this action is still more accurate than if you swing with a square blade into impact.

NORMAL ATTACK – BLADE SQUARE COMING INTO IMPACT

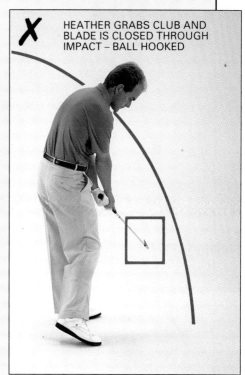

HEATHER GRABS CLUB AND BLADE IS CLOSED THROUGH IMPACT – BALL HOOKED

OPEN CLUBFACE INTO IMPACT

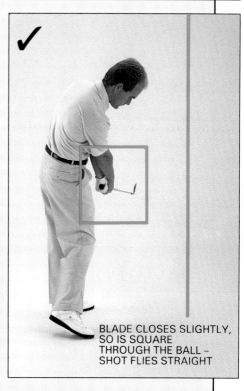

BLADE CLOSES SLIGHTLY, SO IS SQUARE THROUGH THE BALL – SHOT FLIES STRAIGHT

Q When I play on a heathland I find it hard to hit the fairway. My tee shots seem to be shorter and more wayward than usual. Why?

A A heathland can be an intimidating arena, because you know that if you miss the fairway the recovery shot is difficult. The fairways begin to look tighter than they are, and so your confidence sags and your action becomes tentative and stiff.

Your backswing is shorter than normal and your arms and wrists tense. Very little clubhead speed is generated on the downswing and you try to guide the ball down the hole with no release of the hands. You finish high over your head and the ball flies off line.

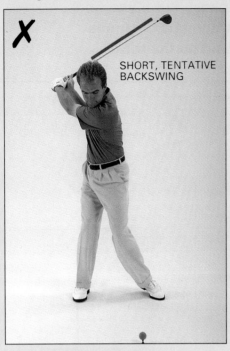

X SHORT, TENTATIVE BACKSWING

X BALL GUIDED DOWN HOLE

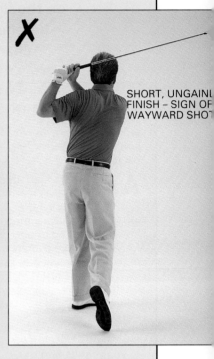

X SHORT, UNGAINL FINISH – SIGN OF WAYWARD SHO

✓ FULL, POSITIVE BACKSWING

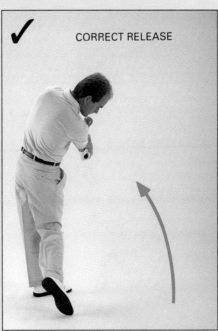

✓ CORRECT RELEASE

✓ FULL, BALANCED FINIS SHOT FIRED STRAIGHT

Free swinging

To conquer a heathland course and keep the ball on the fairways, you must have a free swinging action and confident mental approach. Take care with your aim and alignment and then have the courage to let rip. Make your backswing full and feel relaxed – don't grip the club too tightly. Swing down freely and unleash a powerful strike through the ball, remembering to release your hands after impact.

This flowing action naturally leads you into a full throughswing position and the ball should bisect the fairway.

You should also use this technique on your approach shots. A smooth, controlled swing is critical for accurate iron play, to help avoid the inevitable trouble around the greens.

Lush course struggles

Keeping the ball under control on and around the greens on a
lush US-type course can be a problem for all
standards of golfer. But by using specific techniques you can be
confident of retaining your touch on the fast putting
surfaces and even out of the thick greenside rough.

Q When I miss a green I find it very difficult to play a controlled chip to the hole. Most of the time my ball flies out quite low and running, often rolling well past the flag. Why is this?

A Greenside chipping from bermuda type grass needs a slightly different technique to normal. If you try to play a delicate chip from the thick fringe by aligning square to the target and swinging from in to in, the blade tends to tangle with the grass and close slightly through impact. You can't play the shot with any real force.

Because the clubface shuts, the loft of your wedge lessens and the ball comes out of the grass low and a fraction right of target. It also has no backspin and runs on landing – making it difficult to control.

X NORMAL IN-TO-IN ATTACK
FROM LUSH GRASS – TEND
TO CLOSE BLADE SLIGHTLY

X BALL FLIES OUT
LOW AND RUNNING –
HARD TO CONTROL

Open control

Because the grass is wiry and tough, and the greens fast, you need to play a forceful shot – to make sure the ball comes out – but one that pops up and lands softly. The more lofted the blade is, the more forceful you can be and the higher the ball flies.

To play this shot, align left of target but keep the blade square. This has the effect of opening up the clubface. Play the stroke like a bunker shot – swing along the line of your feet so the attack is from out to in – and hit behind the ball. Take any grass with the shot and hold your blade square for as long as possible through impact. Be forceful – don't quit on the shot. The ball should pop up gently and roll out to the flag.

✓ STANCE WELL OPEN –
OUT-TO-IN ATTACK

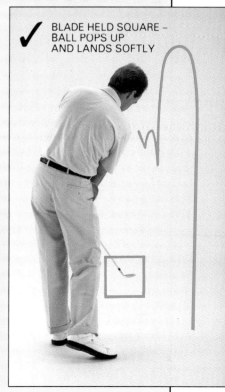

✓ BLADE HELD SQUARE –
BALL POPS UP
AND LANDS SOFTLY

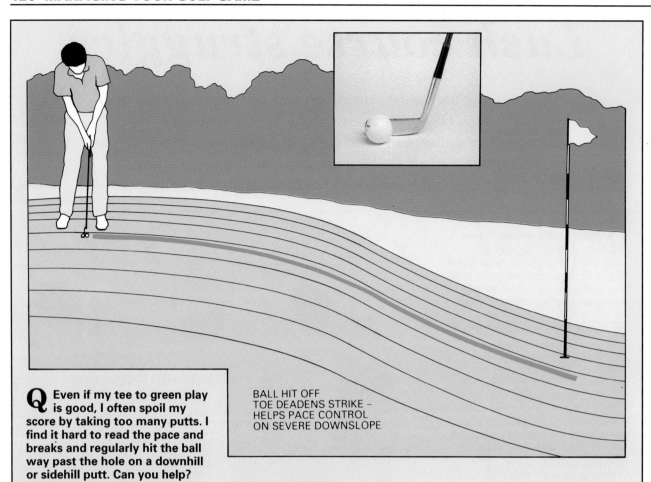

BALL HIT OFF
TOE DEADENS STRIKE –
HELPS PACE CONTROL
ON SEVERE DOWNSLOPE

Q Even if my tee to green play is good, I often spoil my score by taking too many putts. I find it hard to read the pace and breaks and regularly hit the ball way past the hole on a downhill or sidehill putt. Can you help?

A On a fast, steeply sloping green, a downhill putt often just needs to be set off so that the slope takes the ball down to the hole. If you set up normally and strike the putt out of the sweet spot as usual, the ball tends to race off the face too quickly. It gathers pace down the hill and unless it hits the hole can run a long way by.

To guard against the runaway putt you need to deaden the strike so that the ball sets off slowly down the hill. Address the ball with the toe of your putter and use your normal stroke. The ball barely comes off the face so trickles slowly down the hill, making it easier to control.

Your inability to get the ball close on a breaking putt is usually down to miss-reading the slope. On fast, lush greens the ball breaks more than on normal putting surfaces. Because they're slick you have to hit the ball with less force than you usually do.

The ball runs slower than normal so has more time to be affected by the slope. If you find yourself missing on the low side give the ball a wider berth than you expect. You may be surprised how much the ball falls from the top side just when you think it has come to a standstill.

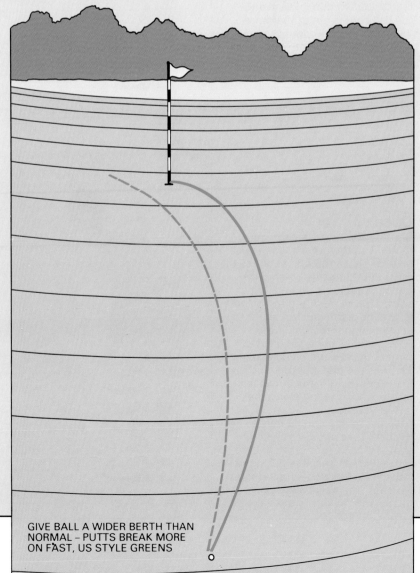

GIVE BALL A WIDER BERTH THAN
NORMAL – PUTTS BREAK MORE
ON FAST, US STYLE GREENS

Where to tee off

You can give yourself an easier and safer shot if you know where best to tee off from. It's the only place on the course you can choose exactly where to stand, so make the most of it.

Always tee up in a position to aim away from hazards on a hole – never towards them. Hit from the left edge of the tee if there is trouble to the left of the fairway. Visualize a spot on the right side of the fairway and fire away. You can then hit away from potential disaster and increase your margin for error.

WITHIN THE RULES

When the greenkeeper places the tee boxes 20 paces apart, use every inch available to you. There's no rule stating you have to stand in the middle of the two markers every time you tee up.

The rules of golf state you can

Even on a straightforward golf hole, it's vital you make your tee shot as easy as possible. With lots of trees and a bunker on the right that's clearly not the side to hit your ball. Tee up on the right and aim to hit the ball down the left side of the fairway.

stand outside the tee markers if you wish, providing the ball itself is positioned between them. It can be placed not more than two club lengths behind the markers.

Be careful where you leave your bag when you walk from a green to the next tee. Try to place it out of sight if you've left it well down the fairway – it's distracting to have a bag in your line of sight when you tee off. You also lose the hole if your ball hits your bag or your partner's bag in matchplay. In strokeplay the penalty is 2 shots.

Never feel pressurized into playing a tee shot you're not ready to hit. If you're distracted on the tee by someone or something, step

MENTAL FEAR
Simply knowing where the trouble is on a hole is often enough to make you hit your ball there. Standing on the left to shoot away from the trees and bunkers makes the tee shot safer – it removes some of the mental fear you may feel about the hole.

away and start your pre-shot routine again. You are unlikely to hit a good shot if your concentration is broken.

CUTTING CORNERS

Think carefully about where you tee off on a dog-leg hole to make sure you gain maximum advantage. When a fairway bends left to right, hit from the left edge of the

TEE TIME

▶CLEAN GOLF BALL
Many courses provide a ball washer on every tee – so keep your golf ball clean whenever possible. A clean ball is more important than you might think – its flight is impaired if the dimples are clogged up with mud and grass. It doesn't fly as far in the air and may veer slightly off line.

BIGGER TARGET
By teeing up on the left you give yourself a larger target area to aim at. The smooth, flat lie gives you the best chance of making clean contact with the ball.

pro tip

Choose a good patch
Always tee up on a good, flat patch of turf with no lumps and bumps behind the ball. Tread down the ground around your ball if you wish – something you can do on the tee only. This helps to prevent the clubhead catching in grass on the backswing. Teeing up on a slope can cause you to hook or slice the ball, so make sure you give yourself an even stance.

RIGHT IS WRONG
Teeing up on the right with trouble lurking on the left is risky here – you're aiming towards the trees and bunkers. The tee is the only place you can choose your lie and your position so select your spot carefully – but don't take so long that you delay play. Place your ball anywhere within the two markers and up to two club lengths behind them.

Watch your shadow
Don't cast a shadow over or near your playing partner's ball when he is about to tee off. If it's ever happened to you, you'll know how distracting shadows can be. Stand well clear and remember the etiquette of golf – keep quiet and still while your partners play their shots. They should show you the same courtesy in return.

teeing area. This helps you cut off more of the corner and leaves you in a better position from which to hit your second shot.

You don't have to flail away with your driver every time you step on the tee of a par 4 or 5. In most cases, good position is more important than distance. Study carefully what's in front of you. If the fairway narrows at around the distance you hit a driver, use a long iron or lofted wood to land the ball short of the trouble. Playing safe is advisable – taking risks often leads to disaster.

Playing a hole in a crosswind can be made easier by knowing where to stand on the tee. In a right to left breeze, hit from the left side of the tee. You can then play a shot with the ball held up into the wind.

If you tee up on the right side, you play with the wind. This is fine if you want maximum distance, but your control over the ball is greatly reduced. A ball curving slightly one way or the other is blown wildly off line.

Where to stand
You risk being hit by a club if you stand directly behind your partner while he plays his shot. The ideal place is to face your partner at address but stand well away and slightly behind his ball. In this way you're in no danger of being hit by a club. You're not in the player's line of vision either.

Playing par 3s

T hink of some courses you know well – you're probably faced with longer shots into greens on par 3s than on most other holes on the course. Few par 5s leave you with more than a mid iron approach into the green, and almost every course has its share of short par 4s.

To add to the challenge, more bunkers often lie in wait around par 3s. Steer clear of the sand and you're handsomely rewarded for finding these closely guarded greens – but you are severely punished for a wayward shot.

While poor technique is sometimes the golfer's downfall, a strategic error is more often the culprit. Simply improving your course management is bound to lower your short hole scores.

Par 3s can measure as long as 250yd (229m) so in a golfing lifetime you come across many that are out of reach from the tee. In

CLOSELY GUARDED
You often make or break your score on the par 3s because these can be the hardest to play. Whether they're protected by bunkers, water or both, the short hole label certainly disguises their difficulty.

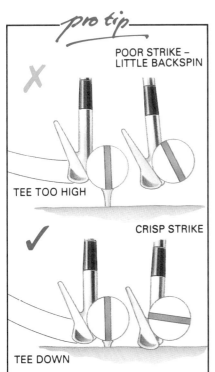

pro tip

POOR STRIKE –
LITTLE BACKSPIN

X

TEE TOO HIGH

✓

CRISP STRIKE

TEE DOWN

Tee down to hit down
Always use a tee peg on a par 3 for the best possible lie. But don't make the mistake of teeing the ball too high (top view) when you use an iron.

The ball should sit only fractionally above ground level to encourage you to strike down into impact (lower view). This is the ideal angle of attack to produce crisp iron shots and generate the backspin you need (see red line).

If you tee up too high for an iron it's impossible to hit down on the ball and strike successfully – you're almost certain to scoop at impact which usually leads to disaster. Miss-hits are more likely – even when you do strike the ball cleanly the flight lacks penetration and backspin is scarce.

these situations forget that the hole is meant to be completed in 3 strokes.

Set yourself a more realistic goal instead. If you lay up short, the worst you're likely to score is 4 – which is far from disastrous, whatever your handicap. With the help of a chip and a putt, occasionally you walk off with a par.

Don't feel intimidated if one of your fellow competitors launches his ball on to a distant green. Swing smoothly and continue to play your own game. It's when you start forcing shots that disaster strikes.

On a par 3 that's in range, try not to be influenced by powerful hitters who take much less club than you. While you can always learn from someone else's shot, it's seldom advisable to stray far from your original choice.

GREENKEEPER'S TRAP

The pin position can alter the degree of difficulty on any hole, particularly a par 3.

If the greenkeeper tucks the flag in behind a bunker, or tantalizingly close to the edge of the green, don't fall into his trap by going for the hole. The center of the green is never a bad position and always sets you up for a 3.

When you fire straight at the pin there's usually more to lose than gain. Unless you're hitting a very lofted club, play the percentages and avoid flirting with danger.

Think before you tee up your ball – don't just casually place it anywhere. What looks difficult from the left corner of the teeing area can often appear easier from the right. Take advantage of any opportunity to make a hole easier – this relieves pressure so you're more likely to make a good swing.

TRIO OF THREES

SHORT PAR 3 – 130yd (119m)

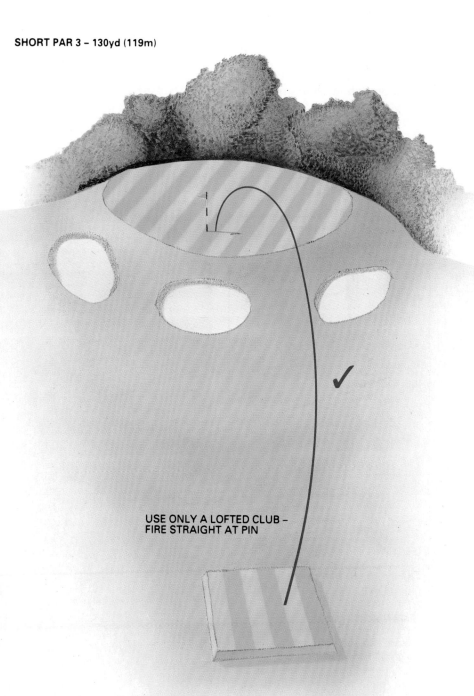

USE ONLY A LOFTED CLUB – FIRE STRAIGHT AT PIN

The choice is yours
When you don't have the honor on a par 3, resist the temptation to tee up on your partner's peg just for convenience. It may not be at the right height for you and there's certainly no guarantee it's in the best place. Always decide for yourself where on the tee to hit from.

SHORT HOLE STRATEGY
The most positive way to look at short par 3s is to imagine you've just hit a fine drive down a tough par 4 – you're in perfect position with the ball lying well.

There's no more than 130yd (119m) between you and the flag. This is the time to attack. Pitch the ball all the way to the flag – strike firmly to avoid the bunkers

guarding the front of the green.

A shot with a lofted iron has plenty of height and should stop pretty quickly. Only when the green is very hard do you need to allow for some bounce and run on landing. Take note of the wind – a high shot is bound to be affected by any breeze that's about so you may need to alter your club selection.

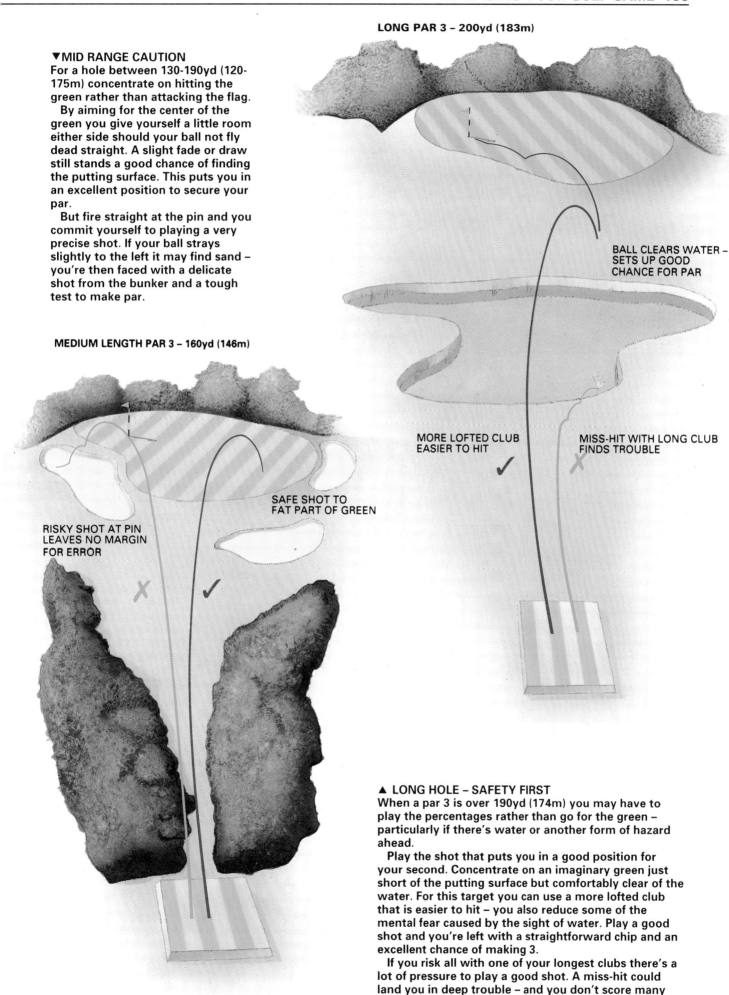

LONG PAR 3 – 200yd (183m)

BALL CLEARS WATER –
SETS UP GOOD
CHANCE FOR PAR

MORE LOFTED CLUB
EASIER TO HIT
✓

MISS-HIT WITH LONG CLUB
FINDS TROUBLE
✗

▼MID RANGE CAUTION

For a hole between 130-190yd (120-175m) concentrate on hitting the green rather than attacking the flag.

By aiming for the center of the green you give yourself a little room either side should your ball not fly dead straight. A slight fade or draw still stands a good chance of finding the putting surface. This puts you in an excellent position to secure your par.

But fire straight at the pin and you commit yourself to playing a very precise shot. If your ball strays slightly to the left it may find sand – you're then faced with a delicate shot from the bunker and a tough test to make par.

MEDIUM LENGTH PAR 3 – 160yd (146m)

SAFE SHOT TO
FAT PART OF GREEN

RISKY SHOT AT PIN
LEAVES NO MARGIN
FOR ERROR

▲ LONG HOLE – SAFETY FIRST

When a par 3 is over 190yd (174m) you may have to play the percentages rather than go for the green – particularly if there's water or another form of hazard ahead.

Play the shot that puts you in a good position for your second. Concentrate on an imaginary green just short of the putting surface but comfortably clear of the water. For this target you can use a more lofted club that is easier to hit – you also reduce some of the mental fear caused by the sight of water. Play a good shot and you're left with a straightforward chip and an excellent chance of making 3.

If you risk all with one of your longest clubs there's a lot of pressure to play a good shot. A miss-hit could land you in deep trouble – and you don't score many pars from water.

PAR 3 PRE-SHOT ROUTINE

Consider the pin position and decide if it's better to go for the flag or play safe to the middle of the green.

Use your yardage chart to check how far it is to carry any hazards such as water.

Take plenty of club if there's more trouble in front of the green than at the back.

Decide on the best position to tee up. By altering the angle of your approach shot you can make a hole easier.

165
PAR 3

CHECKLIST FOR SUCCESS
As well as the more eye-catching characteristics of par 3s there are several less obvious points you should be aware of:
⊃ Note if you're playing from the forward or back tees. Your yardage chart may not take this into account.
⊃ Check the length of the hole. Remember that most yardages are measured to the center of the green.
⊃ Take wind speed into account when you select your club.

⊃ Pitch the ball up to the flag if the greens are holding – allow for a little bounce if the putting surface is firm. Depending on the ground conditions on the day, your club selection may vary by 1 or 2.
⊃ If the teeing area is in poor condition, remember you can go 2 club lengths further back from the markers. Here you may find a patch of ground that has suffered little wear and offers you a better lie.

Exception to the rules
Think twice before you pick and place on par 3s in the winter. Many courses do not allow you this luxury on the short holes, so make sure you check the noticeboard in the clubhouse. If you're in any doubt, play the ball as it lies. It's better to be safe than sorry.

Playing par 4s

Par 4s vary more in length than any other type of hole in golf. They can measure from 250yd (229m) to well over 450yd (411m), so it's important you establish a game plan for each one – whether short, medium or long.

SHORT PAR 4S

These holes are an inviting feature of almost every course. Around the 300yd (274m) mark, they come as welcome relief from some of the longer holes.

While they're definite birdie opportunities, you should still treat short 4s with respect and al-

ways be content with par. The lack of length is sometimes more than made up for by tight fairways which test your accuracy off the tee – and there's seldom much room for error with your approach shot.

Good position off the tee is far more important than hitting the ball a huge distance. A lofted wood is likely to leave you with little more than a lofted iron approach into the green. Be happy to sacrifice distance in order to play your second shot from a good lie on the fairway.

Short par 4s provide great theatre for the public in professional

DRIVING TEST
There's a real mixture of par 4s on every course – they include inviting birdie opportunities, run of the mill holes and severe tests where 4 is quite an achievement. Whichever hole you're on, the drive is often the most critical shot. Successfully send your ball down the fairway and you're in good position to make par on the tough holes – and notch up the occasional birdie on the shorter par 4s.

STARTING OFF ON A PAR 4

1 **PRE-SWING STRATEGY**
Take time to survey the hole and pick out where the danger lies off the tee – this dictates the line you choose. Always aim at a precise spot – imagine where you would like to play your second shot from if you could walk down and place your ball on the fairway. The tree on the left is not in play off the tee but it could cause problems with your approach, so the right side of the fairway is the ideal spot.

2 **DECISION MADE**
Tee up only when you're certain of the shot you want to play. Study the teeing area and decide which is the best side to hit from – make sure you choose a flat piece of ground and an evenly mown patch of grass. But don't dither so long that you hold up other players. A spot close to the right tee marker lets you fire straight down that side of the fairway.

3 **LINING UP**
As you adopt your address position, seek out a mark – perhaps a leaf or bit of mud – a few yards in front of you along the intended line of your ball. This gives you a visual aid to align the clubface correctly. Once you're comfortable with your set-up, centre your attention on the target. Blinker your vision so you see only the landing area down the fairway – try to block out any distractions.

4 **SUCCESSFUL TEE SHOT**
A benefit of the pre-shot routine is to focus your mind on what you *should* do – this encourages you to trust your swing and banish negative thoughts. You begin to feel increasingly confident of your address position – so you can concentrate fully on tempo and make a smooth swing. Stage one of your par 4 strategy is successfully performed.

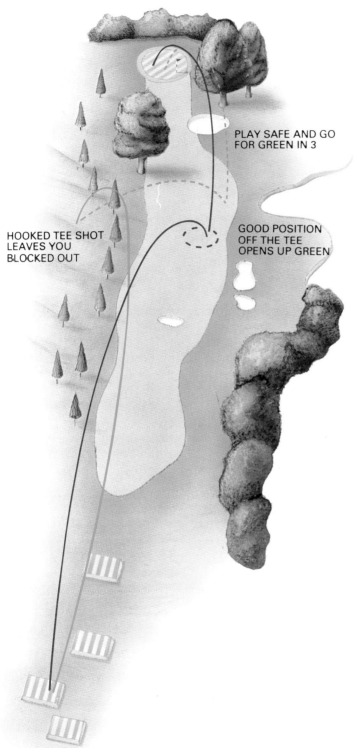

PLAY SAFE AND GO
FOR GREEN IN 3

HOOKED TEE SHOT
LEAVES YOU
BLOCKED OUT

GOOD POSITION
OFF THE TEE
OPENS UP GREEN

ATTACK POSITION

1 **MASTER THE APPROACH**
Intelligent placement off the tee pays dividends on your second shot. You open up the entire green and can thread a path between the hazards instead of picking your way over or under them. From around 140yd (128m) you want maximum control – a 7 or 8 iron lets you swing with ease and helps you avoid forcing the shot. Once you're over the ball try not to let second thoughts creep into your head.

2 **STICK TO BASICS**
When you're faced with a straightforward shot keep it simple – resist the temptation to try anything fancy. You should consider manufacturing a shot only when the wind is blowing hard. Fire straight at the flag – it's positioned in the center of the green which allows you a little margin for error either side.

THE RIGHT LINE

It's important to take the correct line off the tee when you play any hole – this is especially true on par 4s that are comfortably reachable in 2 shots.

Your main aim is to give yourself a clear line into the green. From the right side of the fairway you remove the tree on the left from your path. This paves the way for you to shoot straight at the flag.

If you stray too far to the left you're faced with an extremely tough shot to find the green. You either have to keep the ball very low or high – both are fraught with danger and you're likely to drop a couple of shots if the gamble doesn't pay off. Play out sideways instead and settle for hitting the green in 3.

Losing control
When a par 4 is well out of reach in 2 there's nothing to gain by pulling out all the stops. It's probably a direct road to disaster, as any mistakes are exaggerated when you're hitting the ball hard. It takes only one loose shot to land you in serious trouble – a high score then threatens your card. Swing within yourself.

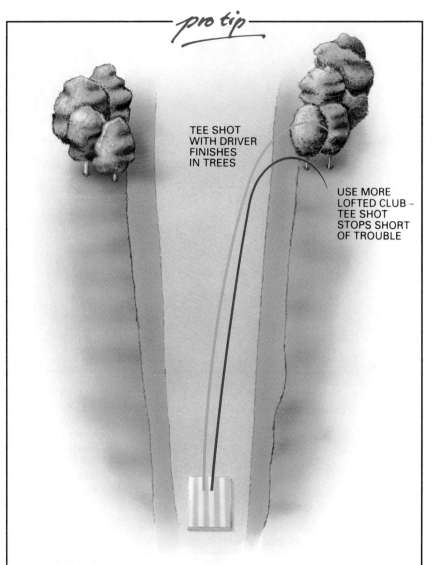

TEE SHOT WITH DRIVER FINISHES IN TREES

USE MORE LOFTED CLUB – TEE SHOT STOPS SHORT OF TROUBLE

tournaments – the Ryder Cup has made the 10th at The Belfry one of the most famous and exciting holes in golf. It's short and invites you to go for the green, but the hole is surrounded by danger. Attempting to imitate the impressive feats of top players is extremely risky.

There are a few exceptions when it pays to pull out your driver and launch the ball as close to the green as possible. For instance, if you're in a relaxed fourball game or looking for birdies in a competition, it can be just the sort of confidence booster you need.

MEDIUM LENGTH PAR 4s

The majority of par 4s range from 330-420yd (302-384m). In calm conditions most of these holes can comfortably be hit in regulation, so don't automatically reach for your driver.

Look at the yardages – it might be wise to step down to a 3 wood or long iron to increase your control off the tee. These percentage clubs help you find the fairway and make your second shot easier.

Fairway bunkers are often strategically placed to catch your drive on a par 4, but careful club selection can prevent you from falling into the course designer's trap. Lay up short of the bunkers and you eliminate the danger. A well placed tee shot still puts you in good position to reach the green, or at least get very close with your second.

Don't risk flirting with fairway bunkers unless you have to – a well struck drive can easily be punished by sand. And if your ball finds a bad lie or rests against the lip of the bunker, trying to salvage par is an almost impossible task.

Cutting your losses
Every golfer knows from painful experience that a wayward tee shot seldom finishes in good shape. But if you're sensible about club selection you can at least limit the damage to your score.

Choose a more lofted club for safety if there is a copse of trees about the range you hit your driver – the loss in distance is unlikely to push the green out of reach in 2. If you stray slightly off line your ball finishes short of the trees and in a position where you can play a recovery shot down the fairway.

With the driver you can hit the ball on exactly the same line, yet find far more serious trouble in the trees. You're likely to be blocked out completely and face no other option but to play out sideways or even backwards. This is severe punishment for just one stray shot.

MASTER THE MONSTERS

Some long par 4s stretch out to well over 450yd (412m) and are arguably the most demanding holes in golf. While psychologically the pressure is on you to take 4 strokes on any par 4 – regardless of length – it's better to decide on a more sensible approach and treat these holes as par 5s.

Keep the ball in play and you're likely to need only a lofted iron for your third on even the longest of par 4s. A good approach shot gives you a real chance of making a 4. You can be pretty confident of dropping no more than 1 shot to par – far from disastrous.

Par 4s that are distant dreams in calm conditions are suddenly in range with a tail wind in your favour. But it works both ways – holes that you usually reach in regulation may be out of range into a head wind, so don't be fooled by past experiences. Play as the conditions dictate.

Playing par 5s

On no other type of hole does the mental attitude between confident and hesitant golfers contrast more than on par 5s – it's the invisible feature that makes the difference between success and failure.

The yardage on the card often intimidates many club players. To the low handicapper and professional, the holes are seen as birdie opportunities – irrespective of length. You can't birdie every hole, but you can take the fear out of all par 5s if you approach them sensibly.

While they're the longest holes in golf, they are often the easiest to play. All but the very longest par 5 can be hit in regulation. And

GOING BOLDLY

Par 5s pose questions every inch of the way – from the moment you step on to the tee until your ball drops into the hole. Usually you must rely on an accurate approach shot followed by a rock solid putt to secure your birdie. But when you're in good position and on top of your game it often pays to seize the initiative and go for the green in 2.

MASTER THE FAIRWAY WOOD

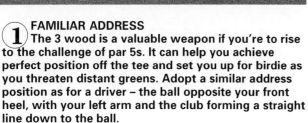

① FAMILIAR ADDRESS
The 3 wood is a valuable weapon if you're to rise to the challenge of par 5s. It can help you achieve perfect position off the tee and set you up for birdie as you threaten distant greens. Adopt a similar address position as for a driver – the ball opposite your front heel, with your left arm and the club forming a straight line down to the ball.

② WIDE AWAY
Sweep the club away from the ball low and wide – concentrate on making a one piece takeaway with your arms and shoulders moving in harmony. This triggers a full shoulder turn which helps you to build a wide arc into your swing. The left hand should dominate the backswing with the right hand helping you to maintain control of the clubhead.

if you play three shots with a 4 iron you can find yourself comfortably putting for birdie on most par 5s.

Pars and birdies are the result of planning your strategy when you stand on the tee – then carrying it through to the end. High scores usually stem from forcing the issue – just because you're on a long hole there's no need to bash the ball as far as possible.

ON THE TEE

Sending a good drive on its way boosts your confidence and puts you in strong position for your next shot. Before you tee up, select an exact spot on the fairway where you want the ball to finish.

Even on the widest of fairways, without a tree or bunker in sight, targeting a mark in the distance ensures you never forget about your alignment. It also helps focus your mind on the task at hand and block out potential trouble from your vision.

Don't fall into the trap of thinking that anywhere on the fairway

will do – this is too careless an approach. If you give yourself a wide and loosely defined landing area to aim at, a sloppy shot often follows. This is likely to put pressure on your next shot.

Resist the temptation to open your shoulders to give the ball a good thump off the tee unless there's a wide fairway stretched out in front of you. Even then, go cautiously. It's possible to miss the most inviting of fairways when you're really striving for extra distance.

SECOND SHOT STRATEGY

There aren't too many par 5s that are comfortably reachable in 2, so usually you're looking for position to play your approach from. You may need to use any club from a mid iron to a 3 wood – making the right choice is almost as important as the shot itself.

Study a yardage chart if you're not familiar with the course, and make careful note of any form of trouble lurking ahead. Lay up short of hazards unless you're sure you

can clear them with ease. The consequences of landing in trouble are often serious – while if the gamble pays off the benefits are not always reflected on your card.

Playing to your strengths is one of the keys to scoring well, so put yourself in positions that generate confidence whenever possible. If your favorite club is an 8 iron, remember this before you hit

pro tip

Keeping your distance
On a par 5 where hazards guard the front of the green, it's a good idea to leave yourself a full shot into the flag. Playing a firm, positive stroke is the best way to fly over trouble and also helps you stop the ball quickly on the green.

If you move closer to the green the shot doesn't necessarily become more straightforward. A half pitch over a hazard is a demanding test and can easily go wrong.

3 SOLID AT THE TOP
At the top of the backswing most of your weight should be on the right side – the right knee is flexed and acting as a brace to help you remain steady over the ball. Note how the upper back faces the target and the left shoulder is tucked under the chin – both are signs of a complete shoulder turn. The clubhead should stop as near to horizontal as possible – a nicely controlled position.

4 DOWN AND THROUGH
It's a long shot but you should always stay in control of your swing – remember, distance is achieved through effortless power not powerless effort. The ball is cleanly swept off the turf rather like a tee shot with a driver. If you have a less than perfect lie, a small divot is almost inevitable. The left wrist remains firm and your arms should extend low through the hitting area.

5 FREE FLOWING
Your right hand applies the power, rolling over the left after impact. The hands and club are moving very quickly through the ball, but you should still be in complete control of your swing. Your right shoulder driving under your chin brings your head up – there's no sign of an early, anxious look for the ball.

6 JUST REWARD
Impeccable weight transfer during the swing enables you to hold the followthrough position as you watch the ball fly towards its intended target. This classical finish is the reward for making the correct moves throughout the swing – it's impossible to achieve if faults have crept in earlier.

SPACIOUS PAR 5

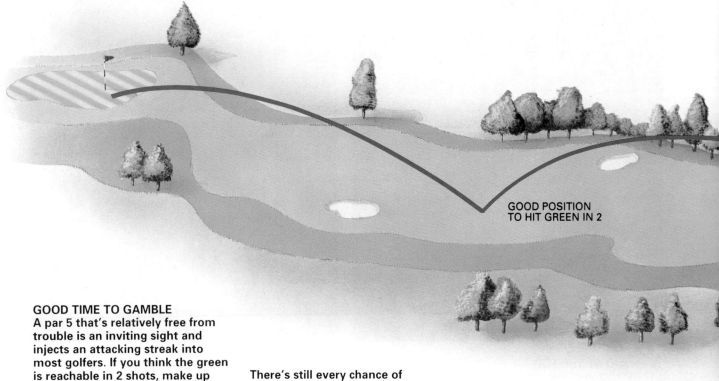

GOOD POSITION
TO HIT GREEN IN 2

DANGEROUS PAR 5 –
TROUBLE EITHER SIDE

PLAY SAFE WITH
LOFTED WOOD OR LONG IRON

GOOD TIME TO GAMBLE
A par 5 that's relatively free from trouble is an inviting sight and injects an attacking streak into most golfers. If you think the green is reachable in 2 shots, make up your mind on the tee exactly how you intend playing the hole.

Have no second thoughts about reaching for your driver – these are the sort of holes to take chances on. If the gamble pays off, your reward is a birdie. If it goes slightly wrong and you hit a wayward shot you're unlikely to find serious trouble.

There's still every chance of salvaging a par.

There's a huge landing area to shoot for and a solid blow puts you in good position. The green is in range and unprotected, so set your sights on the flag and make a controlled swing. Trust your club selection and don't try to force the shot.

your second shot. Try not to leave yourself a sand wedge into the green if that's the club you dislike most.

Some par 5s come into range when conditions are in your favor – perhaps if the ground is hard or a hole is playing downwind. The prospect of going for the green in 2 is often exciting, so take time to compose yourself and build a clear picture in your mind of the shot you want to play.

It's all too easy to pull out a club hurriedly without thinking about distance or potential trouble spots around the green. If the shot goes wrong, from being in ideal position to set up a birdie you're suddenly under pressure just to rescue your par.

WISE APPROACH PLAY

It's satisfying when your first 2 shots go according to plan. Your confidence should be sky high and your eyes firmly fixed on the green ahead.

If you're close enough to the green to be able to use a lofted club, fire at the flag and go for your birdie. Your accuracy should be pretty good from this range so you can afford to be bold.

With a mid iron in your hands, gear your mind towards making par – a birdie using this club is a bonus. Look at the green and the surrounding trouble. When there's a bunker to the right, aim for the left half of the green. If your ball strays slightly off line the worst situation you're likely to face for your next shot is a longish putt or a straightforward chip towards the pin.

From time to time your third

DANGER HOLE

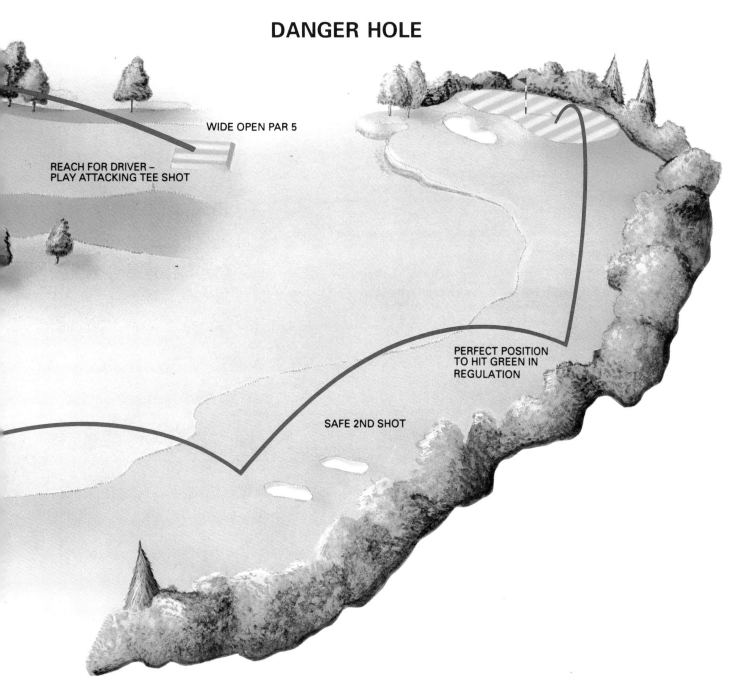

WIDE OPEN PAR 5

REACH FOR DRIVER –
PLAY ATTACKING TEE SHOT

PERFECT POSITION
TO HIT GREEN IN
REGULATION

SAFE 2ND SHOT

shot on a par 5 is a putt. Enjoy the moment, but bring your spirits back down to earth once you set foot on the green. Concentrate on leaving your first putt dead rather than attacking the hole. Few experiences in golf are more frustrating than wasting a golden birdie opportunity through 3 careless putts.

SAFE CONDUCT
A par 5 of exactly the same length but surrounded by trouble requires an entirely different approach. Discipline yourself to hitting the green in 3 and notching up your par. On a tight driving hole it's a good idea to hit a 3 wood for control and accuracy. Just because you're playing a long hole, don't automatically reach for your driver.

Stick to this safety plan all the way along a treacherous par 5. Aim for a safe part of the fairway and

select a club you're confident of hitting straight. It needn't be a long club that threatens the green – just make sure you're able to reach the putting surface with your next shot.

Going for the green in 2 on this type of hole is far too risky – one mistake and you can easily drop a couple of shots to par. While one bad hole may not ruin a score, your morale is bound to take a bit of a knock.

COMPARING THE PARS

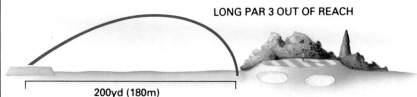

LONG PAR 3 OUT OF REACH

200yd (180m)

LONG PAR 3: They may be the short holes in golf, but many par 3s are out of reach from the tee. The degree of difficulty means birdies are very rare indeed – and while the card states you're supposed to score 3, it's no easy task when a hole measures over 200yd (180m).

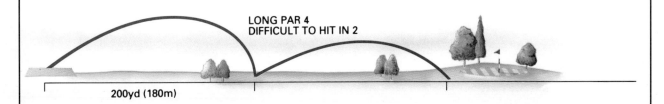

LONG PAR 4
DIFFICULT TO HIT IN 2

200yd (180m)

LONG PAR 4: Many of these holes stretch out well over 400yd (365m) and you sometimes have to accept that hitting the green in regulation is not possible. Even after a solid drive and cracking fairway wood you still need to muster up a chip and putt to secure your par.

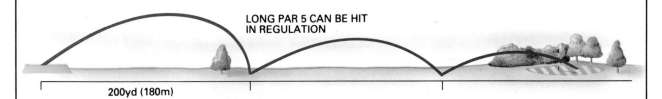

LONG PAR 5 CAN BE HIT
IN REGULATION

200yd (180m)

LONG PAR 5: While it may take a long third shot to find the green on a real monster of a hole, most par 5s can be hit in regulation. While the yardage can often look intimidating, par is always a realistic aim. Play controlled shots with the emphasis on keeping the ball straight – two consecutive shots of 200yd (180m) place you in good position to hit the green.

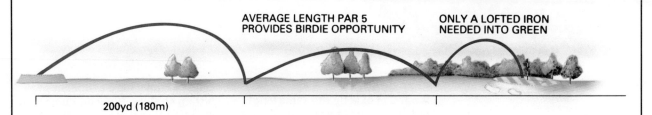

AVERAGE LENGTH PAR 5
PROVIDES BIRDIE OPPORTUNITY

ONLY A LOFTED IRON
NEEDED INTO GREEN

200yd (180m)

AVERAGE PAR 5: Most long holes measure around the 500yd (450m) mark. Adopt the right mental approach and you can step on to the tee with confidence – birdies are a real possibility on holes of this length. A couple of solid shots down the fairway and you're left with just a lofted iron into the green – sometimes no more than a flick with a sand wedge. From this range you can leave yourself with a holeable putt for a 4.

Hazard psychology

Trouble on the course looms in a wide variety of forms, shapes and sizes – usually larger than life if you're playing badly. Bunkers, water, trees, steep banks and cavernous hollows – they're all well known features of golf courses around the world.

Most hazards are designed to look attractive to the eye and enhance the overall appearance of the course – but first impressions often belie the sheer misery they can inflict on the unsuspecting golfer.

The physical presence of a hazard is far from being the main problem. Most bunker shots aren't too terrifying, and knocking your ball into water seldom costs you more than a stroke or two.

Mental torture – the fear of landing yourself in trouble – is a far greater and more damaging obstacle. It's this you must overcome if you want to build a positive hazard psychology into your game. Having the ability to sidestep trouble is, on the whole, far more valuable than any magical talent you might possess to escape from it.

When facing a watery grave, you need to forget that the hazard even exists – imagine the water isn't

FAMILIAR FEELING
Every golfer has experienced a feeling of doubt – perhaps even a state of mild panic – when faced with a shot over several hazards. You often wish you could bypass the hole altogether and walk straight on to the next tee. Golf can be a cruel game though – it makes no allowances for the faint hearted. Try to draw on the good shots you've hit – everyone has a few stored up in the memory bank and they can prove valuable long after the moment. Through experience you can soon develop a positive hazard psychology to help you avoid the sand and water.

PREPARE FOR THE INEVITABLE

① SEMI-BLIND SHOT
You're certain to face greenside bunker shots at some stage – this one always looks a lot harder than it is. Although the lip is high and you can see only the top part of the flag, you really needn't worry – this is the perfect time to use the simple splash bunker shot technique. Before you start, take a moment to stand by the green and visualize the shot.

② OPEN STANCE
As always you should pay close attention to the basics. Make sure your shoulders, hips and feet are aligned left of target with the clubface aimed straight at the flag. Take the club back along the line of your body – this is outside the line in relation to the target, but it's the correct path for this type of shot.

③ RIGHT ANGLE
Unlike most other shots you need to create a steep swing arc when you're in a greenside bunker. This is achieved by breaking the wrists earlier than normal – the ideal moment is as your hands travel past your right knee. At the top of the backswing the shaft of the club and your left arm should form a 90° angle – also make sure the shaft points almost straight up.

④ STEEP DOWNSWING
Your key move on the downswing is to create a steep angle of attack into impact. The clubhead must splash down about a ball width behind the ball itself – this is made easy when you achieve a good position at the top. Pull the club down with your left hand making sure the clubhead never overtakes the hands – this all but eliminates the risk of hitting too cleanly.

(5) SAND BLAST
The clubhead travels from out to in through impact, cutting a trough in the sand under the ball. Combined with the alignment of the clubface the ball floats high in the air and straight at the flag. Even at this stage of the swing you should still keep your hands ahead of the clubhead – this prevents the face closing.

(6) STRAIGHTFORWARD ESCAPE
Always aim to finish high when you hit high from a greenside bunker. This is a good move to work on because it encourages you to complete the followthrough. One of the most destructive faults from any bunker is stabbing the clubhead down into the sand and not following through on the shot – often you're faced with another bunker shot for your next.

pro tip

Praying for guidance

The reputation of a hole can sometimes destroy golfers before they even set foot on the tee. They hear rumours of the nightmare bunker on the left or the water dangerously close on the right. Not surprisingly, the mind becomes awash with negative thoughts, and minutes later another golfer's name is added to the list of victims!

The 3rd at Oakmont – a US Open venue – is a good example. At little more than 400yd (360m) the hole is certainly no monster, but a vast stretch of bunkers known as the Church Pews runs down the left side of the fairway – many golfers look to the heavens for guidance.

The hazards appear bigger, the width of the fairway seems to shrink before their eyes, and the nightmare begins. This happens on golf courses all over the world.

Don't be intimidated by reputation alone – these holes are seldom as frightening as the tales of woe suggest. Approach the hole in a determined frame of mind and you've won more than half the battle. One good shot is often enough to tame the most ferocious looking hole.

there. This is a well worn piece of advice to the club golfer, but it's still an effective one.

There's no short cut to achieving this confident frame of mind – it's simply a case of drawing from past experience. Focus your mind on a great shot you hit earlier in the day, or in your last round, even last month if necessary – just as long as there are positive thoughts running through your mind.

Merely thinking about a cracking good shot helps you concentrate on the right points – rhythm, timing, making a smooth swing and ultimately the perfect result. You force negative thoughts into the background and your supply of golf balls doesn't take a dive either.

KEEP OUT OF THE WOODS

Rows of trees lining both sides of the fairway present a tough driving hole. By definition trees are not true hazards, but they certainly make most golfers' brains work overtime.

You should try to shape the ball with either a fade or a draw when you're aiming at a tight fairway. This constructive approach turns your attentions to the shot rather than the trees. As always, drowning out negative thoughts with a wave of confidence is the most effective way to steer clear of any form of trouble.

Attempting to hit a thunderous blast down the middle is seldom the answer on a tight driving hole. This all out approach is the one most likely to result in the distant clatter of golf ball on timber.

SAND DODGING

Fairway bunkers are one of the easiest type of hazard to avoid – the key lies in sensible club selection. On most holes you should be able to choose a club that doesn't bring the sand into play – unless you're on a bunker strewn course like St. Andrews.

When you select your club, allow some margin for error on the shot so that pinpoint accuracy isn't essential. For example, hitting a driver off the tee isn't a good idea if it means you have to thread your ball between two bunkers in the middle of the fairway – the odds are heavily stacked against you

Sensible club selection
Sometimes one particular hole causes nightmares every time you set foot on the tee. It's hard to put your finger on the exact problem, but hazards that never before came into play seem to suddenly acquire a magnetic pull on your ball – even when you're playing well.

This is a classic example of a mental block and can stem from one disastrous shot into trouble. The memory of that painful moment can linger for months on end, but avoiding the hazard just once is a major step towards playing it out of your system for good.

Next time you play your problem hole, try selecting a different club to the one you usually hit. For example, if your 3 wood has a fatal attraction to the trees, reach for a long iron instead – even on a hole where distance is at a premium. Don't worry if you can't get up in 2 – settle for playing the hole safely so there's no pressure on you.

This change in strategy alters your frame of mind and helps rid you of negative thoughts. You'll be surprised – a fresh approach is sometimes all you need to hit that crucial good shot. And once you've done that you're well on the way to conquering your bogey hole.

and there's more to lose than to gain.

Never underestimate the benefits of playing from a good lie on the fairway – hit a more lofted club and be happy to accept a longer shot into the green. This is the sensible strategy and makes it easier on your score.

Greenside bunkers are the hazards you probably visit more times than any other in a golfing year.

This is true no matter how good an iron player you are, so don't punish yourself if the occasional approach shot lands in a bunker. There's no need to feel that your round is about to fall apart.

Just make sure you find time to work on your bunker technique because there's certain to be a call for it. That way you'll never feel all at sea when you're next in the sand.

Avoiding the water hazard

**This hole is one of the most difficult on the
heathland course: a dog-leg right
with a pond at the angle liable to attract
any stray drives.**

The hole is a 410yd (375m),
par-4, dog-leg right.

There are two bunkers on
the right-hand side of the
green – they'll catch any
stray shots that fall between
the green and the water.

The fairway breaks from
left to right so a sliced
drive lands straight in the
pond, which begins 100 yd
(90m) from the tee.

A large chestnut tree
200yd (180m) from the tee
on the left side of the
fairway means that an
unlucky drive leaves you
with a blind second shot.

The rough on the left is
light but a ball landing here
may settle in the grass. This
makes it difficult to find
clean contact with the ball
and carry the water for the
second shot.

It's a sunny day and there's
a light breeze blowing
across the hole from the
golfer's left.

SAFE SHOT
Left of the water
If you have a high handicap, treat the hole as a short par 5. Hit safely left of the water with your first two shots and set up a short chip on to the green – which still leaves you the chance of a single putt.

The first two shots require a similar set-up, but different clubs. In both you aim slightly left: with the initial drive you need to combat the breeze, and the second shot must avoid the water.
Grip: normal
Stance: square, but aiming slightly left
Ball position: opposite left heel
Weight distribution: even
Swing: full
Swing path: normal
Club: 3 wood for first shot; 3 or 4 iron for second

MATCH WINNER
Draw into the breeze
A perfect tee shot, hit with a slight draw which uses the breeze, gives you a good view of the pin and you may send it close enough for a birdie putt. As the tee shot is tricky, you could use a 1 iron instead of a driver – it's good for accuracy without sacrificing much length.

Grip: normal
Stance: slightly closed
Ball position: opposite left toe
Weight distribution: even
Swing: full
Swing path: in to out
Club: driver or 1 iron

Over water and bunkers
The second shot should skirt the edge of the water and the bunkers and land on the green. To make sure you avoid the hazards, produce an extra high shot with more backspin by placing the ball opposite your left heel.
Grip: normal
Stance: normal
Ball position: midway between centre of stance and left heel *or* opposite left heel
Weight distribution: even
Swing: full
Swing path: normal
Club: 5 or 6 iron

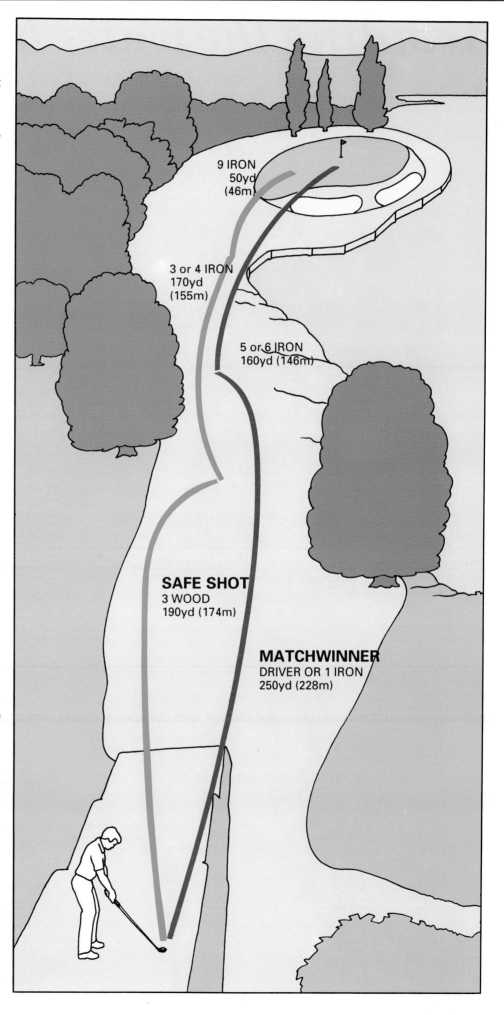

9 IRON
50yd
(46m)

3 or 4 IRON
170yd
(155m)

5 or 6 IRON
160yd (146m)

SAFE SHOT
3 WOOD
190yd (174m)

MATCHWINNER
DRIVER OR 1 IRON
250yd (228m)

Avoiding the trees

Trees are a very common feature of inland heathland courses. At this hole, your view of the pin and the most direct flight path of the ball are partly obscured by leafy branches.

There is no wind. The sun is shining and the greens are firm. The fairways are dried out.

Two trees border the green. They block your view if you try to approach the green from right or left.

A greenside bunker traps loose shots to the right.

The hole is a par 4 of 365yd (333m). The drive from the tee travelled a good distance – about 235yd (215m) – but the ball was sliced into the rough.

A small fairway bunker catches any duffed shots.

The ball is 130yd (118m) from the pin, lying on hard, dry ground under a large tree. The branches block a clear view to the flag, but there is a low line between ball and pin.

SAFE SHOT
Chip and run
A chip and run shot to the left puts the ball back on the fairway for a clear, 130yd (118m) line to the flag and a straightforward 7-iron shot. It might feel like a wasted stroke but it's much better to drop a shot than risk hitting the branches and being even worse off.

Grip: hands slightly lower than usual
Stance: normal
Ball position: center of stance
Weight distribution: just favoring the left side
Swing: half
Swing path: normal
Club: 9 iron or pitching wedge

MATCH WINNER
Low shot to the green
If you are an experienced golfer you can attempt a low-flying shot that lands about 20yd (18m) short of the green and runs on to it. Assuming the ball is on line, this leaves you with the chance of a single putt.

This calculated risk should be based on your knowledge of the distance and height that the ball will travel. Keep your hands ahead of the ball and hit firmly.

Grip: hands slightly lower than usual
Stance: normal
Ball position: halfway between center of stance and right heel
Weight distribution: favoring left side throughout swing
Swing: three quarters
Swing path: normal
Club: 5, 6 or 7 iron

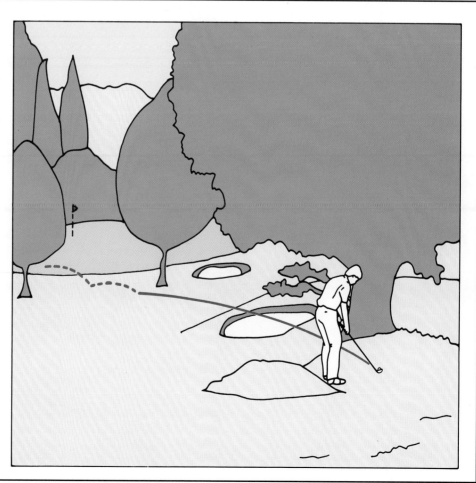

Planning from the tee

As you stand on the tee you can see the hole stretch out before you. You need a strategy that ensures you avoid the danger spots, even if this means taking an extra stroke.

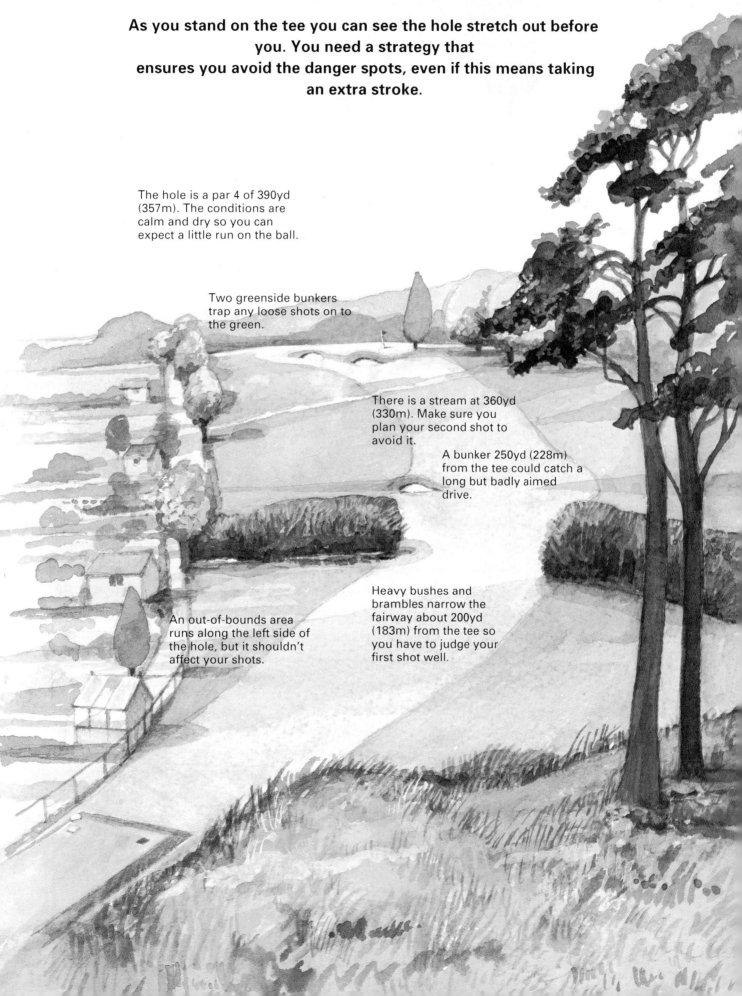

The hole is a par 4 of 390yd (357m). The conditions are calm and dry so you can expect a little run on the ball.

Two greenside bunkers trap any loose shots on to the green.

There is a stream at 360yd (330m). Make sure you plan your second shot to avoid it.

A bunker 250yd (228m) from the tee could catch a long but badly aimed drive.

An out-of-bounds area runs along the left side of the hole, but it shouldn't affect your shots.

Heavy bushes and brambles narrow the fairway about 200yd (183m) from the tee so you have to judge your first shot well.

SAFE SHOT
Take three shots
If you are a high handicapper, plan to send the ball 170yd (155m) so it's short of the bushes. This leaves you a clear second shot of 160yd (146m) that lands short of the stream, followed by a 60yd (55m) pitch or short iron on to the green.

First and second shots
Grip: normal
Stance: normal
Ball position: opposite left heel
Weight distribution: even
Swing: full
Swing path: in to square to in
Club: 3 iron or 4 wood for drive; 4 iron for second shot

Third shot
Grip: normal
Stance: slightly open
Ball position: center of stance
Weight distribution: even
Swing: three quarters
Swing path: normal
Club: pitching wedge or 9 iron

PAR PLAY
Safe drive, long iron to green
You may be a low handicapper but not too confident about controlling the straightness of your drives. If so, choose a 2 iron and aim for the gap 200yd (183m) away. The target area is large enough to ensure that your shot lands clear of the rough. You're then left with a long-iron approach shot of 190yd (174m), but should still reach the green in two – as long as you miss the greenside bunkers – and make par.

Both shots
Grip: normal
Stance: normal
Ball position: opposite left heel
Weight distribution: even
Swing: full
Swing path: normal
Club: 2 iron for first shot; 3 iron for second

MATCH WINNER
Going for a birdie
The confident low handicapper can hit a good 250yd (228m) drive, with a slight fade, that lands beyond the gap, to the right of the fairway bunker. This leaves only a 7- or 8-iron, 140yd (128m) shot to the green and the best chance of a birdie.

Drive
Grip: normal
Stance: slightly open
Ball position: opposite left toe
Weight distribution: even
Swing: full
Swing path: slight out to in
Club: driver (1 wood)

Second shot
Grip: normal
Stance: normal
Ball position: midway between centre of stance and left heel
Weight distribution: even
Swing: full
Swing path: normal
Club: 7 or 8 iron

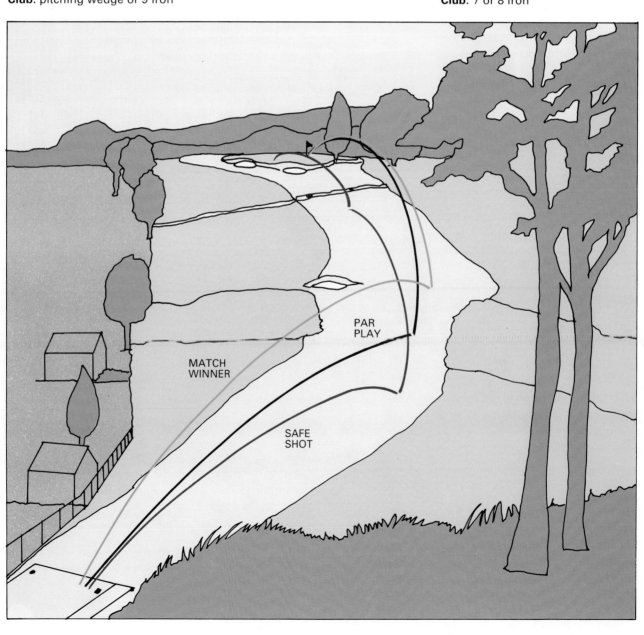

A blind shot

Blind holes – where you can't see the flag – aren't favored by today's course architects but they can still be found on traditional courses. Combine a blind hole with a bit of wind, and you're faced with a tricky shot.

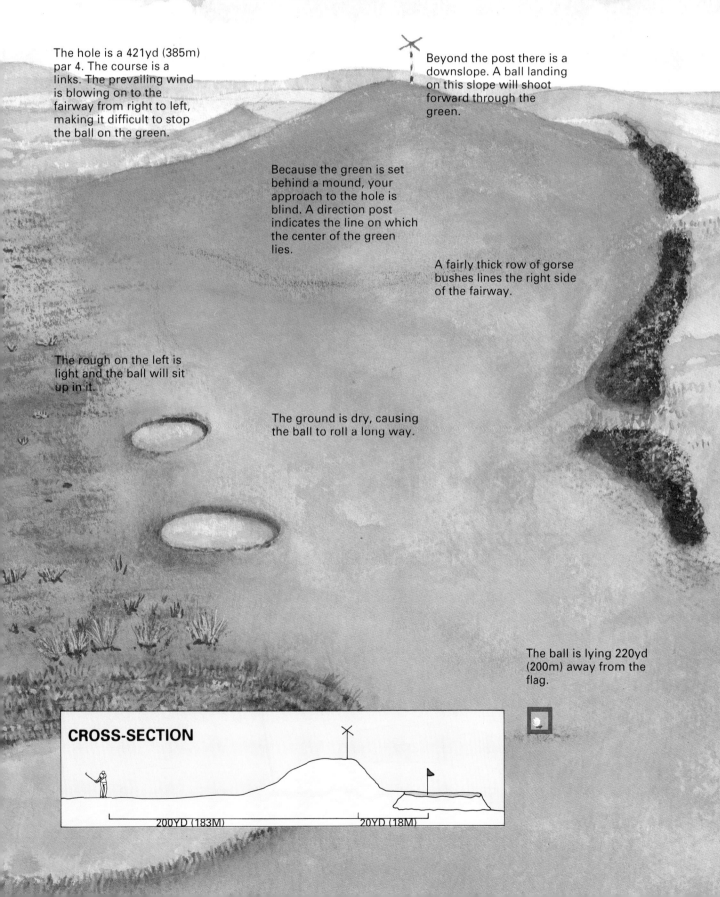

The hole is a 421yd (385m) par 4. The course is a links. The prevailing wind is blowing on to the fairway from right to left, making it difficult to stop the ball on the green.

Beyond the post there is a downslope. A ball landing on this slope will shoot forward through the green.

Because the green is set behind a mound, your approach to the hole is blind. A direction post indicates the line on which the center of the green lies.

A fairly thick row of gorse bushes lines the right side of the fairway.

The rough on the left is light and the ball will sit up in it.

The ground is dry, causing the ball to roll a long way.

The ball is lying 220yd (200m) away from the flag.

CROSS-SECTION

200YD (183M)   20YD (18M)

SAFE SHOT
Left of the mound
Unless you can carry the mound you have no real chance of making a 4 here. However, by playing about 170yd (155m) to the left of the mound you can see the flag with your approach shot.

Even if the wind takes your shot into the light rough the recovery shot is easier than playing a blind shot.
Grip: normal
Stance: normal
Ball position: opposite left heel
Weight distribution: even
Swing: full
Swing path: normal
Club: 4 or 5 wood

Approach shot
Your next shot should be a high wedge to the flag.
Grip: normal
Stance: normal
Ball position: in the center of stance
Weight distribution: even
Swing: three-quarters
Swing path: normal
Club: pitching wedge or 9 iron

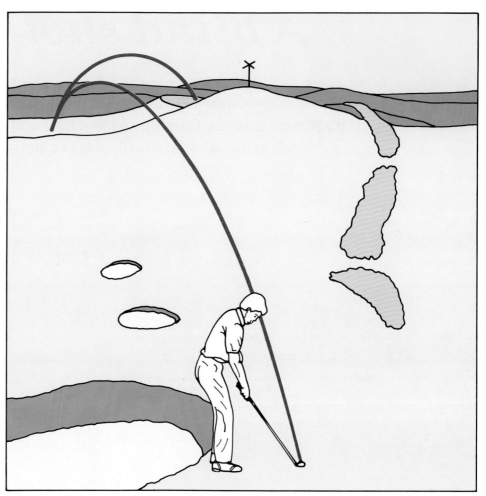

MATCH WINNER
Clearing the mound
You need to carry the ball 200yd (183m) to clear the mound. You must also avoid landing on the downslope as the ball will shoot off and run through the green. Use the marker as a guide – you may also want to walk up and check exactly where the flag is.

Choose a 4 or 5 wood to hold the shot in the wind. Hit the ball high – the height helps to stop the ball on the green.
Grip: normal
Stance: normal
Ball position: opposite left heel
Weight distribution: even
Swing: full
Swing path: normal
Club: 4 or 5 wood

Percentage play

A stiff left-to-right wind and a sloping hole with the pin
tucked into the left side is a true test of
judgement. The varying degrees of risk must be balanced
against your ability.

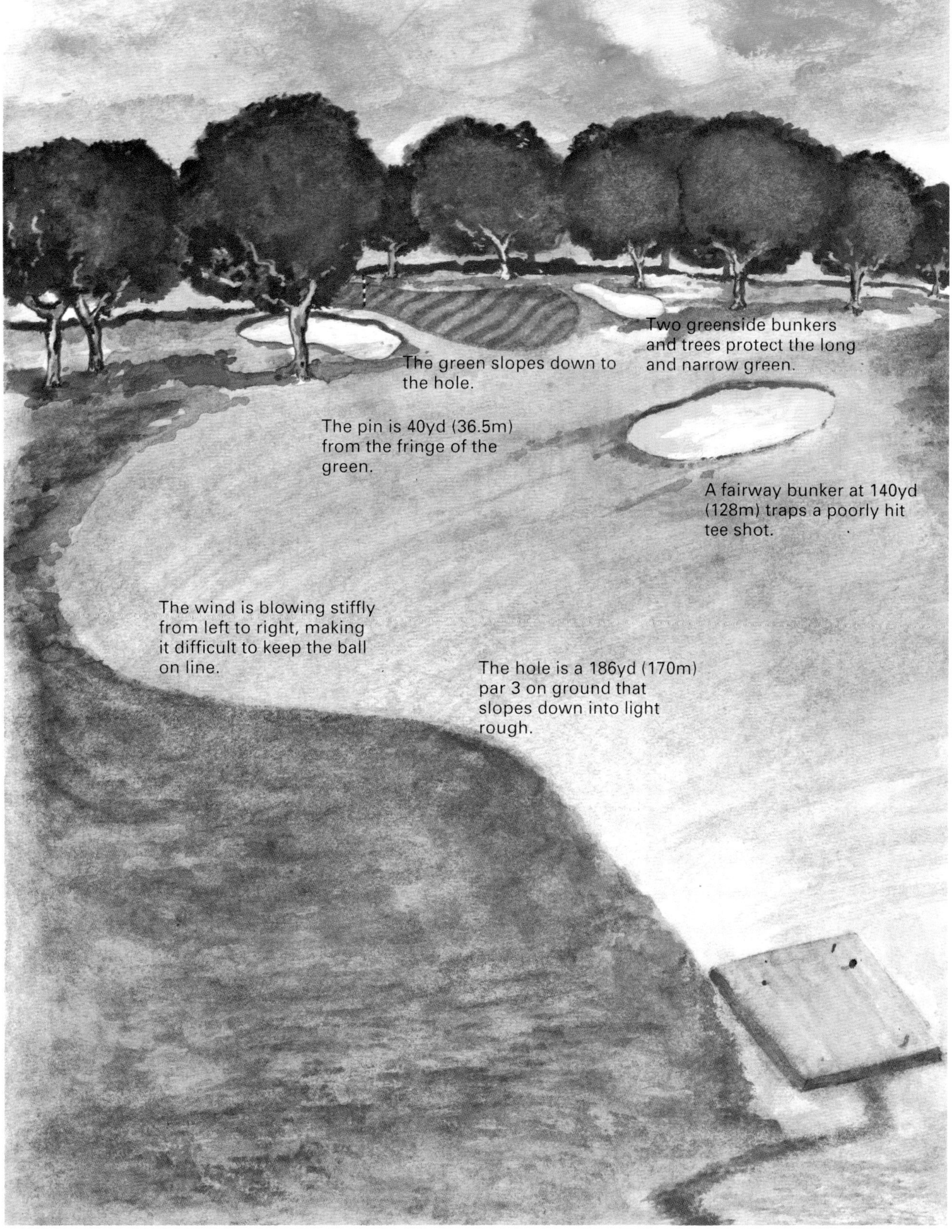

Two greenside bunkers
and trees protect the long
and narrow green.

The green slopes down to
the hole.

The pin is 40yd (36.5m)
from the fringe of the
green.

A fairway bunker at 140yd
(128m) traps a poorly hit
tee shot.

The wind is blowing stiffly
from left to right, making
it difficult to keep the ball
on line.

The hole is a 186yd (170m)
par 3 on ground that
slopes down into light
rough.

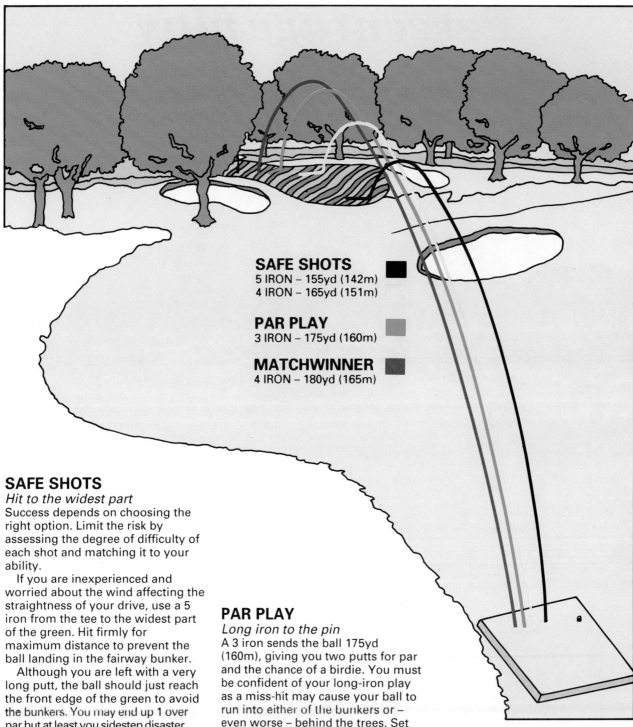

SAFE SHOTS
5 IRON – 155yd (142m)
4 IRON – 165yd (151m)

PAR PLAY
3 IRON – 175yd (160m)

MATCHWINNER
4 IRON – 180yd (165m)

SAFE SHOTS
Hit to the widest part
Success depends on choosing the right option. Limit the risk by assessing the degree of difficulty of each shot and matching it to your ability.

If you are inexperienced and worried about the wind affecting the straightness of your drive, use a 5 iron from the tee to the widest part of the green. Hit firmly for maximum distance to prevent the ball landing in the fairway bunker.

Although you are left with a very long putt, the ball should just reach the front edge of the green to avoid the bunkers. You may end up 1 over par but at least you sidestep disaster.

The more accurate and confident player can use a 4 iron for a 165yd (151m) drive so the ball lands nearer the pin. Hit correctly, the ball rolls up to the middle of the green – this leaves you with a long putt but you still have a chance of making par.

When visualizing this shot make sure you take into account the wind, which could push the ball towards the right greenside bunker.

Grip: normal
Stance: normal
Ball position: midway between center of stance and left heel
Weight distribution: even
Swing: full
Swing path: in to square to in
Club: 5 or 4 iron

PAR PLAY
Long iron to the pin
A 3 iron sends the ball 175yd (160m), giving you two putts for par and the chance of a birdie. You must be confident of your long-iron play as a miss-hit may cause your ball to run into either of the bunkers or – even worse – behind the trees. Set up as for the Safe Shots.

MATCH WINNER
Long-iron draw
The advanced player can take a 4 iron and – using a slight draw to counteract the wind – aim for the right-hand side of the green. A well hit shot lands at the pin with plenty of backspin.

Play the shot with care. Taking plenty of club is risky – if you close the clubface you could hook the shot. The ball may then land in the rough behind the left greenside bunker and – if you're unlucky – the trees as well. From this position you are left with an impossible chip back to the hole.

Grip: normal
Stance: slightly closed
Ball position: midway between center of stance and left heel
Weight distribution: even
Swing: full
Swing path: slightly in to out
Club: 4 iron

Par 3 over water

You need to hit a perfectly flighted shot to avoid the
stream on this testing hole.
To complicate matters a mound makes it dangerous to aim
at the left side of the green.

A ball that lands on this
steep downward slope will
bounce into the water.

A wide stream is marked
by yellow stakes which
indicate a water hazard.

The fairway is hard. A ball
landing here will roll down
into the stream.

The rough is a mixture of
grass and heather.

The hole is a 137yd (125m)
par 3 on a heathland
course. It's a calm day and
conditions are good.

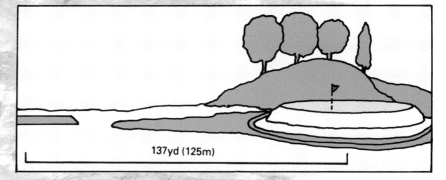

137yd (125m)

SAFE SHOT
Play short of the green
Unless you are confident of reaching the green with a crisp high shot, hit your tee shot about 90yd (82m) to the fairway in front of the stream. As the ground is hard take less club to compensate for the roll on landing.

For your second shot you have an easy chip of 40yd (36.5m) over the water to the green, leaving you with the chance of holding par or two putts for an easy 4.

First shot
Grip: normal
Stance: normal
Ball position: center of stance
Weight distribution: even
Swing: full
Swing path: in to square to in
Club: 9 iron

Second shot
Grip: a little lower than usual
Stance: slightly open
Ball position: center of stance
Weight distribution: even
Swing: half
Swing path: just out to in
Club: pitching or sand wedge

MATCH WINNER
Straight to the flag
For the advanced player this hole allows you to score a psychological victory over your opponent – a less confident golfer is likely to look at the green, the stream and the rough and probably hit the ball into trouble. Despite its difficulties the short par 3 gives a birdie opportunity.

With a sharp angle of attack – taking care to avoid the mound on the left – strike the ball with backspin to the flag. Hit with confidence or your shot may end up in the water.

Grip: normal
Stance: normal
Ball position: midway between center of stance and left heel
Weight distribution: even
Swing: full
Swing path: in to square to in
Club: 7 or 8 iron

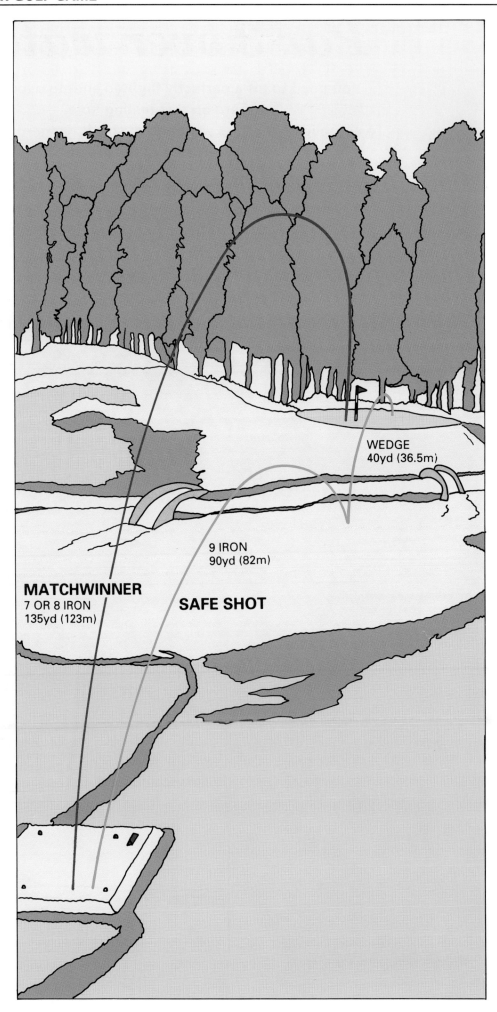

WEDGE
40yd (36.5m)

9 IRON
90yd (82m)

MATCHWINNER
7 OR 8 IRON
135yd (123m)

SAFE SHOT

Links challenge

A short drive on this windswept links has left you in a tricky
situation. You have to contend with sea
on one side and gorse on the other to reach a green protected
by a deep bunker and more heavy gorse.

A strong right-to-left wind
may blow your approach
shot into the greenside
bunker.

A direct shot to the green
– not for the faint hearted
– needs a carry of 180yd
(165m) over the water.

You pick up a penalty if
your ball goes out of
bounds over the cliff.

If you aim for the fairway
and the shot pulls, your
ball is in danger of landing
in the bunker.

Deep gorse lines the
fairway on the left. A stray
ball landing here is not
only unplayable but
difficult to find.

The ball is lying in the
middle of the fairway and
is 220yd (201m) from the
pin.

The dog-leg hole is a par 4
of 420yd (384m). The drive
from the tee was short
and only traveled 200yd
(182m).

SAFE SHOT

Play away from the shore

If you don't feel confident of clearing the water play safe for a bogey – you avoid the risk of going out of bounds over the cliff and you could even make par.

Take a short iron and with a smooth three-quarter swing aim to land the ball about 100yd (91m) along the fairway.

Play a little to the right to counteract the crosswind and avoid the bunker. Don't make a full swing or your ball may land in the gorse.

Your next shot is fairly straightforward. Use the direction of the wind to your advantage and aim to the right-hand side of the green. The crosswind will blow your ball back, leaving you with a couple of putts to finish.

Both shots
Grip: normal
Stance: normal
Ball position: center of stance
Weight distribution: even
Swing: three-quarters
Swing path: in to square to in
Club: 8 or 9 iron first shot, 7 or 8 iron second shot

MATCH WINNER

Punch fade to the green

The advanced player faces a true test of skill for a birdie on this hole. The shot to play is a punch fade with backspin which carries the ball straight in the wind all the way to the green. If played with confidence you are left with a short birdie putt.

A high shot is risky. The strong right-to-left wind may make the ball bounce left into the greenside bunker.

Grip: a little lower than usual
Stance: slightly open
Ball position: midway between center of stance and left heel
Swing: three-quarters
Swing path: just out to in
Club: 3 iron

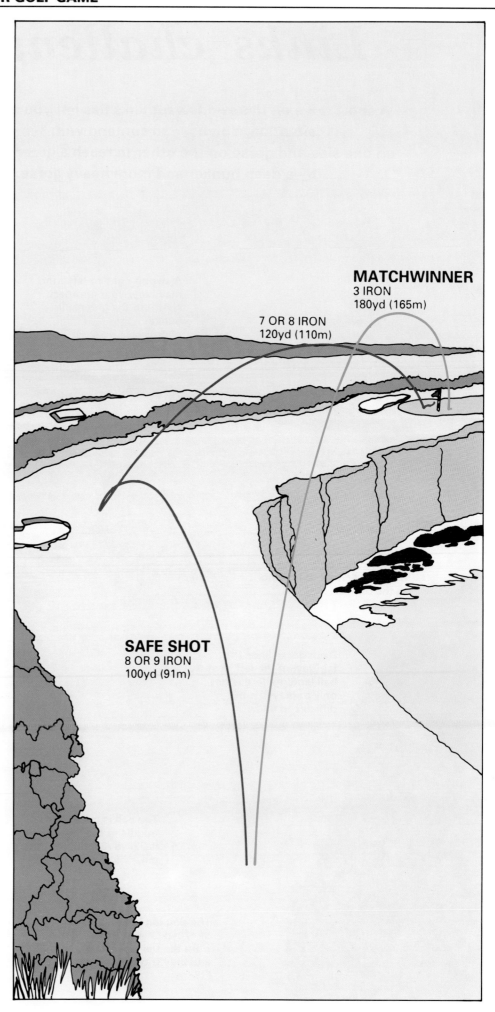

MATCHWINNER
3 IRON
180yd (165m)

7 OR 8 IRON
120yd (110m)

SAFE SHOT
8 OR 9 IRON
100yd (91m)

Dog-leg water hazard

**The high risk of hitting water on this testing
hole more than makes up
for the absence of bunkers. You need to play very
carefully to avoid a watery grave.**

If you land in the lateral water hazard you incur a 1-stroke penalty.

To reach this point on the fairway from the tee is virtually impossible with a carry of 270yd (247m).

You need a carry over the water of at least 220yd (201m) to land on the fairway from the tee.

Conditions are good – the fairway and green are firm. There is a slight breeze from the right but it doesn't affect your play.

This dog-leg left on parkland is a par 4 of 472yd (432m) from the middle tee.

SAFE SHOT
Three steps
Treat the hole as a par 5. Choose a 3 wood and make a straight shot of about 190yd (174m) to land on the fairway. From here you require another good shot of 170yd (155m) to leave you with a medium iron over water to the green.

First and second shots
Grip: normal
Stance: normal
Ball position: opposite left heel
Weight distribution: even
Swing: full
Swing path: in to square to in
Club: 3 wood for first; 4 or 5 wood for second

Approach shot
Grip: normal
Stance: normal
Ball position: center of stance
Weight distribution: even
Swing: full
Swing path: in to square to in
Club: 7 iron

MATCH WINNER
Two shots over water
If you decide to go for the carry over water you must produce one of your best drives. Settle for a shot of at least 250yd (229m) to clear the water and land safely on the fairway. Don't be over ambitious – if you attempt a carry of 270yd (247m) and just miss-hit you'll probably find water.

Hit a powerful drive with a slight fade to avoid the trouble. Even if your aim isn't perfect your ball should still land on the fairway.

To make par you have to carry the water yet again. Play a high shot of about 200yd (183m) to hold on the good green.

First and second shots
Grip: normal
Stance: just open for first; normal for second
Ball position: opposite left heel
Weight distribution: even
Swing: full
Swing path: slightly out to in for first shot; normal for second
Club: driver for first; 5 wood for second

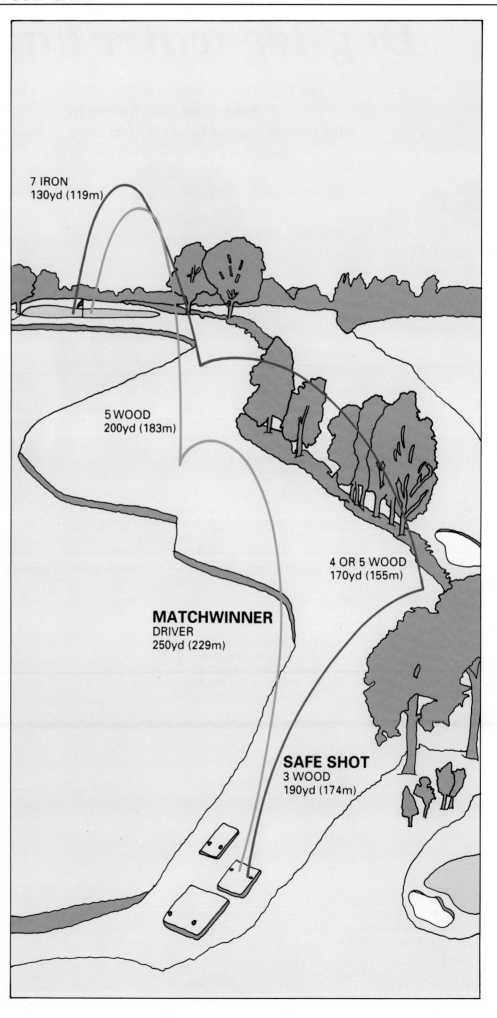

7 IRON
130yd (119m)

5 WOOD
200yd (183m)

4 OR 5 WOOD
170yd (155m)

MATCHWINNER
DRIVER
250yd (229m)

SAFE SHOT
3 WOOD
190yd (174m)

Penal par 3

Regarded by some golfers as unfair, penal holes often feature on U.S. and Australian courses and are starting to form part of the U.K. golf landscape. On this do or die approach there's no easy path home – the only way to go is over the water.

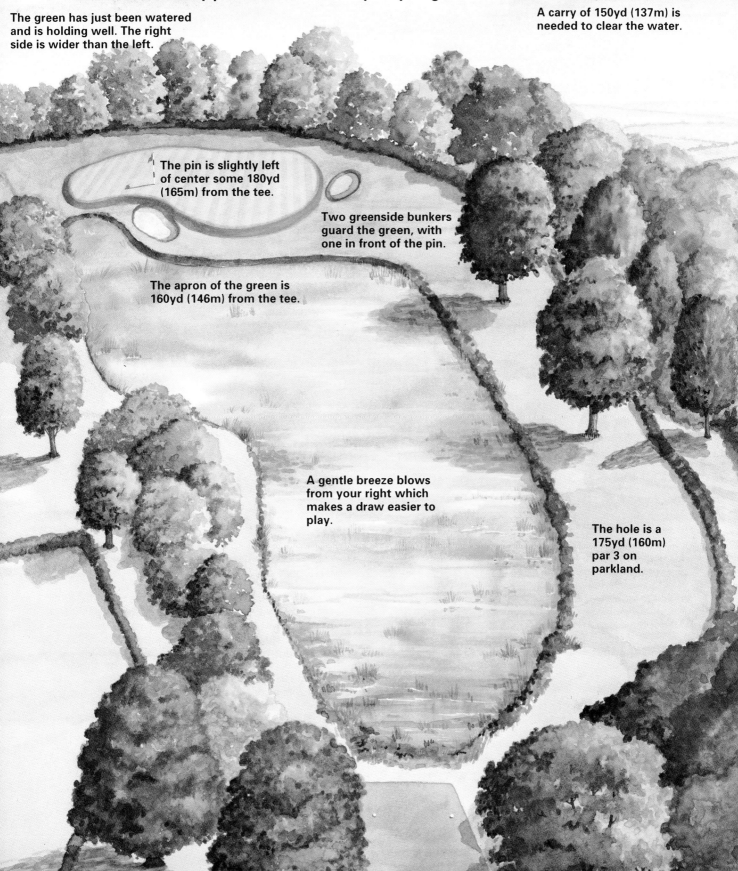

The green has just been watered and is holding well. The right side is wider than the left.

A carry of 150yd (137m) is needed to clear the water.

The pin is slightly left of center some 180yd (165m) from the tee.

Two greenside bunkers guard the green, with one in front of the pin.

The apron of the green is 160yd (146m) from the tee.

A gentle breeze blows from your right which makes a draw easier to play.

The hole is a 175yd (160m) par 3 on parkland.

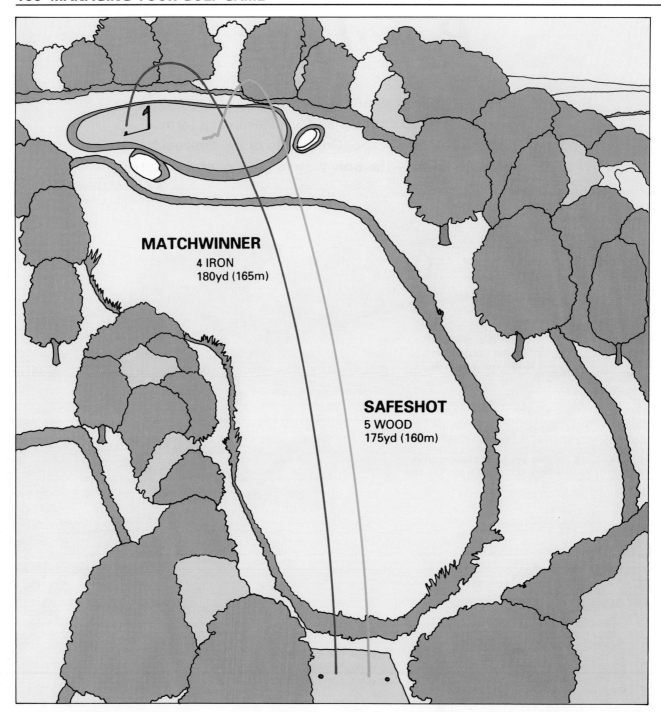

SAFE SHOT

Strike firm to center of green

The lack of fairway leaves little room to maneuver, but fix your mind only on making a smooth swing – blot out that large expanse of water. Don't dally on the tee and let doubts creep in. Strike crisp and firm with a club you're sure carries you over the water.

A straight shot of 175yd (160m) leaves you safely on the wide central part of the green – go long rather than risk finding water, as the ball holds on the watered green. Be content with a respectable par by laying up your first long putt close to the pin.

Grip: normal
Stance: normal
Ball position: opposite inside left heel
Weight distribution: even
Swing: full
Swing path: normal
Club: 5 wood

MATCH WINNER

High draw to pin

With a confident stroke and a cool nerve you can set up a birdie opportunity. Using a long iron, aim for the middle of the green to avoid the risk of the greenside bunker in front of the pin. Take advantage of the slight breeze to draw the ball back towards the flag.

Because of the drawspin the shot rolls a little on landing but on the well watered green the ball should sit down close to the pin. You are left with a short putt for a possible birdie.

Grip: normal
Stance: slightly closed
Ball position: opposite inside left heel
Weight distribution: even
Swing: full
Swing path: slightly in to out
Club: 4 iron

Approach off hard ground

As the seasons change, so does the golf course. Even if you play mainly on the same course you face a variety of experiences. A course covered in frost or baked hard by hot sun flatters your drives but threatens the accuracy of approach play. Proceed with caution on this iron hard par 5.

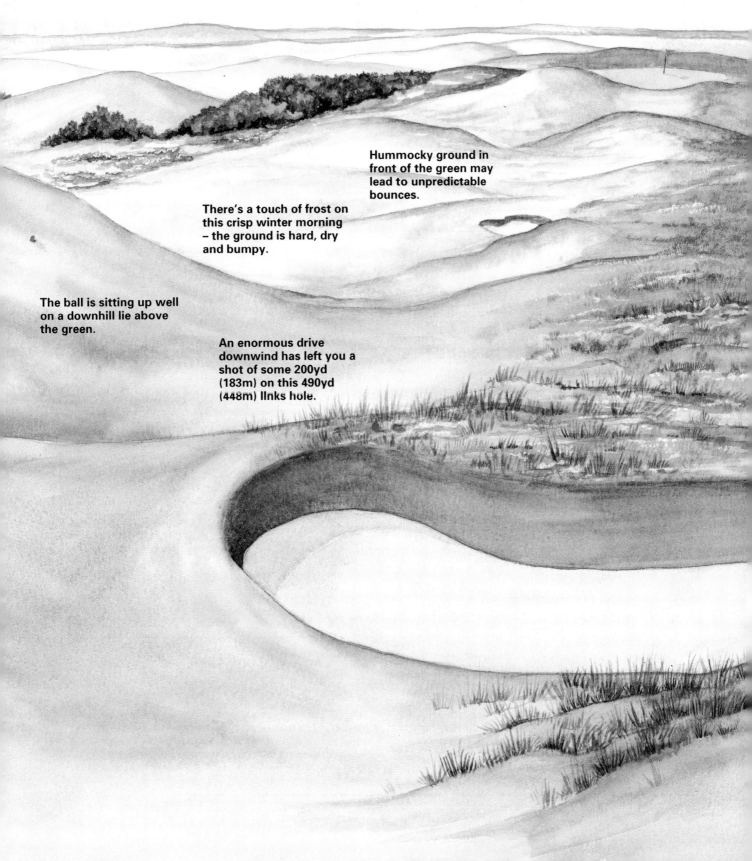

Hummocky ground in front of the green may lead to unpredictable bounces.

There's a touch of frost on this crisp winter morning – the ground is hard, dry and bumpy.

The ball is sitting up well on a downhill lie above the green.

An enormous drive downwind has left you a shot of some 200yd (183m) on this 490yd (448m) links hole.

SAFE SHOT

With the combination of a downhill drive and a following wind you've had the satisfaction of seeing your ball sail a massive 290yd (265m) down the fairway. Now there's a good chance of coming off as well as the low handicapper, but approach with caution – don't be greedy.

Make sure you use a club that suits the conditions. On a calm day a 200yd (183m) approach calls for a 4 wood – with a helping wind take two clubs less. But before you reach for your 4 iron take into account the iron hard ground and drop down to a 5 iron.

Make a smooth swing. If you avoid a cruel bounce you can watch the ball roll towards the putting surface. Be content to take 2 putts for your birdie 4.

Grip: normal
Stance: normal
Ball position: midway between left heel and center of stance
Weight distribution: even
Swing: full
Swing path: normal
Club: 5 iron

MATCH WINNER

Sometimes there's just one way to play a shot – only the club differs. The stronger player needs less club to hit the ball the same distance. Fly your approach up to, but short of, the green. Though it's downwind and downhill all the way, this isn't the time to go flat out for the pin. In frosty conditions you won't manage backspin on the ball to stop quickly on the green.

Hard ground can lead to an unpredictable bounce so be content to finish on the right of the green to avoid the worst of the humps and hollows. With luck a 6 iron will bounce just before the green and roll up towards the flag, leaving you 2 putts for a birdie.

Grip: normal
Stance: normal
Ball position: midway between left heel and center of stance
Weight distribution: even
Swing: full
Swing path: normal
Club: 6 iron

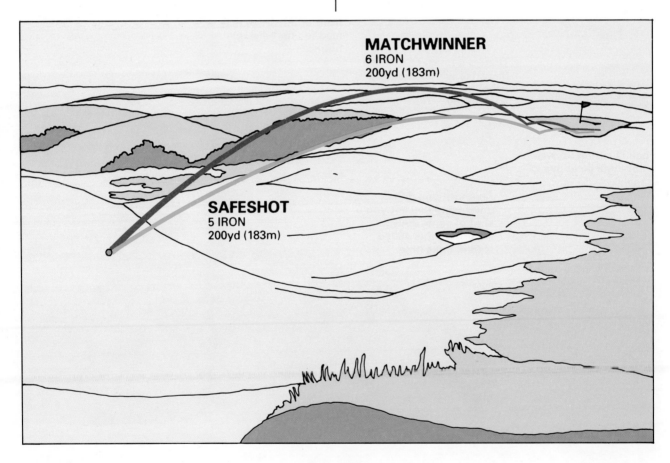

Hard ground

Whether it's the result of a severe frost or baking hot sun, playing off iron hard surfaces is a lottery. You have to accept unpredictable bounces. Be careful with club selection – although the ball rolls a long way on hard ground, it doesn't fly as far in cold winter air.

You can make winter play easier by using a colored ball when there's a dusting of snow or frost on the ground. If you're playing in freezing conditions avoid the misery of cold hands and uncontrolled shots by wearing mitts. Use hand warmers in severe weather – but remember the rules forbid you to warm your golf balls with a mechanical aid.

Cross hazards

Rain starts to fall and the wind gathers force
on this par 4 450yd (411m) links hole.
Some precise golf is needed if you're to clear
the trouble and limit any damage.

Strong wind blowing
from the sea makes the
hole play much longer.

A pot bunker guards the
approach area some 30yd (27m) short
of the putting surface, and two
greenside traps protect the flag.

A large bunker –
14ft (13m) deep
and reinforced
with sleepers –
stretches the
width of the
fairway.

Long grass and deep
gorse may trap a ball hit
wide of the fairway.

Cross bunkers are
fiendishly placed to catch
an incautious stroke off
the tee.

SAFE SHOT

Play within yourself
It's time to appraise your game realistically. If your average drive goes 180yd (165m) forget about trying to carry the cross bunkers. It's all too easy to let wind and rain upset your tempo so leave your driver in the bag – sacrifice a little distance in the interests of accuracy. Concentrate on good rhythm and play a fairway wood or long iron from the tee.

Your second shot must fly over the cross bunkers. To be sure of carrying the sand play a 4 iron to the middle of the fairway.

You then have to play over the large bunker for your third shot. Take the 4 iron again – with the wind blowing you won't reach the little bunker just short of the green. Having hit your third you are left with a 40yd (37m) pitch to the green. With 2 putts you card a 6 – give thanks it's not more in such conditions.

First, second and third shots
Grip: normal
Stance: normal
Ball position: opposite inside of left heel off tee; slightly further back for next two shots
Weight distribution: even
Swing: full
Swing path: in to in
Club: 4 wood or long iron off tee; 4 iron for second and third

MATCH WINNER

Steady as you go
With the misery of rain and a strong wind to contend with, this par 4 plays like a 5. The hole dog-legs left – the drive is hit into wind though on your approach the wind blows from the right.

The carry of 180yd (165m) should not be too difficult – but beware a low shot which may thud into the fairway bunkers.

After a short drive into wind the green is unreachable. When you plan your second shot you must be careful to avoid the little pot bunker 30yd (27m) short of the green.

Take a club that won't reach the sand and content yourself with a chip and the possibility of a single putt. A 4 on this hole feels like a birdie – a 5 still represents good golf.

First and second shots
Grip: normal
Stance: normal
Ball position: normal for drive; midway between left heel and center of stance for second
Weight distribution: even
Swing: full
Swing path: in to in
Club: driver off tee, then 3 iron

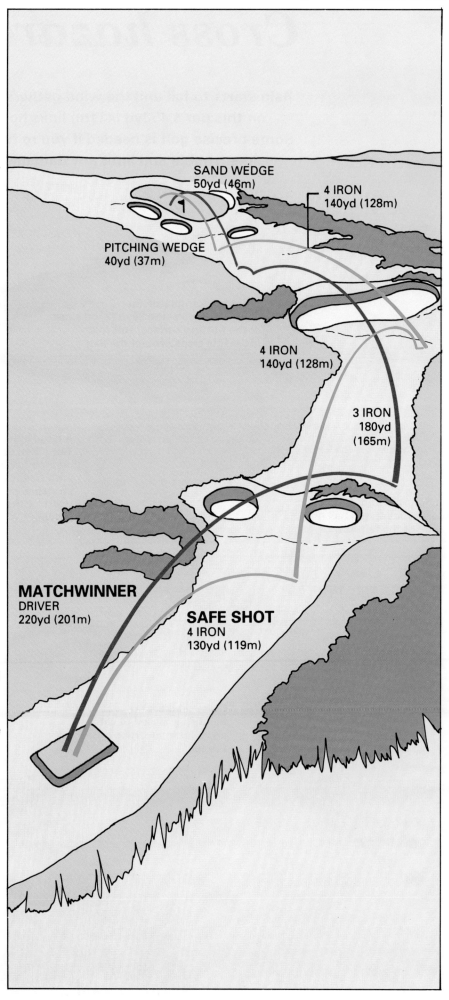

SAND WEDGE
50yd (46m)

4 IRON
140yd (128m)

PITCHING WEDGE
40yd (37m)

4 IRON
140yd (128m)

3 IRON
180yd
(165m)

MATCHWINNER
DRIVER
220yd (201m)

SAFE SHOT
4 IRON
130yd (119m)

Difficult pin placement

With two pars needed to reduce your handicap, it is tempting to aim your tee shot directly at the pin on this 173yd (158m) par 3 17th. But, as the butterflies flutter, it is easy to forget about tempo and lose your ball in the water.

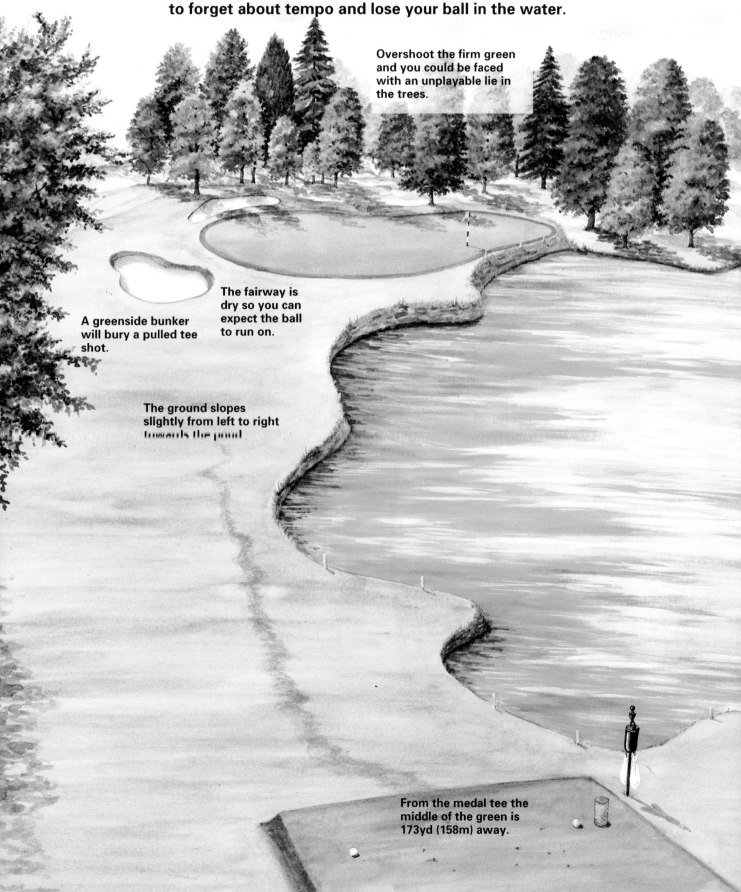

Overshoot the firm green and you could be faced with an unplayable lie in the trees.

The fairway is dry so you can expect the ball to run on.

A greenside bunker will bury a pulled tee shot.

The ground slopes slightly from left to right towards the pond

From the medal tee the middle of the green is 173yd (158m) away.

SAFE SHOT
Go for the green not the flag
Since you need a par here and at the 18th, it is important not to take too high a risk.

Ignore the flag and make your target the left side of the green, thereby avoiding the threat of the lake.

Choose a 4 iron as it is easier to get a clean strike than with your 3. Concentrate on making a smooth swing – don't hurry.

A very good shot with the 4 will hold the putting surface leaving you with two careful putts for par. Even a reasonable strike will run along the firm fairway to the green.

Grip: normal
Stance: square
Ball position: opposite inside left heel
Weight distribution: even
Swing: full
Swing path: normal in-to-in
Club: 4 iron

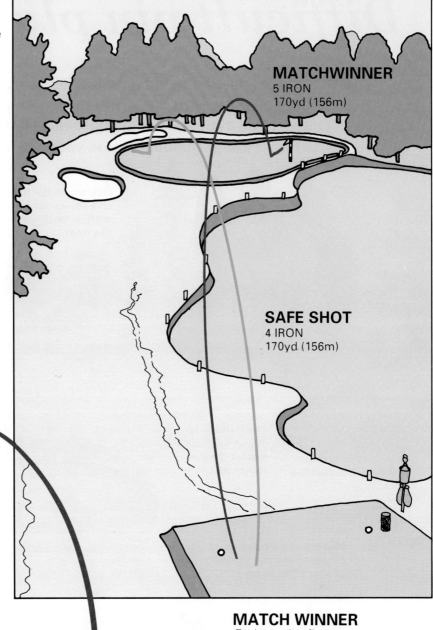

MATCHWINNER
5 IRON
170yd (156m)

SAFE SHOT
4 IRON
170yd (156m)

Play the percentages
You will often be faced with a range of strategies. You can make the choice easier by thinking in terms of the chances of success.

Go to a range and hit 10 balls at a target. If you land two within 5yd you have a 20% chance of shooting that accurately on the course. Similarly, if you land four within 10yd, and eight within 20yd you have 40% and 80% chances of repeating those shots.

Where you need a steady par go for an easier shot – one with at least a 50% chance of success. When the chips are down though, go for the good bet, the 20% chance. As Tony Jacklin once said, "Play the game to the limits of your ability and anything is possible."

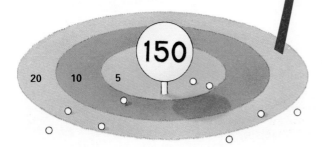

MATCH WINNER
Fade to the flag
This is the sort of hole that can make the difference between you looking like an accomplished golfer or a complete duffer!

Because the pin is so close to the lake, shoot a slight fade for the centre of the green.

The ball will come round towards the pin with enough backspin to hold the dry green and leave you with two easy putts for par, and a good birdie chance.

Grip: normal
Stance: align left of target line
Ball position: midway between left heel and center of stance
Weight distribution: even
Swing: full
Swing path: slightly out-to-in
Club: 5 iron

Preferred lie

Preferred lies, often called winter rules, are used to protect the course but you can make them work to your advantage. On this par 4 it's surprising what a difference a preferred lie could make to your second shot.

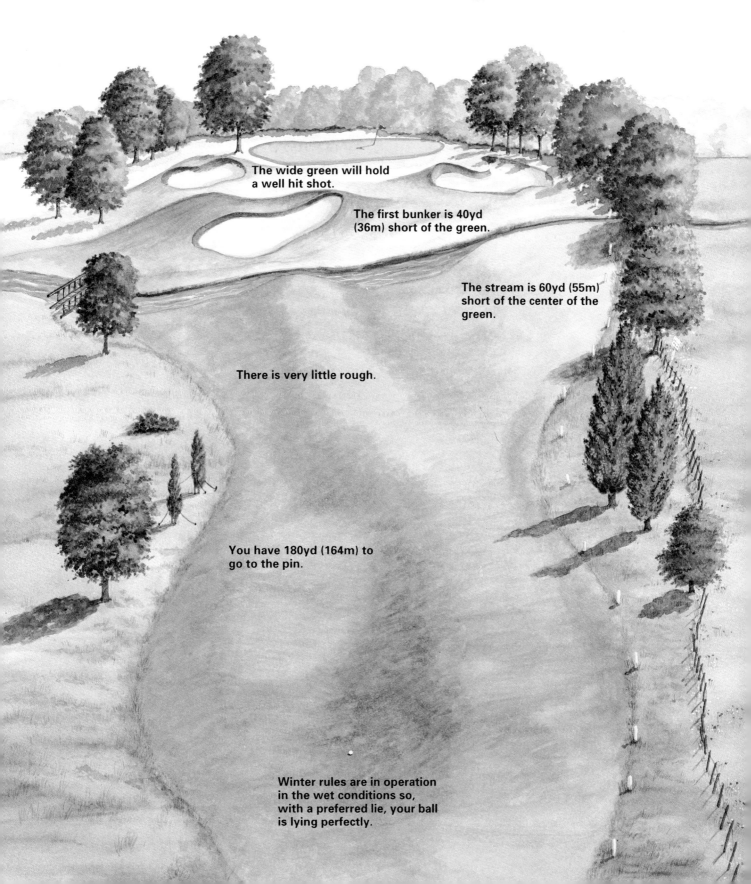

The wide green will hold a well hit shot.

The first bunker is 40yd (36m) short of the green.

The stream is 60yd (55m) short of the center of the green.

There is very little rough.

You have 180yd (164m) to go to the pin.

Winter rules are in operation in the wet conditions so, with a preferred lie, your ball is lying perfectly.

SAFE SHOT
Make the most of the new lie
Under normal playing conditions, this is a difficult approach shot. It is all too easy to linger on visions of your shot plopping into the stream or bunkers.

The out of bounds threatens all along the right hand side so the safe route to this green is a shot laid up short of the water hazard, followed by a wedge into the green (dotted line).

But you should take advantage by adopting the preferred lie rule. After marking, lifting and replacing your ball you have a perfect lie. It is now worth trying to fly the ball all the way to the green.

Take a 5 wood and aim for the flag. If you are unlucky enough to hit a complete duff, your ball will not reach the stream and so you will be playing from about the same spot as if you had decided to lay up short of the water.

As always, it is a case of playing the percentages – sometimes it is worth taking the risk.

Grip: normal
Stance: normal
Ball position: opposite inside of left heel
Weight distribution: even
Swing: full
Swing path: normal
Club: 5 wood

pro tip

Rules reminder
Preferred lies are often misunderstood by club golfers. You do not simply roll the ball over. You should mark, lift, clean and replace your ball within 6in (15cm) of your marker but not nearer the hole.

MATCH WINNER
Attack the pin
If the greens are good and you are hitting the fairways, a preferred lie can give you a distinct advantage.

It doesn't really matter that the fairway is wet and the hole is playing longer, or that the heavy lie would normally make the shot tricky.

With a preferred lie you can approach with a straight attack to the pin by confidently hitting a long iron from what would have been a nasty tight lie.

The greens are holding so you can fly a high ball all the way to the pin – you might expect to pick up a birdie.
Grip: normal
Stance: normal
Ball position: opposite inside of left heel
Weight distribution: even
Swing: full
Swing path: normal
Club: 4 iron

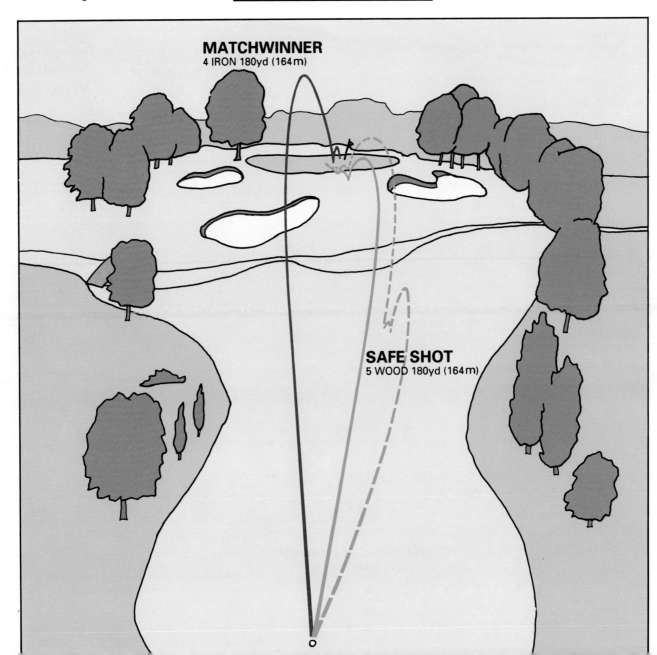

MATCHWINNER
4 IRON 180yd (164m)

SAFE SHOT
5 WOOD 180yd (164m)

Saucer green

You can just see the top of the flag but the hole is hidden
by the slope leading to the green. How can you
be sure of finding your ball nestling near the cup? The real
problem here is club selection.

Conditions are calm with
almost no wind to affect
your shot.

Light rough covers the
rise behind the green.

A ball landing in the trees
is likely to be unplayable.

The large tree is 150yd
(137m) from the front of
the green and your ball is
a further 5yd (4.5m) away.

The fairway slopes uphill
although your ball is lying
well on a flat piece of
ground.

SAFE SHOT
Fairway flyer
Conditions are calm and the hole will never play more easily. You have 165yd (150m) to the hole and a wide fairway to play with. If you have been hitting the ball well it is worth having a go for the green with a fairway wood.

Concentrate on making a good shoulder turn and imagine your ball sailing over the hill. Don't even think about the trees.

The accommodating green will hold your shot even if it's a little long. Two good putts will see you safely home with a solid par.
Grip: normal
Stance: normal
Ball position: opposite inside left heel
Weight distribution: even
Swing: full
Swing path: normal
Club: 5 wood

MATCH WINNER
Choose carefully
The essence of the matchwinner is choosing the right club to match the calm conditions and the unusual shape of the green. Calculate the distance carefully.

From the large tree you have 150yd (137m) to the front of the green (a 6 iron). Add 1 club to reach the pin and another ½ club to take account of the distance between your ball and the large tree.

A full 4 iron is the correct club as a slightly long shot will be gathered in by the slope on the back of the green. The ball should roll back towards the hole leaving a birdie opportunity.
Grip: normal
Stance: normal
Ball position: opposite inside of left heel
Weight distribution: even
Swing: full
Swing path: normal
Club: 4 iron

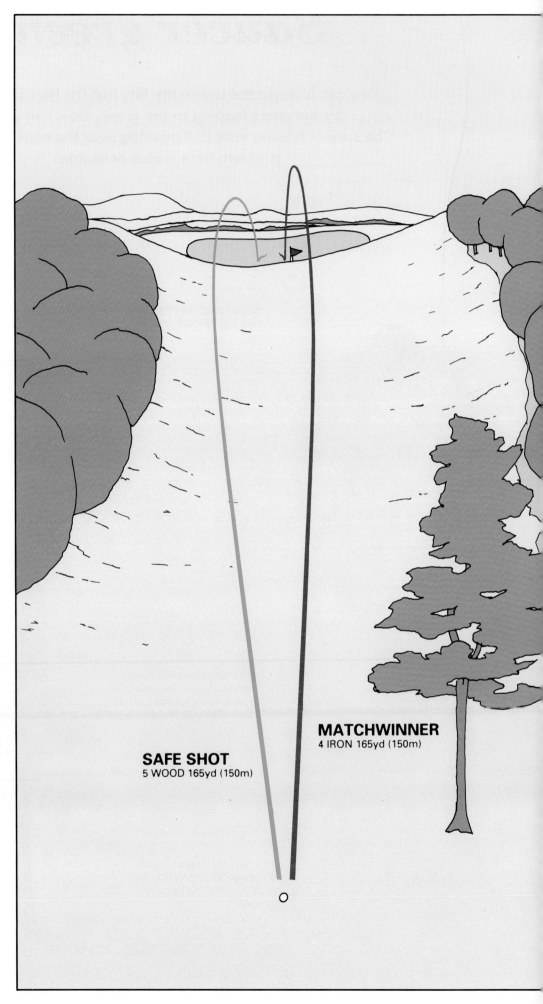

SAFE SHOT
5 WOOD 165yd (150m)

MATCHWINNER
4 IRON 165yd (150m)

When to attack

You have 130yd (118m) to go on this par 4. With the
wind, the lie, and everything else seemingly
against you, is there any way you can attack the pin
to set up a birdie chance?

A strong wind blows
from right to left.

Beware of a hard kick on
the green causing the ball
to run out of bounds.

Thick gorse lines the left
side of the fairway.

The wind and sun-dried
fairway produce
unpredictable bounces.

A sloping lie means the
ball is sitting below your
feet.

SAFE SHOT
Easy lay-up
There are times when so many factors conspire against an approach directly at the green that only an ultra-cautious strategy provides a safe and dependable option.

In this case the breeze, the rough, the traps and the lurking out of bounds mean that a lay-up in front of the bunkers is the only banker.

Take a wedge, flex your knees a little more than normal to allow for the ball being below your feet, and with a three-quarter swing pitch up to a position short of the bunkers.

Aim slightly left as the awkward stance produces an upright swing causing the ball to fade right. The wind has little effect on such a short shot.

An easy pitch will bring you safely to the putting surface in 2 and a chance of making par.

First shot
Grip: normal
Stance: slightly open
Ball position: center of stance
Weight distribution: favoring heels to combat slope
Swing: three quarter
Swing path: normal
Club: pitching wedge

MATCH WINNER
Use the wind
Despite the complications there is a backable matchwinner here.

The ball lying below your feet tends to put your swing on a more upright plane, sending the ball to the right. However, the wind is blowing to the left so you can use the awkward stance to your advantage.

Flex your knees and address the ball 1in (2.5cm) further right in your stance. Correct club selection is vital. You have 130yd (118m) to the flag – an 8 iron in calm conditions. Take a 7 iron to keep the ball low and hit firmly but with a three-quarter length swing.

Take care not to over compensate for the wind or your hands will turn over as you hit through the ball, pulling the shot left – and into the out of bounds.

A well struck shot should be held on the wind and stop on the putting surface to give you a birdie chance – if you have calculated the effects of the wind and the slope correctly.

Grip: slightly lower than normal
Stance: normal
Ball position: slightly towards right foot
Weight distribution: favoring the heels
Swing: three quarter
Swing path: normal
Club: 7 iron

MATCHWINNER
7 IRON 130yd (119m)

SAFE SHOT
FIRST SHOT – PITCHING WEDGE 80yd (73m)
SECOND SHOT – SAND WEDGE 50yd (45m)

pro tip

Concentration cap
Some players find wearing a woolly hat to cover the ears improves concentration and balance in cold and windy conditions – it insulates you against the hissing of the breeze and cuts you off completely from the inclement conditions.

Out of reach

For most golfers a pin 230yd (210m) away is out of reach.
After a good drive over dry ground on this 480yd (438m)
par 5, you have a difficult choice of strategy to tackle both
the distance and the traditional heathland terrain.

The raised green slopes
down on both sides to two
large bunkers.

The brook is 185yd (169m)
away and will bury any
weak approach.

Heather has been allowed
to grow into the center of
the fairway.

You're likely to lose a ball
landing in the trees lining
the right side of the
fairway.

SAFE SHOT
Lay up before the brook
The heather growing in the middle of the fairway is unusual but is a common feature on older heathland courses.

Fearing a bad lie in the middle of it, you may be tempted to smack a fairway wood over the brook. Think again. Even with the advantage of dry ground the green is out of reach. If you carry the brook you still have an awkward chip to a raised green. Miss-hit your fairway wood and you might pick up a 1 stroke penalty after visiting the water.

Make par by taking the safe route. Take a 4 iron – you will hit it consistently better than your 3 iron and it will leave you short of the brook. From behind the water you have a straightforward wedge. Safely on the green in 3 you have 2 putts for par.

First shot
Grip: normal
Stance: square
Ball position: opposite inside of left heel
Weight distribution: even
Swing: full
Swing path: normal
Club: 4 iron

Second shot
Grip: normal
Stance: square
Ball position: center of stance
Weight distribution: even
Swing: three quarter
Swing path: normal
Club: pitching wedge

MATCH WINNER
Raking 1 iron
The stronger player can take advantage of superior length and go for the green on this long approach.

From 230yd (210m) however, a well hit 3 wood on to the bone hard green has less chance of stopping than a pitch on to the dining room table!

And if it lands short, there is a danger of your shot running out of steam on the bank leaving you with a delicate chip.

You need to manufacture a long low shot that will hold its line and run on to the green. This is a perfect situation for a raking 1 iron. Hit solidly it will fly 200yd (182m), clearing the burn.

On the dry ground the ball should then roll up the bank between the bunkers leaving you 2 putts for birdie.

Grip: normal
Stance: normal
Ball position: opposite inside left heel
Weight distribution: even
Swing: full
Swing path: normal
Club: 1 iron

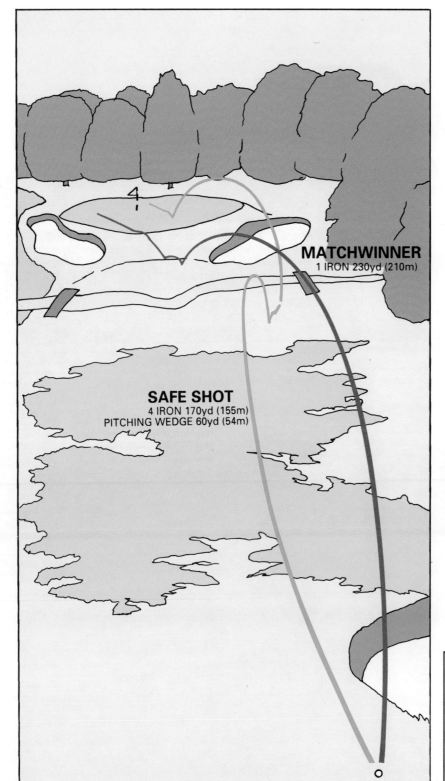

MATCHWINNER
1 IRON 230yd (210m)

SAFE SHOT
4 IRON 170yd (155m)
PITCHING WEDGE 60yd (54m)

pro tip

Bespoke stroke
It is not always a good idea to play the full shot – it might look good but it doesn't necessarily get good results. Always keep in mind a manufactured stroke that is better designed for the particular shot you're required to play.

Know your yardage

On the card this par 3 measures a tame 135yd (123m). However, a closer inspection reveals a much longer and more testing shot.

There is no wind to worry about.

The air is cold and damp so don't expect your shots to fly as far as usual.

A ball landing on the slope rolls back down again – possibly into the water.

Rough surrounds the green and is tricky to get back from if you land wide.

From the tee the hole is slightly uphill.

SAFE SHOT
Pitch to the front

Measuring 135yd (123m), this is not a long hole so you should be confident of setting up a chance for par.

However, like all good short holes there is a penalty if you miss the green. Water guards the right so you must be sure of carrying the ball all the way if you play for the flag.

With the bunker eating into the left, the middle of the green – usually a safe option – is narrow and demands good accuracy.

By ignoring the pin position you have a very safe route to the lower section of the green which reduces the danger of the hazards.

The front of the green is 125yd (114m) from the tee so even allowing for the cold damp air you only need an 8 iron. You should be confident of reaching the target and having 2 putts to make par.

Grip: normal
Stance: normal
Ball position: center of stance
Weight distribution: even
Swing: full
Swing path: normal
Club: 8 iron

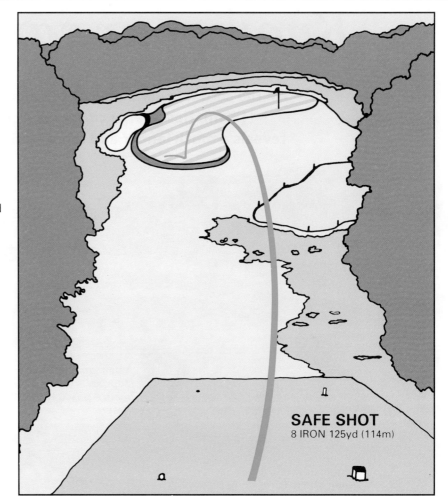

SAFE SHOT
8 IRON 125yd (114m)

MATCH WINNER
Calculate wisely

Look closely at this green and you notice that you have a bigger target if you go for the flag – the green is twice as wide at the back as it is at the front.

The danger is that by going for the target you bring the bunker into play on the left. You must also be confident of carrying the ball all the way to avoid pitching into the slope on the right.

The essence of the shot is in calculating the yardage. As you size it up consider all the factors which affect your choice of club.

A shot of this length – 135yd (123m) – usually needs a 7 iron. However the hole is slightly uphill which means the ball won't reach as far, and the dank, heavy air also dampens your firing power.

Take an extra club and, as long as you keep it on line, your ball should finish close to the pin for a possible birdie.

Grip: normal
Stance: normal
Ball position: mid way between left heel and center of stance
Weight distribution: even
Swing: full
Swing path: normal
Club: 6 iron

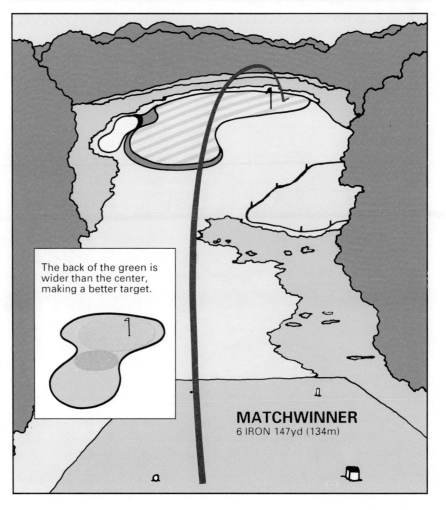

The back of the green is wider than the center, making a better target.

MATCHWINNER
6 IRON 147yd (134m)

6

IRON PLAY

It is good iron play that sets up birdie opportunities. Likewise, it is bad iron play that leaves you struggling to string-together a good score. There's more to it than that, of course, but that's the bottom line. Two-time U.S. Masters champion Bernhard Langer is one of the best iron players of his generation. From the short irons all the way up to the long irons, his efficient and repeatable swing rifles the ball at the flag with unerring accuracy. This ability comes not just from trusting his swing, but also from knowing how far he hits the ball with each club, and playing the right shot at the right time – an art you can learn in this chapter.

Master the long bunker shot

If there's one thought to concentrate on when playing a full shot from a fairway bunker, it's to hit the ball before the sand. This is undoubtedly the key to success at long shots from sand. If the clubhead makes contact with the sand first, you lose a great deal of distance on the shot.

Before setting foot in the bunker, look at the distance between you and the green and judge which club you need. Then, providing there's enough loft to clear the lip in front of you, take one more club. The small adjustments you need to make in your swing mean that the ball doesn't travel quite as far as a shot from grass.

Always remember – if the lip in front of you is so high that you can't use a club long enough to reach the green, resist the temptation to try anything adventurous. It usually ends in disaster. Just accept that you can't attack the pin this time – make sure of your escape and go for the green with your next shot. In these situations a cagey approach keeps you out of trouble.

SOUND TECHNIQUE

Work your feet into the sand just enough to give yourself a firm footing. Put a little more than half your weight on your left foot. This promotes a steeper swing arc which helps you strike the ball cleanly. Grip slightly further down the club as an extra precaution against the fat shot.

Play the ball further back in your stance than for a shot from grass. This helps ensure the clubhead is on a downward path into impact. Make a three-quarter backswing for maximum control – the choice of one more club removes any doubts about distance.

Make sure your head remains very still on the downswing. Dipping down is likely to cause a heavy shot. If you come up off the ball – even just slightly – you're in real danger of hitting a thin. Keep your hands ahead of the clubhead in the hitting area and your eyes on the ball – your only concern should be how close to the flag the shot finishes.

CLOSE SHAVE
Step into sand with confidence – regardless of the distance from the green – with a clear understanding of the techniques of fairway bunker play. Shave the ball as cleanly as possible off the sand – the clubhead creates only a small puff of sand rather than the explosion you often see from a greenside bunker. The red stripe shows early signs of backspin.

FAIRWAY BUNKER CLOSE-UP

(1) POISED TO STRIKE
As with every bunker shot, hover the clubhead about 1in (2.5cm) above sand level. This gives you enough leeway to ensure you don't shave the sand during the early stages of the swing. If you make even the tiniest contact with sand on the backswing you incur a penalty stroke. With a relatively long club such as a 5 iron, grip a little further down than normal.

Costly mistake
Take a cautious approach if you're in any doubt whether you can reach the green from a fairway bunker. Many world class golfers have gone for the gamble and paid the price.

The young American star Bobby Clampett led after two rounds of the Open at Troon in 1982. But midway through the third round, Clampett came to grief in a fairway bunker. An ambitious recovery shot sent the ball thudding into the lip in front of him and Clampett's championship hopes disappeared. Your mistake won't be as costly, but it's an experience every golfer could do without.

2 CLEAN CONTACT
The arc of your swing is slightly steeper than normal, delivering the clubhead to the ball on a downward path. The precise moment of impact shows the club making contact with the ball fractionally before it touches the sand. This guarantees that you don't lose any distance by hitting the sand first.

KEY POINT
Concentrate on rhythm and swing down smoothly.

(3) SIGNS OF SPIN
As the ball is launched on its way the red line (indicating spin) starts to rotate backwards – it's completed a half revolution already. This is the first evidence of the backspin generated from a well struck fairway bunker shot. The ball climbs quite quickly and always lands softly.

KEY POINT

Keep your head rock steady and level – don't dip down or come up off the ball.

4 SAFE ESCAPE
Contact with the sand is inevitable because the clubhead travels down into impact. But note that the club hits the sand *after* the ball is on its way. The clubhead leaves a very shallow trough in the sand as the ball is clipped away – the strike should feel crisp and perfectly under control.

pro tip

Leg action
In a fairway bunker it's essential you work your feet into the sand – but don't bury them too deep or you restrict body rotation and reduce the amount of power you're able to generate. You also lower the arc of your swing and risk hitting sand before the ball.

Take plenty of club and keep your weight fairly central throughout the swing. Make a three-quarter backswing for control – it's when you start forcing the shot that your feet are likely to move around.

AVOID THE THIN
A thin from a fairway bunker is certainly one to eliminate from your game. The shot – shown above just after impact – is usually caused by anxiety. The swing speeds up, rhythm is lost and the leading edge of the clubhead strikes the middle of the ball, sending it shooting low along the ground.

Try to set aside your sand fears. A shot from a fairway bunker is very similar to playing from grass – there's just a little more pressure on you to strike the ball cleanly. Concentrate on rhythm and control – both help you achieve success out of a fairway bunker.

Using casual water

When rain makes your grips wet and the ground soggy, it's all too easy to despair, lose your patience and increase your scores. However, you can use a waterlogged green to your advantage.

The hole is a par 5 of 502yd (459m). It has been raining for several hours, and puddles have started to appear on the course. Conditions are heavy underfoot but there is little wind.

The green is considerably wider at the front. It slopes from back to front.

A pond catches any shot that is hooked or pulled left. A shot that doesn't carry all the way to the pin falls back into deep rough.

The fairway slopes from the green down to where the ball is lying.

After the second shot, the ball is about 140yd (128m) from the pin.

SAFE SHOT
Hit to the right
There is a large section of green to the right of the flag. The high handicapper is safer to aim over here, rather than straight at the flag, where a ball landing short of the green would roll back towards the pond.

You can afford to take one more club than in normal conditions – even a ball with no backspin will hold on the green because the puddles prevent roll. Use a favorite mid-iron or even a 5 or 6 wood. Concentrate on a good, clean strike that then leaves you a medium-length putt.

Grip: normal
Stance: normal
Ball position: opposite left heel to give shot extra height
Weight distribution: even
Swing: full
Swing path: in to square to in
Club: 3 iron, 5 wood or 6 wood

MATCH WINNER
Straight for the pin
Good players can take even greater advantage of the wet conditions, and play straight for the flag. As is often the case when it's raining, there is very little wind. Combined with the softness of the green, a high ball will stop instantly. This bold shot would not be possible if the ground was dry and the shot was traveling downwind.

Hit confidently with a 7 or 8 iron. The ball should land and stop at the flag leaving a birdie putt.

Grip: normal
Stance: normal
Ball position: center of stance or slightly left of center for extra height
Weight distribution: even
Swing: full
Swing path: in to square to in
Club: 7 or 8 iron

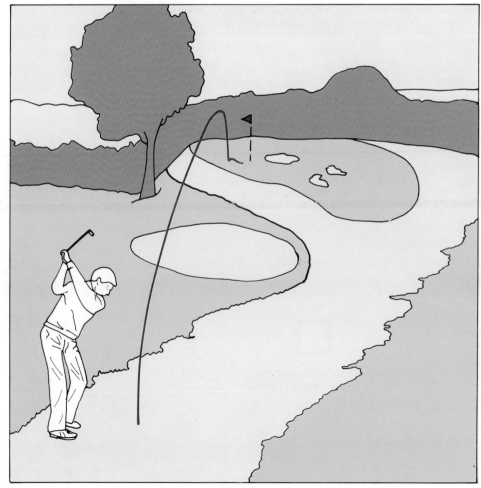

Gorse gully

Natural gullies and mounds – originally created as the seas
and oceans fell back – have become the links of today.
Even after a fine drive you are left with a tricky approach
to a narrow, windswept plateau green.

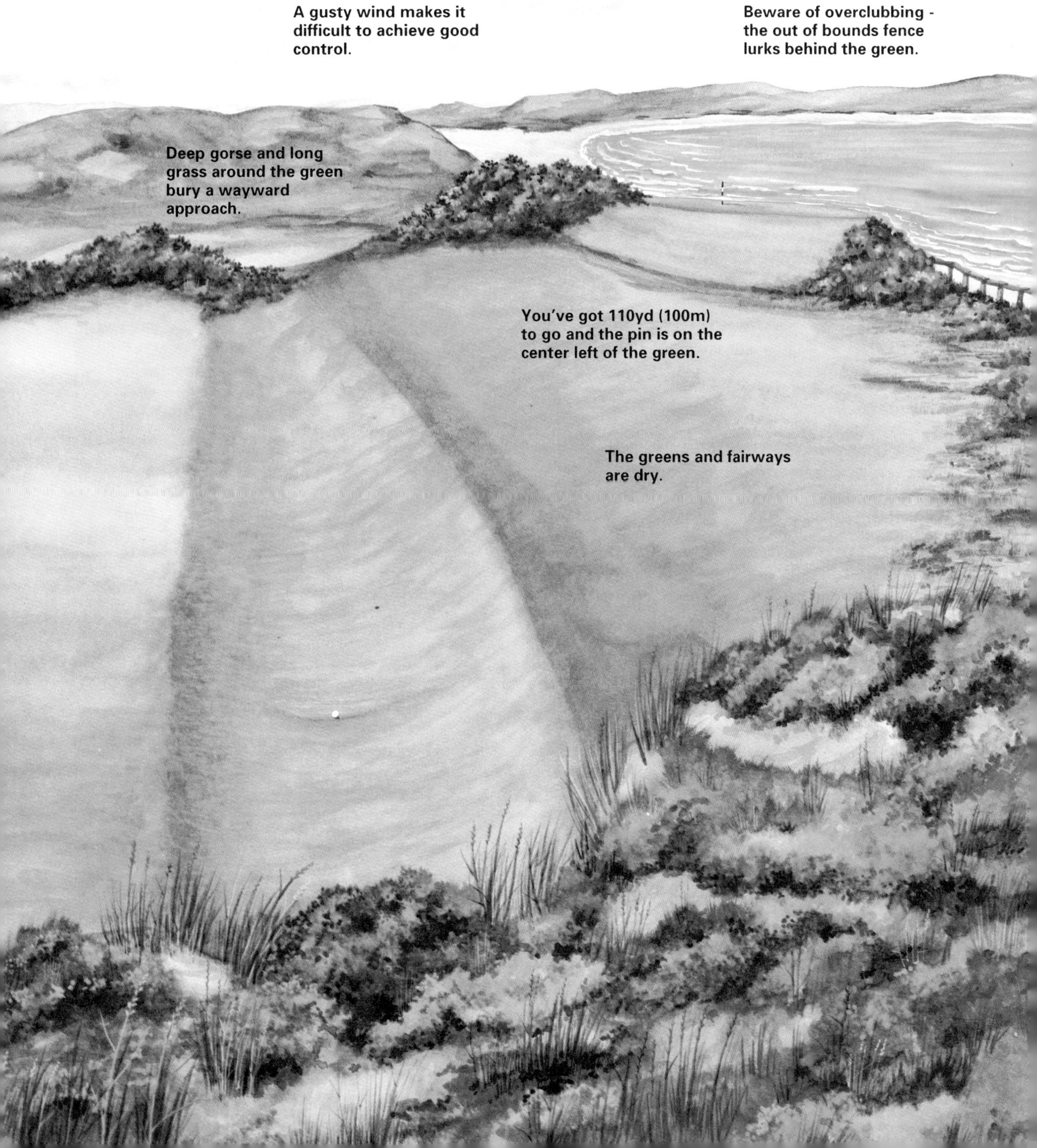

A gusty wind makes it
difficult to achieve good
control.

Beware of overclubbing -
the out of bounds fence
lurks behind the green.

Deep gorse and long
grass around the green
bury a wayward
approach.

You've got 110yd (100m)
to go and the pin is on the
center left of the green.

The greens and fairways
are dry.

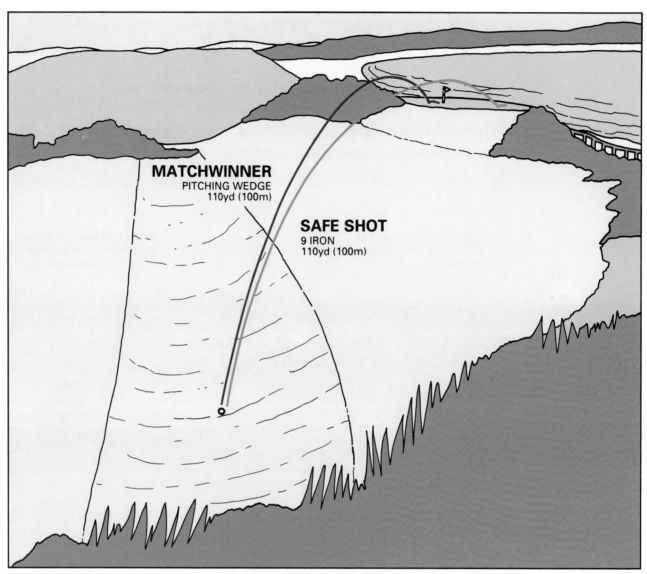

SAFE SHOT

Crisp 9 iron approach

You don't want to waste a good drive by dumping your approach shot into the gorse or – even worse – out of bounds.

There's no point in just hoping your ball will run up the bank – it is too steep. Don't delay play, but walk towards the pin and give yourself a good idea of the size of the landing area – it looks much larger and therefore give you more confidence.

Try to picture your shot landing on the green. A crisp 9 iron approach will hold the putting surface, leaving you a comfortable 2 putts for par.

Grip: normal
Stance: square
Ball position: center of stance
Weight distribution: even
Swing path: normal
Club: 9 iron

MATCH WINNER

Capitalize on your long drive

Take a good look at the green. From the gully the target looks frighteningly small. If you walk quickly up the fairway you will have a better idea of the landing room available. In your mind the green now looks larger. You can rely on a solid wedge holding the wind and stopping quickly on the putting surface, giving you a birdie chance.

Grip: normal
Stance: square
Ball position: center of stance
Weight distribution: even
Swing path: normal
Club: pitching wedge

pro tip

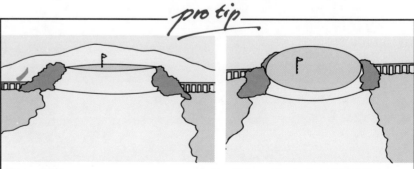

Target tip

From below the green you see a narrower target. A closer inspection of the green reveals a bigger landing area. If you can, take a good look at the pin and the green. It's surprising how your view of the shot changes – an intimidating task can become much more attractive. The growth in confidence helps you play positively.

Deceptive distance

What could be easier than a simple iron shot into
this large green? But beware – long
shadows dance across the putting surface and the flat
fairway makes correct club selection vital.

There is only a very
light wind.

The pond is up to 50yd
(45m) across.

The small trees on the left
are shown on the
scorecard as being 120yd
(180m) from the center of
the green.

A ball landing in the pond
will cost you a penalty
shot.

The ball is lying well after
a 230yd (207m) drive on
this 370yd (333m) par 4.

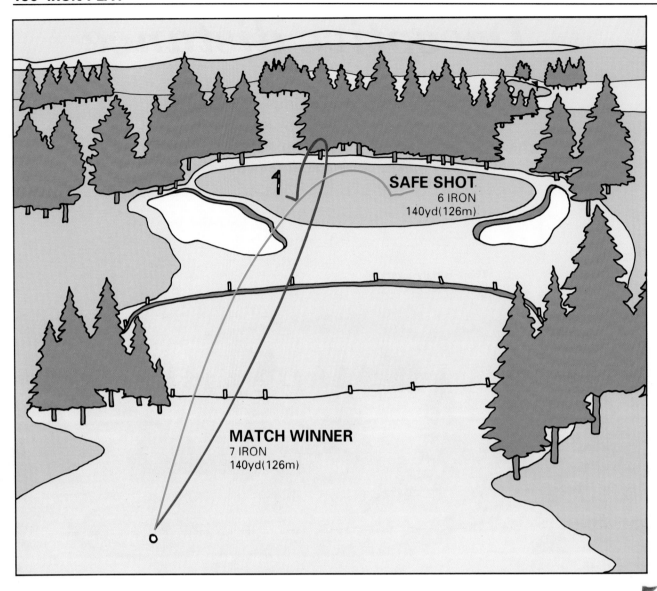

SAFE SHOT

Bunker-free route

After a good drive of 230yd (207m), it's easy to become greedy and end up dumping the ball into the bunkers, or – even worse – into the pond.

Consciously put the pond out of your mind. Only a duff will land there so concentrate on your rhythm and selecting the right club.

The scorecard shows the trees on the left are 120yd (108m) from the middle of the green. If you are 20yd (18m) from the trees, an easy 6 iron is the club.

Take the bunker-free route and play for the middle of the green.

Grip: normal
Stance: normal
Ball position: between center of stance and inside of left heel
Weight distribution: even
Swing: full
Swing path: in-to-in
Club: 6 iron

MATCH WINNER

Ignore the shadows

If you know that you usually drive 230yd (207m) and the hole measures 370yd (333m), you should have a 7 iron of 140yd (126m) to the middle of the green.

However, because of the flat ground and the shadows, the approach shot looks much shorter than it is – more like a wedge of 110yd (99m).

Ignore the shadows and, wary of the flat fairway, confirm the yardage on the scorecard.

With 140yd to go, you should confidently start right of the flag and play a gentle draw around the trap into the flag. Even if the ball doesn't draw you are still on the green.

Grip: normal
Stance: slightly closed
Ball position: center of stance
Weight distribution: even
Swing: full
Club: 7 iron

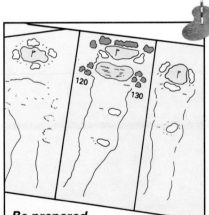

Be prepared

On your home course, you should never be caught in a position where you don't know how far you are from the flag.

Get to know how far particular trees or landmarks are from the center of the green on each hole.

With careful preparation you should never be fooled into underclubbing because of flat fairways or shadows on the greens and fairways.

Tiger tee

Multiple tee positions give players a variety of challenges.
From the front, this par 3 requires a
little flick with a short iron – but from the back tee it
becomes a monster and you need a new strategy.

The green is soft and will hold most shots. It slopes to the left.

A strong breeze is blowing from right to left.

There isn't much fairway but a ball will bounce off the slopes towards the center.

A wild shot is unplayable from the gorse left and right of the fairway.

The raised tiger tee at the back is 210yd (192m) from the green.

MATCH WINNER
Bore through the wind

The yardage indicates either a 1 iron or a lofted wood. Consider the wind and the shape of the hole. Although the green will hold a high floating shot with the wood, there is a danger it will come in with the wind, roll to the left and disappear into the greenside bunker.

If you can hit a low boring shot with the 1 iron it is more likely to hold its line.

Aim for the center of the green as the ball will spin slightly left due to the wind and the slope of the green.

Grip: normal
Stance: normal
Ball position: opposite inside of left heel
Weight distribution: even
Swing: full
Swing path: normal in to in
Club: 1 iron

SAFE SHOT
Play it as a par 4

After playing a 7 iron from the front tee, it comes as quite a shock to discover you now need a full hit with the driver to reach the green.

However, taking the driver is risky as a wild hook or push will end up in the gorse.

Your scorecard will look better if you take the safe option of playing this as a par 4.

Select a club that will not reach the right hand bunker. This gives you the full width of the fairway to aim at.

Visualize a shot landing in the left centre which will leave you with a safe little pitch.

Play the percentages and your scores will come down.

First shot
Grip: normal
Stance: normal
Ball position: midway between center of stance and left heel
Weight distribution: even
Swing path: normal
Swing: full
Club: 5 iron

Second shot
Grip: 1in (2.5cm) below normal
Stance: normal
Ball position: center of stance
Weight distribution: even
Swing path: normal
Swing: three quarter
Club: pitching or sand wedge

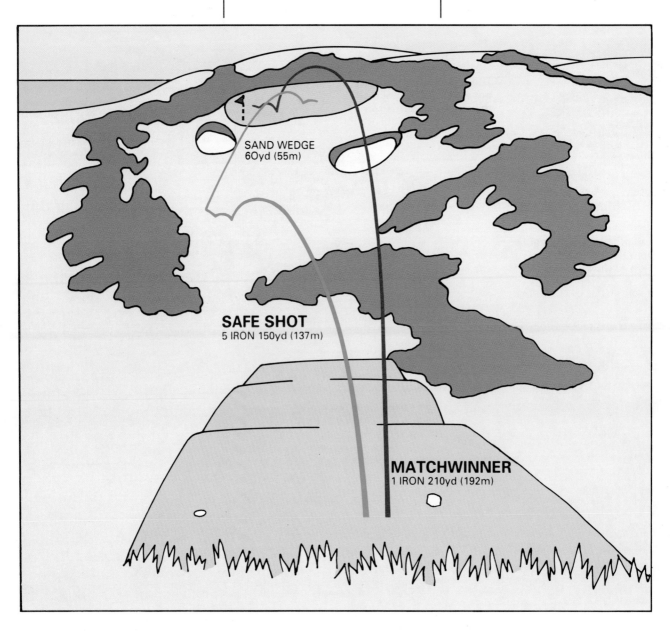

SAND WEDGE
60yd (55m)

SAFE SHOT
5 IRON 150yd (137m)

MATCHWINNER
1 IRON 210yd (192m)

7

SHORT GAME SECRETS

The expression "drive for show and putt for dough" perhaps doesn't quite capture the essence of what makes a good golfer, but it does highlight a view shared by professionals all around the world – namely, that a great score is put together on and around the greens. Corey Pavin's short game is so hot that he aims to hole virtually every chip, putt or bunker shot that he looks at. He is that confident. This chapter represents a comprehesive guide to shots on and around the green. Study the techniques, practice them, and you too can find yourself developing a similarly cavalier attitude to the short game.

Uncontrolled chipping

**Poor striking and command around the greens can have many
different causes – perhaps bad set-up or
club selection – but often an uncontrolled backswing is to
blame. A consistent short game stems from good
clubhead control achieved by a firm and rhythmical swing.**

Q On short chips I often fluff or stab the ball, even though I know my set-up is sound. Why?

A The main reason for fluffing a chip is quitting on the shot and not attacking the ball with purpose. This deceleration is frequently an effect of too long a backswing.

If you take the club back a long way (**1**), you naturally become worried that the ball will fly too far after impact. You react to this feeling by slowing down into impact and don't attack the ball firmly with authority.

This loose, unconfident action with a stunted followthrough (**2**) means that you either hit weakly behind the ball – a fluff – or stab the shot.

The only time your backswing should be full for a short chip is when you have to play a deliberate cut up shot – perhaps over trouble. But even for this shot you must be firm through the ball – don't quit.

X **①** BACKSWING TOO LONG

X

X **②** SLOWS DOWN INTO IMPACT AND QUITS ON SHOT

X BALL FLUFFED OR STABBED

Q Even from a good lie I regularly thin a short chip way past the flag or hit it weakly and don't reach my target. What am I doing wrong?

A One of the main ways to hit a thin is to force the shot and not swing with rhythm. A common cause of a forced stroke is to have too short a backswing (**1**).

This leaves you no room or time to find a good rhythm for the downswing. To compensate for this short action you thrust down with your hands, and the club attacks the ball in a jerky, scooping action. Trying to flick the ball into the air with too much wrist action (**2**) to ensure reaching the target means you can easily thin the ball.

The shot that fails to reach the target comes from not being able to attack the ball with enough power – another legacy of too short a backswing.

① BACKSWING TOO SHORT

HARD TO FIND GOOD RHYTHM

② FORCED DOWNSWING SCOOPS AT BALL

LIKELY TO THIN

Chipping with purpose

BACKSWING LONG ENOUGH TO FIND RHYTHM – NO NEED TO FORCE SHOT

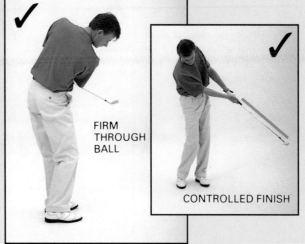

FIRM THROUGH BALL

CONTROLLED FINISH

The perfect length of backswing needs to be long enough to be able to attack the ball with rhythm and conviction, but short enough so you don't feel like slowing down into impact for fear of hitting the ball too far.

Take the club back smoothly with an easy tempo, to a point from where you can swing down with the same rhythm. Attack the ball firmly and make sure you follow through into a controlled finish position. Keep steady throughout the stroke to lessen the risk of a thin.

Putting puzzles

Putting is so important to your scoring that it's essential to master the art. If you don't seem to be holing as many putts as you should be, try to find a cure.

Q I keep missing short and medium length putts I expect to hole. What could I be doing wrong?

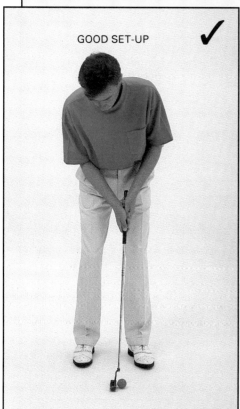

GOOD SET-UP ✔

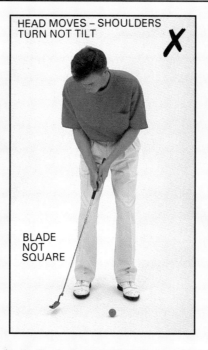

HEAD MOVES – SHOULDERS TURN NOT TILT ✗

BLADE NOT SQUARE

LIFTING SHOULDERS THROUGH IMPACT ✗

BALL PUSHED OR PULLED

SHOULDERS TILT PROPERLY ✔

HEAD STILL

HEAD KEPT DOWN – BLADE ON LINE ✔

A The two main reasons for missing a putt are a misjudgment of pace and line or moving excessively during the stroke. It's crucial to stay still on a putt and minimize the amount of moving parts if you're to keep the blade square to the target.

If you're too eager to follow the progress of the ball towards the hole, it's all too easy to come off the shot. Even from a good set-up, watching the clubhead on the backswing can lead to this jerky action as you tend to look at the club throughout the stroke. Your head and shoulders start to lift up just before impact. The blade doesn't stay square through impact and you either push or pull the ball.

Pendulum putt

A good putting stroke is based on a pendulum action of your arms and shoulders while keeping your wrists firm.
○ Resist the temptation to look up and follow the ball.
○ Don't move your head or raise your shoulders until well after the ball is on it's way.
○ Swing with a slow smooth rhythm and be firm through the stroke.
○ Don't jerk the putter back after impact – hold the followthrough position.

Q I know that I keep still on my putts and have a good stroke, so I can't understand why the ball keeps slipping past the hole. What could be wrong?

A Your grip may be poor. There are several putting grips so even if yours is good it may not be ideal for you. Make a fresh start and experiment with your grip. Almost anything goes as long as it's comfortable and most importantly your hands and blade are square to the target line. This is essential if you're to have a chance of keeping the blade square throughout the stroke.

Try out some of these famous players' grips.

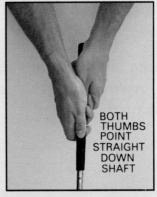

BOTH THUMBS POINT STRAIGHT DOWN SHAFT

◀ Ben Crenshaw

He points both thumbs straight down the center of the grip to ensure that his hands are square with the blade. His right palm and the back of his left hand face the target – this increases the chance of the blade returning square at impact.

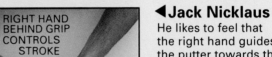

RIGHT HAND BEHIND GRIP CONTROLS STROKE

◀ Jack Nicklaus

He likes to feel that the right hand guides the putter towards the hole and so places his right palm squarely behind the grip. He locks it there by cocking his wrist. The left hand is there to steady the putter and is also square to the target.

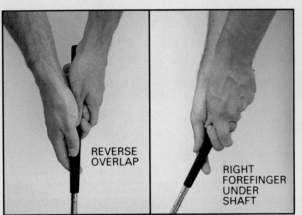

REVERSE OVERLAP

RIGHT FOREFINGER UNDER SHAFT

▲Faldo and Ballesteros

They both use the classic reverse overlap grip – where the left forefinger is placed over the fingers of the right hand. Also their right forefinger points downwards and curls comfortably underneath the grip to help guide the putter.

▶ Bernhard Langer

For short putts, the German uses the cross-handed grip. He feels that it locks the left wrist and so stops the right hand taking over through impact, which can lead to a pull. This is quite a drastic measure but can work if you suffer from the yips.

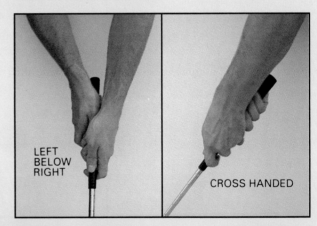

LEFT BELOW RIGHT

CROSS HANDED

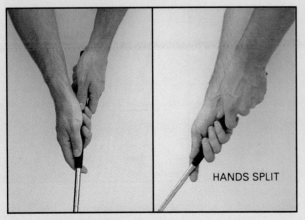

HANDS SPLIT

▲ Hubert Green

This double major winner uses a split-handed method. It helps lessen the chance of swinging with any unnecessary wrist action. The right hand becomes the dominant force in the putting stroke – this can help guide the club directly at the hole.

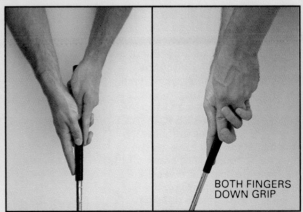

BOTH FINGERS DOWN GRIP

▲ Mark McNulty

He points both his forefingers down the shaft. He overlaps his left forefinger with the second and third fingers of his right hand to reduce wrist action. The right forefinger gives Mark extra feel for the stroke – especially for judging distance.

Bunker blues

**Even if you practice hard at greenside bunker play, faults can creep into your game. A fairly
simple recovery shot often turns into a disaster even if your
technique is only slightly wrong.**

Q I'm catching the ball well, but my shots are flying out of the bunker on too low a trajectory and going left of target. Often the ball scoots through the green. Why?

A You are probably using a normal pitching method, instead of the specific greenside bunker technique. If you swing normally and attack the ball on an in-to-in path it's difficult to slide the club under the ball with the maximum amount of loft on the clubface.

You tend to release your hands and close the blade slightly through impact, and so the ball flies out lower than it should and left of target. Little backspin is produced – combined with the low flight it's hard to hold the green.

Sliding through sand

Keep your swing smooth and follow the line of your feet. You should be aligned slightly left of the target with the blade square, and so your swing path should be out to in. Lead with the left hand into impact so the opened up blade slides under the ball.

If you resist releasing your hands and hold the blade square to the target for as long as possible, the ball flies out high, on line and with a good deal of backspin.

X

NORMAL IN-TO-IN
ATTACK

X

RELEASED TOO EARLY

BALL FLIES
LOW AND LEFT

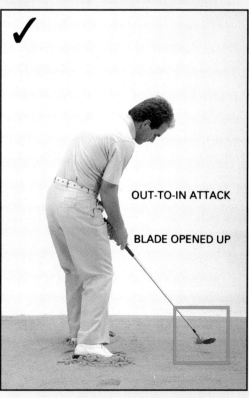

✓

OUT-TO-IN ATTACK

BLADE OPENED UP

✓

BLADE STILL SQUARE TO TARGET

BALL FLIES HIGH
AND STRAIGHT

X TOO STEEP AN ATTACK

X DIPS INTO IMPACT

BALL FLUFFED

Q **Why do I regularly take too much sand and leave the ball in the trap?**

A The most likely cause of this problem is digging down into the ball in an effort to lift it out of the sand. Even if you are perfectly set up and make a good backswing, forcing the downswing means you

attack the ball from too steep an angle.

Instead of sliding under the ball the club digs deep into the sand and the shot is fluffed. If you attack too steeply and take too much sand the ball can't fly as normal however much effort and power goes into the shot.

✓

CONTROLLED SWEEPING ARC SLIDES CLUBHEAD UNDER BALL

✓ BLADE STAYS SQUARE

Floating action

The sand wedge is designed to slice under the ball and loft it out of a trap – it doesn't need any extra effort on your behalf. If you set up correctly and swing with a smooth steady action – so that the opened up blade takes a sliver of sand from under the ball – the shot should float out of the bunker

without a problem.

Stay balanced and still throughout the stroke and remember to hold the blade square to the target for as long as possible. This simple action is reliable even from a tricky lie, so have confidence in your method at all times.

Wedge worries

One of the more frustrating aspects of golf is not being able to hit your wedge close to the hole – especially with a basic pitch. If you keep your technique neat and simple, you can iron out any inconsistencies.

DOWNSWING TOO WRISTY

FLICKING ACTION LEADS TO THIN

Q I keep thinning the ball with my wedge, even though I'm sure that my set-up is sound. What could I be doing wrong?

A Your action is probably too wristy. Picking the club up quickly with quite a lot of wrist break, and then flicking at the ball on the downswing in an attempt to lift it off the turf makes swing co-ordination difficult. This action dramatically reduces

the chances of timing the ball sweetly.

If you're not lucky enough to strike the ball exactly at the bottom of your swing arc, you're likely to catch it on the up and blade the shot. Even if you do strike the ball well, the narrow arc you create often leads to a weak trajectory shot that doesn't fly as far as you've planned.

CONTROLLED INTO IMPACT

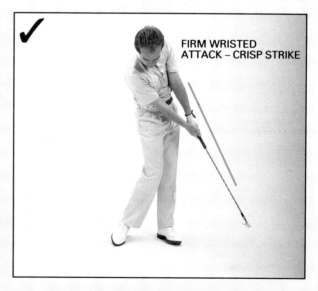

FIRM WRISTED ATTACK – CRISP STRIKE

Firm wrist control

To keep your swing sweet and consistent, the back and downswing must be controlled and compact. To gain this commanding and authoritative strike, swing with a rhythmical, firm-wristed action. Make sure you strike down on the ball, but never chop down too hard.

Never try to lift the ball off the turf by flicking the wrists – let the natural loft of your wedge do the work. Swing through firmly and resist releasing the hands too quickly – keep your wrist break to a minimum to add to your control.

Q I can't understand why I keep overshooting my target. What could I be doing wrong?

A Your problem could stem from poor ball positioning. If you place the ball too far forward (1), you have to reach for the ball and are likely to catch it too clean – even if your swing is rhythmical and controlled. Instead of striking down on the ball you tend to hit it slightly on the up (2). Though you may not hit an out and out thin, the ball still flies low and can easily skid through the green.

If you play the ball from too far back in your stance (3) you tend to chop down forcefully on the ball (4). The clubface naturally becomes delofted and though you can sometimes produce quite a lot of backspin the ball often flies too low and doesn't check on the green.

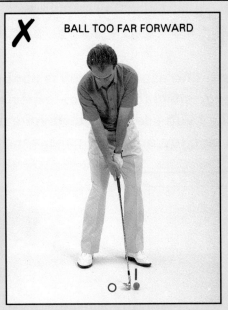

X BALL TOO FAR FORWARD

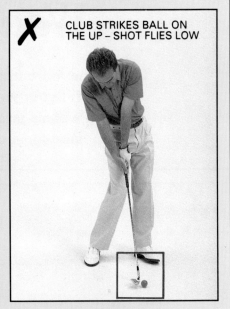

X CLUB STRIKES BALL ON THE UP – SHOT FLIES LOW

X TOO FAR BACK IN STANCE

X CLUB DELOFTED AT IMPACT – BALL SHOOTS LOW

Central strike

Position the ball centrally in your stance to ensure a crisp strike and a consistently well flighted pitch. If your swing is sound, this placement means that you attack the ball with a firm downward blow and the swing path is not too steep.

At impact the blade is perfectly angled to flight the ball on a good, high yet strong trajectory, and also to produce plenty of backspin – both adding to your control and accuracy.

✓ CENTRAL PLACEMENT

✓ CRISP STRIKE – WELL FLIGHTED PITCH

Short putt slip-ups

**Failing to hole short putts is not only annoying but is damaging to your scorecard. It can be a
mental problem, but is just as likely to be caused by a slight
fault in your putting stroke.**

Q **I struggle to hole short, breaking putts – I tend to pull a right to lefter, and push the one from left to right. And even my straight putts are erratic in a strong wind. Can you help?**

A The most common cause of missing short, breaking putts is if you guide the ball at the hole. Even if you aim your blade right of the hole for a right-to-left breaker, the natural tendency is to close the blade slightly into impact in an attempt to hit the ball directly at the hole. A pulled putt to the left is the result.

You don't mean to, but it is something built into the brain that tells you to aim straight at the hole. To avoid this mishap, you must concentrate on striking the ball at a point wide of the hole and let the slope do the work. Set up and aim the blade square to the intended path, and then stroke the ball straight towards your imaginary target. If you have judged the break and weight well, the ball should take the slope and drop in.

The problem with putting in a strong wind is that you can be blown off balance easily. And because a short putt stroke is such a small and precise swing, the tiniest body movement can ruin your action. Two adjustments help your balance and short putt technique in a wind. Adopt a wider stance than normal to give yourself extra stability, and grip down the putter to give you more control over the clubhead.

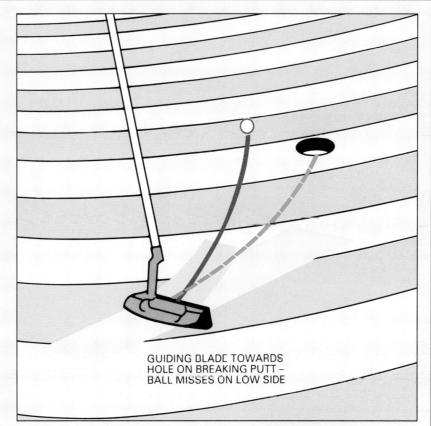

GUIDING BLADE TOWARDS
HOLE ON BREAKING PUTT –
BALL MISSES ON LOW SIDE

WIDER STANCE
IN STRONG WIND

GRIP DOWN FOR
EXTRA CONTROL

Q I tend to pull my short putts even if there is no break. Why?

A Your putting stroke is almost certainly incorrect. If you take the putter back slightly on the inside and then swing through impact on an in-to-in path – like a micro version of a full swing – there is only a very precise point when the blade is square.

If you're lucky the blade returns exactly square at impact. But it's also very possible that your clubface is a fraction crooked. Because you swing back to the inside you are likely to have a slightly closed blade through impact and that is why you pull your putts.

Straight back and through

To be sure of holing out from a short distance, you must have a square blade at impact. The only way you can be positive of achieving this is to swing with the blade square throughout your action.

Take the club back on a straight path along the ball-to-target line. If you now swing into and through impact along the same line while keeping your blade square, the ball rolls straight at the hole. The only way the ball won't drop is if you have misjudged the pace or something in its path knocks it off line.

PUTTER TAKEN BACK ON INSIDE LINE

PUTTER SWINGS STRAIGHT BACK ON BALL-TO-TARGET LINE

BLADE RETURNS SQUARE IF LUCKY

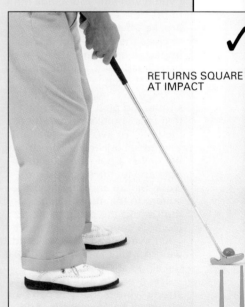

RETURNS SQUARE AT IMPACT

SWINGS TO INSIDE – LIKELY TO PULL BALL

CLUB SWINGING THROUGH ON TARGET LINE KEEPS FACE SQUARE – BALL ROLLS STRAIGHT

Mid-range muddles

The awkward length bunker shot – 30-60yd (27-55m) – is one of
the trickiest of all to judge. Poor striking and
gauging of distance are common faults, but they can be
eliminated with confidence and the correct technique.

Q I swing fully to try to power the ball out of sand and reach the target, but my shots nearly always fall short. Why?

A Taking too much sand is the most common reason for shots out of a mid-range bunker landing short of the target. The main cause of this is using your normal greenside bunker technique.

Aligning too far left and opening up the blade creates an out-to-in swing path, and you naturally hit behind the ball and take sand with the shot. This action combined with your usual follow-through – holding the blade square for as long as possible – floats the ball out softly. It is almost impossible to hit a ball 40yd (36m) if you use this greenside method.

Square and clean
Play these tricky mid-rangers like you would a normal pitch shot from the fairway. Align and aim square and try to pick the ball crisply and cleanly off the sand. This alignment helps to promote an in-to-in swing path and a full release through the ball – both useful if you need to gain distance.

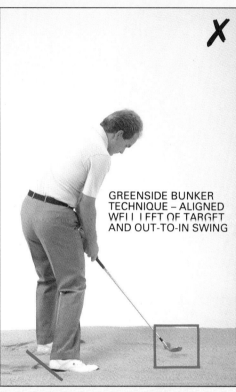

GREENSIDE BUNKER TECHNIQUE – ALIGNED WELL LEFT OF TARGET AND OUT-TO-IN SWING

HELD BLADE SQUARE FOR TOO LONG

BALL POPS OUT BUT NO DISTANCE

SET-UP SQUARE AND INSIDE ATTACK

RELEASE THROUGH BALL

SHOT FLIES GOOD DISTANCE

Q I set up square, position the ball centrally and concentrate on clipping the ball cleanly, but often hit a flyer through the green. Can you please help?

A You are probably preoccupied with striking the ball cleanly and worried about hitting behind it. If you are deliberately trying to avoid a fat shot your body tends to move up and out of position at impact.

By striving not to hit the sand first, the blade attacks the ball on the up and catches it thin. A flyer through the green is often the result.

Hit down, stay down

It is essential to catch the ball before the sand, but you must strike down to achieve this, not catch it on the up. Concentrate on playing the pitch-style shot with conviction and strike down on the ball firmly. Then, and only then, should you take sand. To ensure you don't lose momentum through impact don't dig down too hard – only a sprinkling of sand should be taken.

Stay with the shot through the ball – to avoid coming up and off it – and release fully. This action eliminates the thin from your list of miss-hits and ensures you reach the target.

WORRIED ABOUT FAT

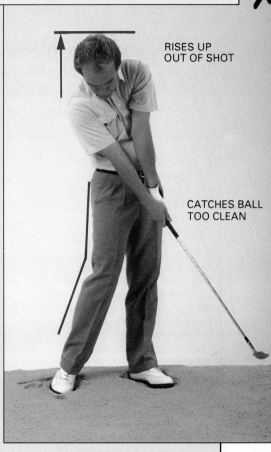

FLYER THROUGH GREEN

RISES UP OUT OF SHOT

CATCHES BALL TOO CLEAN

CONFIDENT, CRISP, DOWNWARD ATTACK

STRIKES BALL BEFORE SAND

STAY WITH SHOT THROUGH BALL – WELL FLIGHTED PITCH

Sharpen your short game

The club golfer probably receives more snippets of advice on the short game than any other aspect of golf. Wise words inform the frustrated player that half the shots in a normal round are putts, and that you make your score around the greens.

This sort of advice alone is seldom enough to end the misery of the golfer who suffers from a poor short game. Knowing how to do it is one thing – putting it into practice is another.

Everything you do around the greens needs to be more precise and repeatable than on the other shots because there's less margin for error. For this reason alone it's essential to keep your technique as simple as possible.

OPTIONS OPEN

The quickest route to a complete short game is to develop a wide repertoire of shots around a variety of clubs. From close range always practice with a selection of clubs – you can then approach every situation with a choice of shots in your bag.

Some golfers practice around the greens with just one club, feeling this is the quickest route to proficiency and consistency. But if you restrict yourself to a favorite club for chipping you make the short game even more difficult for yourself.

For example, it's extremely hard to manipulate the flight and roll of a pitching wedge from a variety of lies and situations – you need impeccable feel and magical hands. The occasional master stroke is bound to come off, but there are likely to be more times when you struggle to hit the ball close.

TARGET PRACTICE
Knocking your short game into shape isn't simply a case of hitting pitches and chips on the practice green – the often neglected greenside bunker shot is equally important. Grab a bag of golf balls and flip them on to the green from different lies. Try the hard shots as well as the easy and remember the basics – open stance with the clubface pointing at the flag.

HOW TO STAY IN CONTROL

1 FUNDAMENTAL RULES
Every time you approach a pitch shot think of control – try saying the word to yourself if necessary, as long as it's the uppermost thought in your mind. Stand relaxed to the ball in a comfortable address position – for a wedge shot the ball should be central in your stance.

2 STROKE AND DISTANCE
The backswing serves more purpose than just setting the club in the ideal position from which to attack the ball. The length of backswing determines the distance you want to hit a pitch shot. Halfway back gives you lots of control and enough time to generate clubhead speed.

Destructive force

Every golfer enjoys being in a situation where attack is the best policy. After all, shooting for the pin is a far more exciting prospect than playing safely to the middle of the green.

From perfect position some golfers can be too impetuous, swinging the club with such force and aggression that they seem to be trying to bash the cover off the ball. This tactic is ill-advised from any range, but with a pitching wedge in your hands it's perhaps the worst fault of all.

Coordination can easily desert you as the followthrough becomes a frantic flail with your arms. A solid strike can't be ruled out, but you cannot possibly judge distance or accuracy on a consistent basis if you're trying to hit the ball too hard.

The most effective way to hit your ball close is to swing within yourself – your short game is certain to benefit. Factors such as brute force and aggression are potentially disastrous in the golf swing.

3 IMPACT MIRRORS ADDRESS
The position of the left arm and club at impact is almost exactly the same as at address helping to ensure that the clubface returns to square. You can only achieve this consistently if your downswing is unhurried – clubhead speed is built up gradually rather than suddenly.

4 PUNCHED FOLLOW-THROUGH
You achieve this compact follow-through position by driving the back of your left hand towards the target. This helps keep the clubface square for as long as possible. Note how the follow-through is the same length as the backswing – a good habit to build into your game.

ESSENTIAL INGREDIENTS

The fundamentals are the same for most short shots:
○ slightly open stance;
○ hands positioned ahead of the ball at address;
○ light but secure grip;
○ length of swing that enables you to accelerate the clubhead smoothly into impact;
○ clean contact with the ball.

Tempo and rhythm are just as important from close range as they are for the full swing – this is vital to a reliable short game. Tempo varies from one golfer to another. Study the top players and see how their tempo – although it differs from pro to pro – remains constant from tee to green.

Tom Watson has a brisk swing and keeps the same tempo all the way down to his putting stroke.

Fred Couples wields his driver with a slow, almost lethargic ac-tion – but like Watson, he too keeps the same rhythm for his short game.

You must also adopt a sound strategic approach to the short game – the mechanics without the mind is no guarantee of success.

SHORT SHOT STRATEGY

Every golfer should have a pre-shot routine, whether preparing to hit a drive or weighing up a chip from close to the green. Whatever system you choose, try to make it such an integral part of your game that it never varies.

A study carried out by the U.S.P.G.A. found the time it took some professional golfers to pre-pare for each shot – after the club was selected – varied by less than one second.

This is not so much a conscious effort on the part of the player – it's almost impossible to time your-self so precisely. This consistency results from good habits on the practice ground.

Part of your pre-shot routine for the short game should always be to visualize the stroke you want to play. Never hit a pitch or a chip without first targeting a precise landing area.

GAUGE THE BOUNCE

Make it easy to predict how the ball reacts on landing. Bear in mind that you're likely to get an even bounce if you pitch your ball on the green rather than off it. And whenever possible, land your ball on a flat area, not a slope.

With good mechanics and a sound approach you have the recipe for success. Both of these qualities lead to good feel – and it's feel that can make the crucial difference between a sharp short game and an untidy one.

Imaginary target

Firing approach shots into the pin is one of the spectacular benefits of having a sharp short game – not only do the shots look good, they do wonders for your score and your confidence.

While very few golfers are blessed with the ability to do this every time, everyone is capable of achieving this result a couple of times in a round. Whenever club golfers struggle with pitch shots, the problem is often something to do with length – the ball usually falls on the shy side rather than too long.

If you find this happens to you, it's not necessarily a flaw in technique – more a slight error in judgment. A bit of visualization can help you out.

Next time you're faced with a shortish approach into the green, picture an imaginary flag at the point where you intend landing your ball – probably just short of the flag in most cases. Try to pitch your ball on top of the imaginary flag. In your mind you are then playing an attacking stroke – albeit at a target that doesn't exist!

Using your imagination should enable you to get the ball up to the flag more often. It's also a great morale boost because it helps cut out the frustration of seeing endless approach shots fall short of the mark.

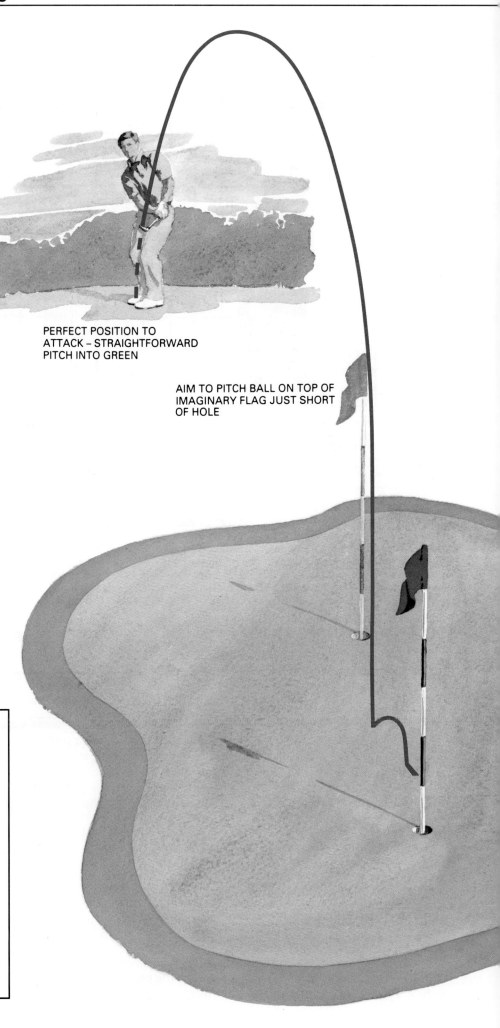

PERFECT POSITION TO ATTACK – STRAIGHTFORWARD PITCH INTO GREEN

AIM TO PITCH BALL ON TOP OF IMAGINARY FLAG JUST SHORT OF HOLE

Subtle adaptation

Before you choose which ball to use make a decision – do you play one that spins, or adapt your approach shots to allow for bounce and run? Sensible ball selection is often neglected by club golfers, at great expense to their scores. Make sure you play the right type of ball at all times.

A ball with a wound construction and soft cover is much easier to control than a two piece ball with a hard cover. Even Seve Ballesteros would struggle to stop a solid ball quickly on a firm green, so don't attempt to do so yourself.

Raised green with bunker

**A common situation facing the golfer
is a raised green combined with a bunker. You want to
avoid the bunker at all costs, and there are two ways of
going about it.**

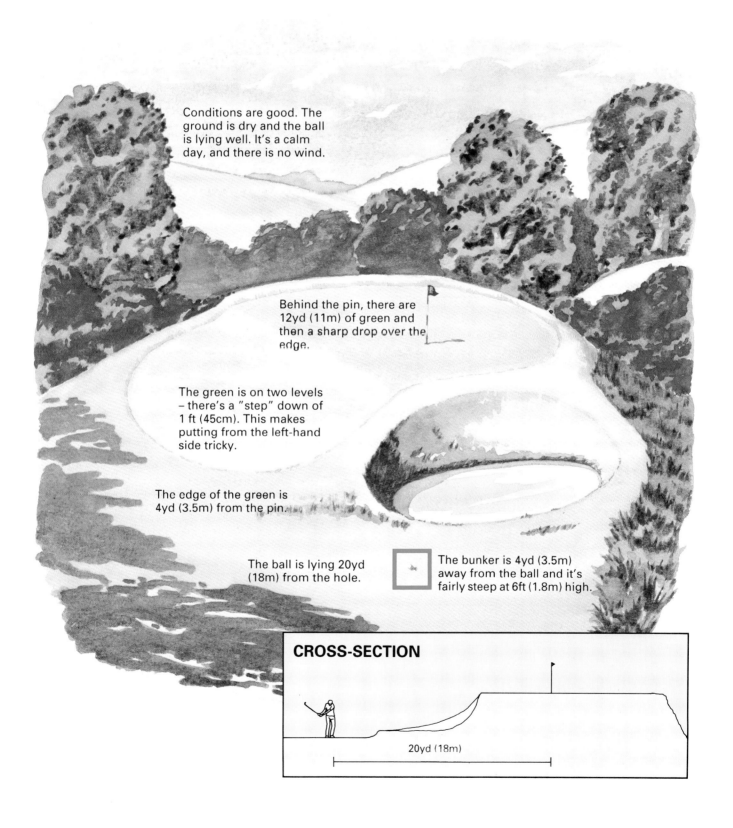

Conditions are good. The ground is dry and the ball is lying well. It's a calm day, and there is no wind.

Behind the pin, there are 12yd (11m) of green and then a sharp drop over the edge.

The green is on two levels – there's a "step" down of 1 ft (45cm). This makes putting from the left-hand side tricky.

The edge of the green is 4yd (3.5m) from the pin.

The ball is lying 20yd (18m) from the hole.

The bunker is 4yd (3.5m) away from the ball and it's fairly steep at 6ft (1.8m) high.

CROSS-SECTION

20yd (18m)

SAFE SHOT
Chip to left
If you have a high handicap this is the best shot as it avoids the bunker. However, it leaves you with a difficult putt and maybe at least two putts – one to negotiate the level change and one or more to hole the ball. In a strong downwind, even the scratch player is wise to chip to the left.

Grip: hands a few inches lower than usual
Stance: normal
Ball position: center of stance
Weight distribution: favoring the left
Swing: half
Swing path: normal
Club: 9 iron

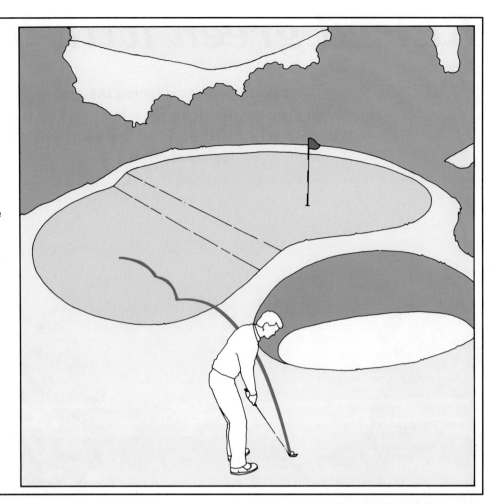

MATCH WINNER
Cut-up wedge or pitch
This stroke or par saver takes confidence and practice. You must hit high enough to avoid the bunker and short enough not to overshoot and lose the ball over the back of the green. Height, rather than backspin, causes the ball to stop.

Grip: hands a few inches lower than usual
Stance: open
Ball position: center of stance
Weight distribution: even
Swing: three quarters
Swing path: out to in
Club: sand iron

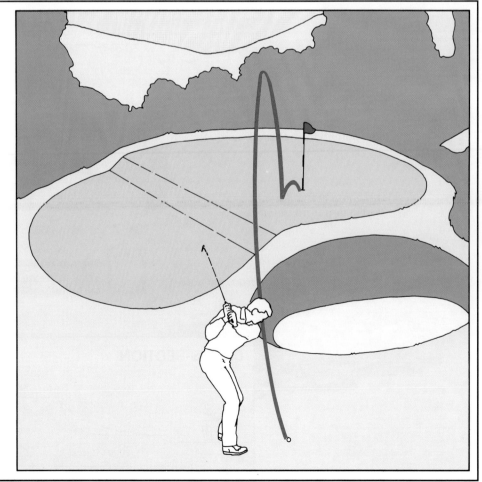

Deep greenside bunker

**An ambitious approach shot straight to the flag unfortunately
overshot – the ball trickled into the
back bunker because of lack of backspin on the dry, flat green.
Your aim now is to try to get down in two shots.**

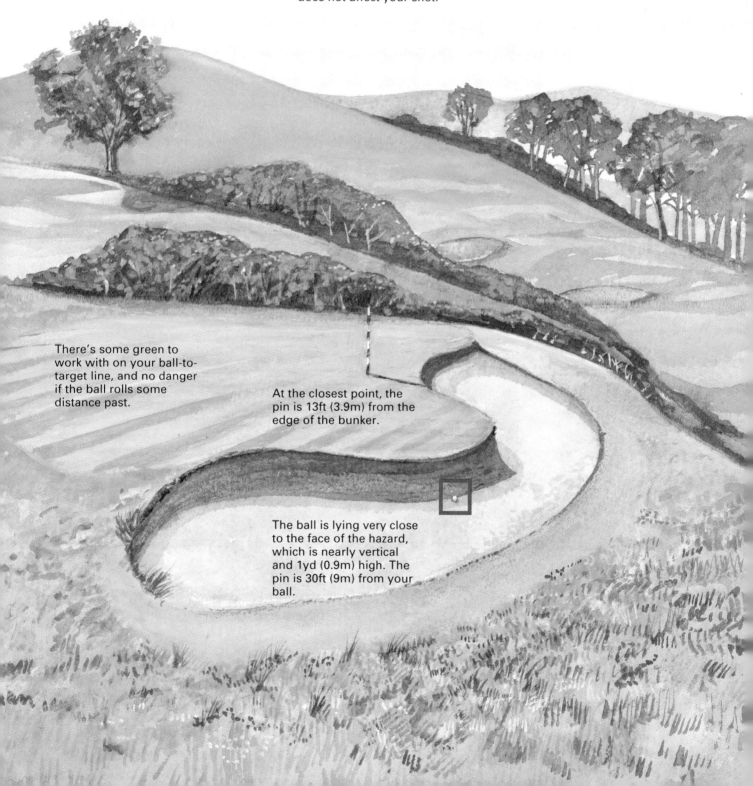

The hole is a par 4 of
362yd (331m). It is a calm
day and the slight wind
does not affect your shot.

There's some green to
work with on your ball-to-
target line, and no danger
if the ball rolls some
distance past.

At the closest point, the
pin is 13ft (3.9m) from the
edge of the bunker.

The ball is lying very close
to the face of the hazard,
which is nearly vertical
and 1yd (0.9m) high. The
pin is 30ft (9m) from your
ball.

SAFE SHOT
Play well left

Take advantage of the extra space on the left side of the bunker, where there is more room between the ball and the face of the hazard. Aim well left to give yourself a better chance of clearing the bunker.

This leaves you a long putt of 40ft (12m), but you achieve your main purpose. You can escape from a stubborn lie at the first attempt, without dropping a stroke, and also give yourself a fighting chance of holing the putt.

Because you have lessened your worries about leaving the ball in the sand, you are free to make a confident stroke.

Grip: hands slightly lower than usual
Stance: very open
Ball position: center of stance
Weight distribution: even
Swing: three-quarters
Swing path: out to in
Club: sand wedge

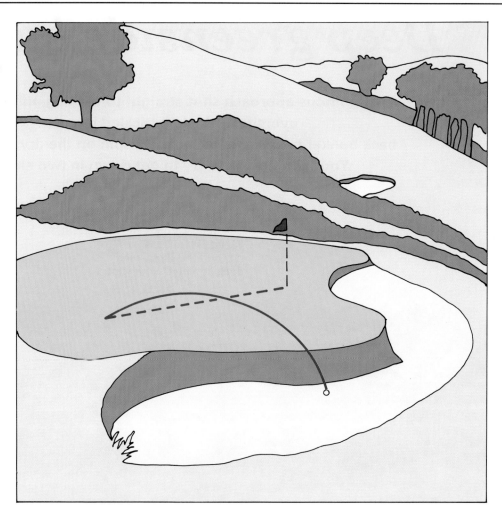

MATCH WINNER
Cut-up splash shot

An experienced player can play this shot to perfection. As the ball is so close to the face of the hazard, the chances are that it has just trickled into the bunker and is sitting up well in the sand.

Hit positively 2-3in (5-7cm) behind the ball. The cut-up splash shot throws the ball high out of the bunker on a carpet of sand. Despite the dry conditions, the ball lands gently, close to the flag, leaving a short putt.

Grip: hands slightly lower than usual
Stance: very open
Ball position: center of stance
Weight distribution: even
Swing: three-quarters
Swing path: sharp out to in
Club: sand wedge

A split-level green

On this long par 5 your approach shot has rolled off the split-level green, leaving you with a delicate feel shot to the hole. Accuracy is needed if you're to make par.

The green is dry and in good condition. There's a slight wind but this shouldn't affect the shot.

If you fluff the shot, sending the ball short, it may land on the bank and roll down to the lower level. You're left with a tricky putt to the pin.

If you scull the shot and overshoot the hole, the ball will roll down the gentle slope behind the green.

The flag is 8ft (2.5m) from the top of the step.

The green is on two levels with a step down of 2 ft (75cm). A putt aimed at the left of the green is risky.

The green slopes down from the step to the back of the putting surface

After your third shot, the ball is lying on a sandy patch just off the right side of the green.

SAFE SHOT

Aim right of flag

You don't want to risk rolling back down the bank, leaving a tricky uphill putt over the step. Aim your shot slightly to the right of the flag.

Use your putter or a 5 iron – which plays like a slightly lofted putter – and firmly putt the ball on to the top level. You are left with a long putt and it's still the safest way to save par.

Grip: hands slightly lower than normal. With a 5 iron use the reverse overlap grip for greater control
Stance: normal
Ball position: center of stance
Weight distribution: even
Line of shot: 6ft (1.8m) to the right of the flag
Club: putter or 5 iron

MATCH WINNER

Chip left of flag

From a sandy lie the experienced player can play a chip to the left of the pin with a pitching or sand wedge.

Visualizing the shot is essential for accuracy. The ball must be hit crisply or you risk a fluffed short shot which leaves you awkwardly placed on the lower level.

Finish with a simple tap-in shot – unless you manage to hole out for a birdie.

Grip: hands lower than usual
Stance: slightly open
Ball position: center of stance or towards left heel
Weight distribution: just favoring the left side
Line of shot: 2ft (60cm) to the left of the flag
Club: pitching or sand wedge

Downhill to the green

After 2 good shots on this 496yd (453m) par 5,
your ball has settled on a bare lie.
Walk down to the green to have a look at the options
from a different angle.

Your ball is lying on a downhill slope 50yd (45m) from the hole. The lie is bare.

The raised green, which slopes down towards the bunker at the back, is dry and firm. Conditions are good, with little wind.

Along the ball-to-flag line there's 26ft (8m) of green between the hole and the water, and another 8ft (2.5m) behind the flag.

A pond guards the front of the green and a bunker lies behind.

SAFE SHOT
Low strike
Consider your options carefully. Success in these cases doesn't always depend on a high shot – an accurate low shot is needed here. Use a putter from this bare downhill lie and play a Texas wedge to the fat part of the green. Alternatively, use a mid iron like a putter and play a low chip and run.

Concentrate on a clean hit – not too hard or you may end up in the bunker. This shot is just as effective as a pitch – you're safely on the green and can take 2 putts for par.

Grip: reverse overlap (normal if you use a mid iron)
Ball position: center
Weight distribution: even
Swing: short back and throughswing with smooth tempo
Club: putter or 6 iron

MATCH WINNER
Attack the flag
Walk down to the green to check how much landing room you have. A precise stroke off this bare lie should give a chance for a birdie putt. Hit cleanly to avoid the danger of sculling the ball from this downhill lie – a thin shot will land you in water.

Throw up a high pitch with a sand wedge – preferably one with a narrow sole as it's less likely to bounce – and aim to land the ball on the front of the green.

As the green slopes towards the back, you should get a nice roll down to the pin.

Grip: hands about 1in (2.5cm) lower than usual
Stance: slightly open
Ball position: opposite inside left heel
Weight distribution: even
Swing: three-quarters
Swing path: slightly out to in
Club: sand wedge

Final approach

At the 18th hole you may well be feeling tired and off your guard. An out of bounds behind the green, strong gusty winds and bumpy ground make your last approach shot a very challenging one.

The sight of the clubhouse directly ahead is likely to distract you.

The green is wider at the front. There's 8ft (2.5m) behind it but beyond the white fence is out of bounds.

The face of the bunker is 4ft (1.2m) high and is likely to trap any shots that fall short.

It's very cold – particularly in the gusts – which leads to less feeling and control in your hands.

The fairway is dry and bumpy and slopes left towards the bunker.

This 18th hole is a par 4 of 442yd (404m). The wind is behind you with occasional strong left-to-right gusts. The ground is dry and conditions are firm underfoot.

Because of the strong wind and a poor second shot the ball has landed 40yd (36.5m) from the flag. The lie is good.

SAFE SHOT
Chip and run
To prevent any possibility of your ball landing in the bunker, play safe and aim to the right of the flag. Play a very low chip and run aiming to land your ball 5yd (4.5m) away from the fringe of the green. The ball will bounce on landing and roll up to the level of the pin leaving you with an 8-10ft (2.4-3m) putt to save par.

Don't be tempted to thrash the ball at the green. As it's the end of the round and you're cold, your concentration and control are probably not at their peak. The crosswind will play havoc with a high ball and a bad bounce on the dry bumpy ground could lead to disaster.

Grip: hands about 2in (5cm) lower than normal
Stance: normal
Ball position: center of stance
Weight distribution: favoring the left
Swing: half
Swing path: normal
Club: 7 or 8 iron

MATCH WINNER
Punch shot
If you're feeling confident play a low punch shot with a 7 or 8 iron, landing the ball 5yd (4.5m) short of the fringe. The ball will roll up to the pin leaving you with a short single putt.

At first a lofted pitch may seem a good idea. But with the strong wind there is a real danger of the ball landing on hard bumpy ground and shooting forward through the back of the green and into the out-of-bounds area.

Grip: hands about 2in (5cm) lower than usual
Stance: slightly open
Ball position: midway between center of stance and right heel
Weight distribution: favoring the left side
Swing: half
Swing path: normal
Club: 7 or 8 iron

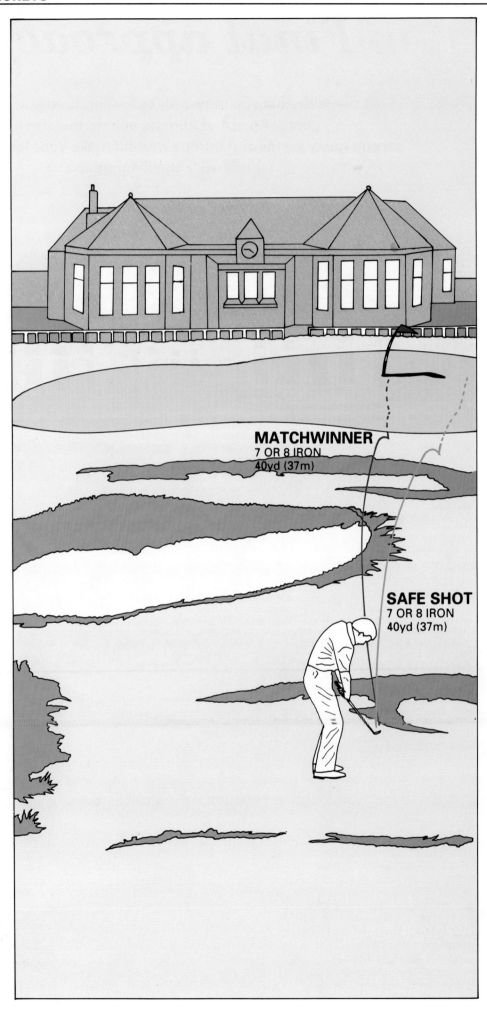

MATCHWINNER
7 OR 8 IRON
40yd (37m)

SAFE SHOT
7 OR 8 IRON
40yd (37m)

Bunker to plateau green

The dry parkland ground has caused your approach shot to roll
over the raised green and into a
deep greenside bunker. The two-tiered green makes recovery
even more difficult.

The hole is a par 4 of
390yd (357m). Your
second shot is lying well
on soft sand in the
greenside bunker.

There is a slight breeze
which does not affect
your play.

The green is dry and firm,
making the ball run on
landing.

The lower half of the green is longer
than the top, giving you more room
to work with.

The face of the bunker is
6ft (1.8m) high.

The ball is 10yd (9m) from
the pin.

SAFE SHOT
Hit to bottom tier
Your most important consideration is to lift the ball out of the bunker on your first attempt. Concentrate on a good greenside technique and pop the ball over the shallower part of the bunker on to the bottom level of the green. This larger area gives you more chance than the top tier of staying on the green in these dry conditions.

A long uphill putt of 11yd (10m) means a second tap-in putt for a bogey. Take care with your first putt – look behind the hole as well as in front to judge the distance and slope. Make sure you strike firmly to send the ball up the raised green.

First shot
Grip: slightly lower than usual
Stance: open
Ball position: opposite left heel
Weight distribution: even
Swing: three-quarters
Swing path: out to in
Club: sand wedge

Putt
Grip: reverse overlap
Stance: square
Ball position: center
Weight distribution: even
Swing: back and throughswing with smooth tempo
Swing path: normal
Club: putter

MATCH WINNER
Splash shot to pin
To salvage par you must get the ball on to the top tier. From the bottom level a single putt is most unlikely. Play your best splash shot over the highest part of the bunker face, landing just before the flag. Open the blade a little to give the ball height and minimize roll on landing. A short tap-in putt completes a successful recovery.

Grip: slightly lower than usual
Stance: very open
Ball position: opposite left heel
Weight distribution: even
Swing: three-quarters
Swing path: extreme out to in
Club: sand wedge

pro tip

Controlled ball
In tricky situations coupled with dry conditions a balata ball – often used by top amateurs and pros – gives an advantage over the more common surlyn ball. Though costly, balatas have softer covers, allow more control and so are easier to stop. If you're a low handicapper, it's worth investing in some for days when you know the ball is going to roll on dry ground. High handicappers are unlikely to reap the benefits.

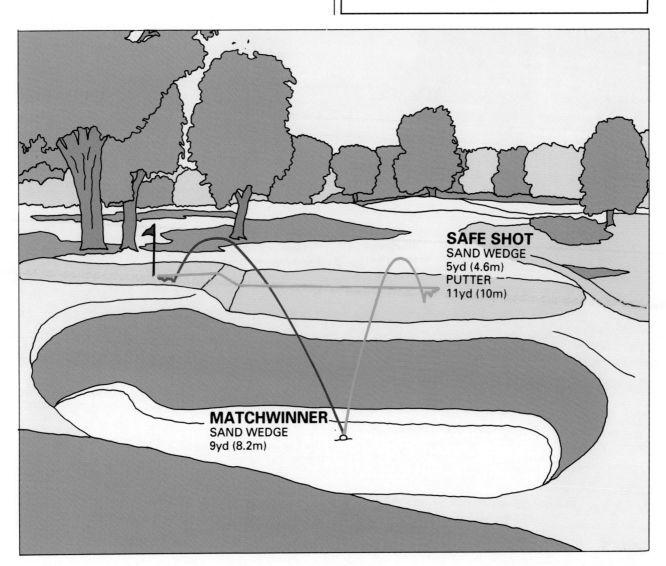

SAFE SHOT
SAND WEDGE
5yd (4.6m)
PUTTER
11yd (10m)

MATCHWINNER
SAND WEDGE
9yd (8.2m)

Gully approach

Although this exposed par 4 hole on a coastal
links is downwind, underclubbing
on your approach shot has left the ball awkwardly
short in a greenside gully.

A strong wind gusts
towards the flag.

The ball will roll when it
lands on the fast, dry
green.

The slope from gully to
green is 6ft (1.8m) high.

Though the lie in the gully
is tight the ball is sitting
up well

There is a distance of 15ft
(4.5m) between the flag
and the fringe.

SAFE SHOT
Roll up to the green

As the hole is downwind this is by no means an easy shot. Your priority must be to reach the green – it's all too easy to hit an over delicate chip which runs back down the slope, leaving you once again in the gully.

Treat the shot as a long putt – think of an imaginary hole about 6ft (1.8m) behind the pin, and make a firm stroke with your putter. The ball should roll past the pin but finish close enough to give you a chance of a single putt for par.

Grip: reverse overlap
Stance: normal
Ball position: normal
Weight distribution: even
Swing: quarter
Swing path: normal
Club: putter

MATCH WINNER
Punch into bank

Play a little sand wedge out of the gully – punch the shot crisply into the bank. The ball will hop up on to the green, land softly and roll on the fast, dry surface. It should stop close to the pin, leaving a simple tap-in putt to save par.

Grip: a little lower than normal
Stance: slightly open
Ball position: inside of right heel
Weight distribution: favoring left side
Swing: quarter
Swing path: normal
Club: sand wedge

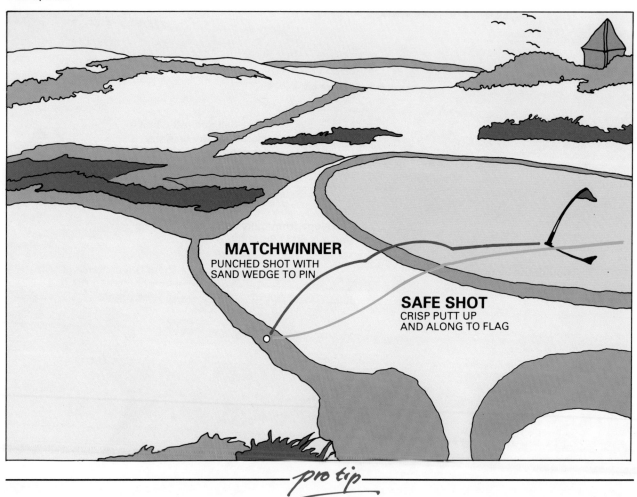

MATCHWINNER
PUNCHED SHOT WITH
SAND WEDGE TO PIN

SAFE SHOT
CRISP PUTT UP
AND ALONG TO FLAG

pro tip

Read the wind
Always take wind direction into account when considering your options – particularly when playing an exposed course. A mid to high handicapper would be wise to putt out of the gully regardless of wind direction, but an experienced player can adapt tactics – still using the sand wedge – to suit conditions.

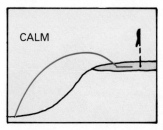

High chip runs slightly on landing.

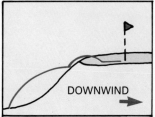

Low punch into bank runs to pin.

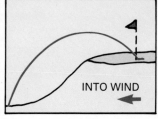

High pitch to flag stops quickly.

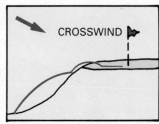

Low punch into bank runs to pin.

A holeable putt

**The golfer prepared to rise for an early breakfast may be
rewarded with a quiet course and a speedy 18 holes.
But it's not all easy work – damp, early morning greens
can be uncomfortably slow.**

Conditions are good –
it's a dry morning with
little wind though at this
early hour the green is
covered in large droplets
of dew.

Remember that dew is not
casual water – there's no
relief. You must putt over
even heavy dew – never
attempt to brush the moisture
away with your hand or
putter.

The uphill putt on the
rolling green measures
20ft (6m), with the pin
near the crest of a slope.

A solid approach shot
gives you a definite birdie
opportunity on this 378yd
(347m) par 4.

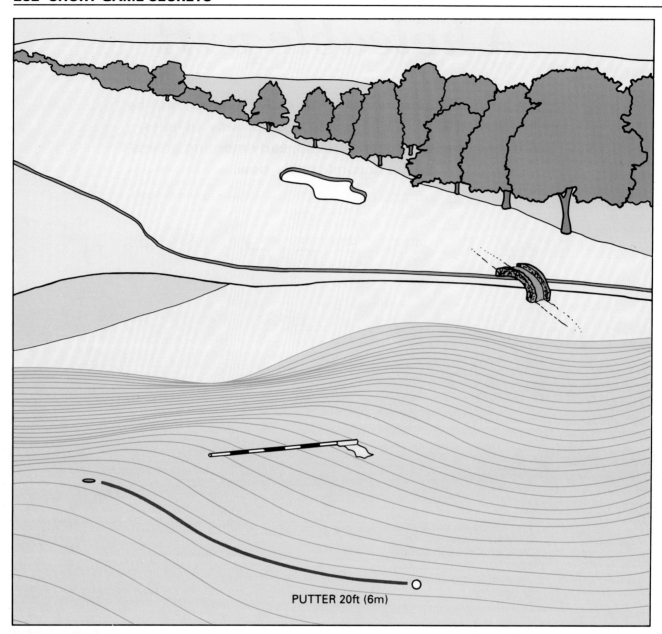

PUTTER 20ft (6m)

SAFE WINNER
Slow but sure

The game of golf is sometimes a great leveler. Whether you're a massive hitter or you struggle after distance you don't need strength to finish off the job by dispatching the ball into the hole – and that's what counts.

All golfers can be good putters, but experience helps when you putt on unusual greens. This rolling surface is made trickier by early morning dew – the greenkeeper hasn't been round to switch the greens.

You can count on having a slow putt. It's uphill, and the green is wet. Even if you go past the hole the putt back is uphill – "never up, never in" is certainly good advice this time.

Aim for the center of the hole, make a smooth stroke and give the ball a firm rap up the slope. To help you judge the distance, try visualizing a hole about 3ft (1m) beyond. Putt for this imaginary hole. With luck the putt will drop in for a fine birdie 3.

Grip: reverse overlap
Stance: normal
Ball position: just right of inside of left heel

Weight distribution: even
Swing: smooth tempo
Swing path: in to in
Club: putter

pro tip

On the pro side
Look around the hole when you're faced with a tricky putt. Take in every little detail – at a quick glance a putt may look flat, but is there a subtle borrow or break?

Inspect the cup carefully. If one side of the hole is worn away it will help you find what's termed the professional side of the hole.

Not all greenkeepers use a board to keep the area around the cup as flat as possible when they're cutting the hole, so putt with care to avoid your ball hopping or jumping at the last minute.

Off the green

With bunkers to the front, trees at the back and a narrow,
two tiered green, this par 3 is a potential
card wrecker. You're left with a tricky chip up the bank
– but don't just hit and hope.

A slight breeze blows
from right to left – helpful
if you need backspin.

A shot running through the
green will be lost in the
copse.

Conditions are good,
although a ball landing on
the fast dry green may roll
a long way.

The ball is almost 3ft
(90cm) below the
putting surface but is
sitting up well. The
longish fluffy grass
may cling to the
clubhead when you
try to chip.

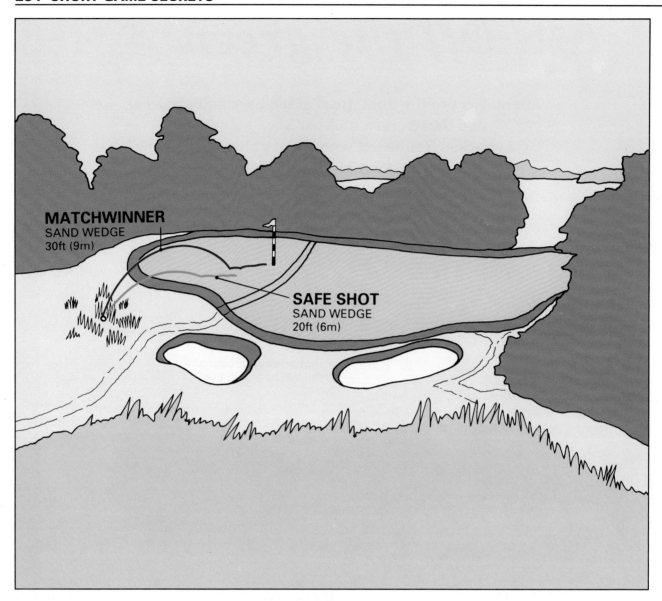

MATCHWINNER
SAND WEDGE
30ft (9m)

SAFE SHOT
SAND WEDGE
20ft (6m)

SAFE SHOT

Go warily into this one. Played too daintily you'll fluff the shot. If you overhit, the ball is likely to disappear into thick copse at the back of the green.

Even a reasonable chip hit just a touch too strong may roll down the green, leaving you in trouble in the 3 putt zone.

Be prudent – concentrate on keeping your ball on the upper level. Play safe with a little firm wristed chip. The ball will hop on to the putting surface, leaving you 2 putts to keep your card going.

Grip: 1½-2in (4-5cm) down the shaft
Stance: square
Ball position: center of stance
Weight distribution: favoring left side
Swing: quarter
Swing path: in to in
Club: sand wedge

MATCH WINNER

A delicate little stroke is required. You have to play it like a bunker shot, although you risk going completely underneath the ball – resulting in a fluffed shot which won't even reach the green.

Confidence and a sure touch are essential. Take advantage of the slight breeze – it gives you a little more backspin. Open the blade of your sand wedge and drop the ball precisely at the pin. The height helps to stop the ball – it shouldn't roll more than 3-4ft (90-120cm). A solid putt salvages par.

Grip: 1½-2in (4-5cm) lower than normal
Stance: open
Ball position: opposite inside of left heel
Weight distribution: favoring left side
Swing: three-quarter
Swing path: extreme out to in
Club: sand wedge

pro tip

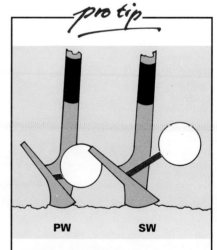

PW   SW

Wedge choice
With its extra loft, heavy sole and low center of gravity, a sand wedge helps get the ball airborne quickly – it's the ideal club for a delicate little chip on to a green. A pitching wedge also gives height but the wider flange of the sand wedge works well out of long grass.

Uphill bunker shot

A slightly loose tee shot to this par 3 sits annoyingly
on the steep upslope of the greenside bunker. The
awkward stance makes a few hacks in the sand – with several
shots dropped to par – a clear possibility.

The ball is 28ft (8.5m)
from the hole.

Landing on the lower tier
of the green leaves you
with a very difficult putt.

The ball is perched on firm
dry sand on the slope at
the back of the bunker.

You must be careful not
to dig the clubhead into
the sand.

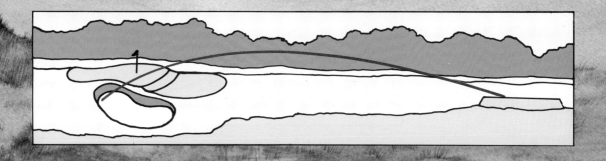

SAFE SHOT
Escape safely
Finding your ball lying on the upslope is undoubtedly irritating. You have been left with an awkward shot and may feel that you have been heavily penalized after playing a tee shot which was only a few feet left of target.

This is a very tricky lie so make life easier by playing out sideways, towards the back of the green. By doing so you can place both feet in the bunker and play it as a normal bunker shot. There is no reason to fear it provided you follow basic bunker technique.

Aim well left of the pin to send the ball directly over the back slope. Hit the sand 2-3in (5-7cm) behind the ball and you should see it lobbing safely on to the putting surface. Down in 2 gives you a respectable bogey from a difficult position.

Grip: 1½in lower than normal
Stance: aligned towards back of green
Ball position: center of stance
Weight distribution: even
Swing: three quarter
Swing path: out to in
Club: sand wedge

MATCH WINNER
On your knees
With imagination, confidence and an unorthodox attitude you can still get up and down in 2.

By standing in the bunker you would have to aim well left of the pin leaving a long putt for par. With one foot in and one foot out and an out-to-in swing, you're in danger of hitting your left foot as you try to spin the ball from left to right.

The only option if you want to go for the pin with any degree of confidence is to hit the shot from a kneeling position outside the bunker.

Make sure the clubface is open and aiming straight at the flag. You will be aligned left of the pin but an extreme out-to-in swing – to avoid clipping the lip on the backswing – and the open clubface will compensate and send the ball spinning towards the hole.

Maintain your balance throughout the shot. You need good hand action as you pick up the club very quickly on the backswing. It is very much a feel shot. Aim 2-3in (5-7cm) behind the ball and blast it out.

Grip: 1½in lower than normal
Stance: kneeling, aligned left of target
Ball position: center of stance
Weight distribution: even
Swing: three quarter
Swing path: extreme out to in
Club: sand wedge

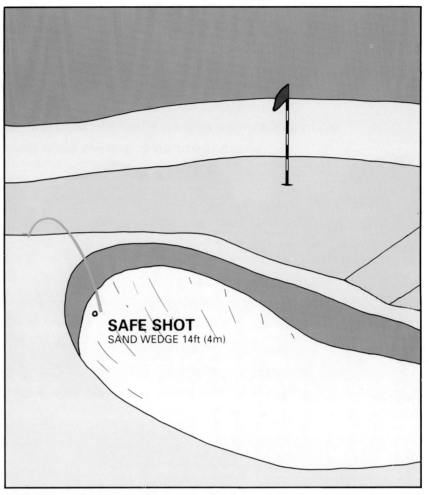

SAFE SHOT
SAND WEDGE 14ft (4m)

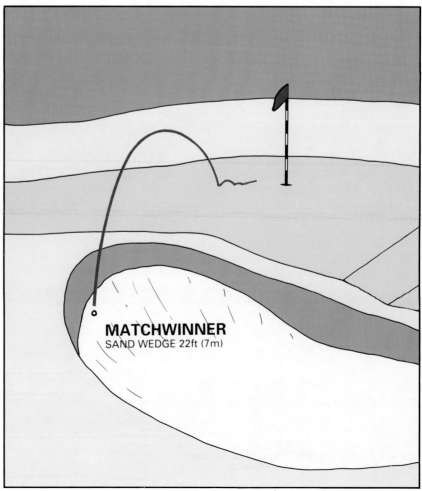

MATCHWINNER
SAND WEDGE 22ft (7m)

Slippery slope

A bold approach has skipped through the green
and nestled on an awkward downslope. A
delicate touch is now required if you are going
to save par on this short par 4.

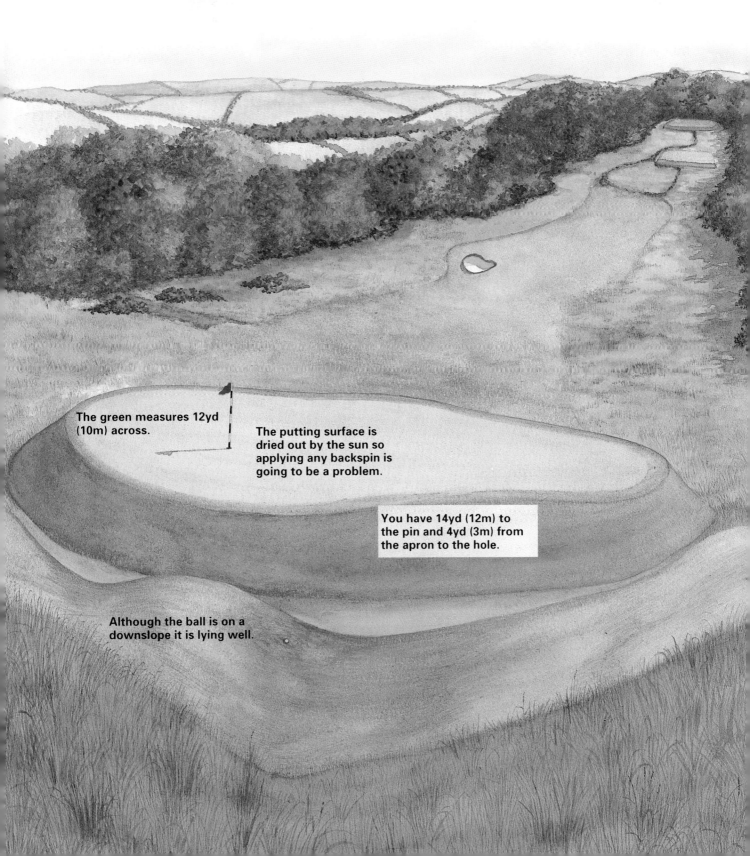

The green measures 12yd
(10m) across.

The putting surface is
dried out by the sun so
applying any backspin is
going to be a problem.

You have 14yd (12m) to
the pin and 4yd (3m) from
the apron to the hole.

Although the ball is on a
downslope it is lying well.

SAFE SHOT
Chip from a level position
If this was a shot from a flat lie to a flat green, it would be no problem. However, it is complicated by the awkward stance with the ball below the level of your feet. You must also master the delicate 10yd (9m) carry across the dip to the green.

You won't get much backspin on the dry green, so if you aren't confident of playing a cut-up wedge shot you should take the safe option.

Play a conventional chip to the heart of the green and you are at least able to have both feet on the same level.

Keep your knees well flexed to make sure you crisply strike the ball below your feet. There is enough green to hold your chip and, though you have a long putt back, you should limit the damage to your score.

Grip: 1in (2.5cm) lower than normal
Stance: square
Ball position: center of stance
Weight distribution: balanced on heels
Swing: half
Swing path: normal
Club: sand wedge

MATCH WINNER
Cut-up wedge
There is no point in playing a conventional chip as you won't get the ball to stop close enough to the pin.

The shot you need is a cut-up wedge. It is very difficult in this situation as you have to adopt a very open stance, forcing you to to place your feet on different levels with the right below the left.

There are a few essentials to this shot: like the safe shot you must keep your knees well flexed throughout; you mustn't lift your head even a fraction or you risk thinning the ball and sending it scuttling across the green; and you mustn't swing too much from out to in or you could hit the ball off the socket producing a horrendous shank.

The secret of the shot is practice. It requires a delicate touch and nerves of steel. Don't be too delicate either or you will fluff it into the dip.

Use your bunker technique. Take a sand wedge and align left of the pin. Keep the clubhead square to the hole and with an out-to-in swing drop the ball gently beside the pin. Good height stops the ball despite the lack of backspin.

Grip: 1in (2.5cm) lower than normal
Stance: aligned left, clubhead square
Ball position: center of stance
Weight distribution: balanced on heels and towards left side
Swing: three quarter
Swing path: extreme out to in
Club: sand wedge

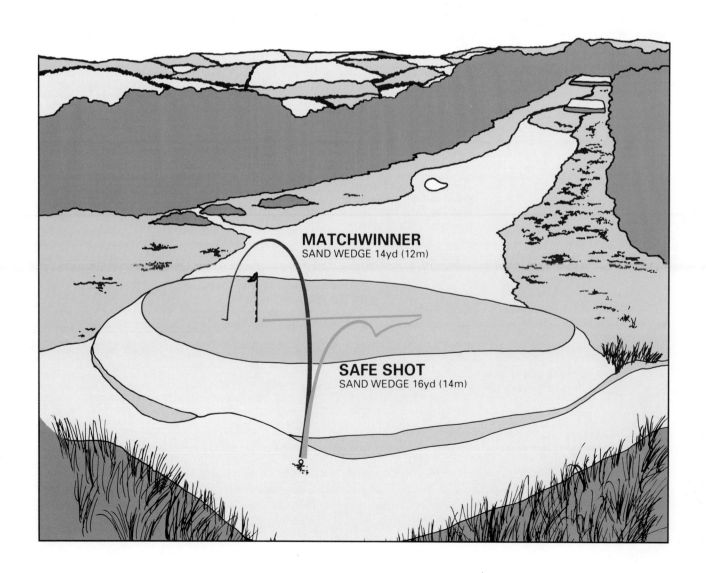

MATCHWINNER
SAND WEDGE 14yd (12m)

SAFE SHOT
SAND WEDGE 16yd (14m)

8

LONG GAME LESSONS

Power drives and dynamic fairway woods arc the most impressive, and perhaps the most satisfying, shots in golf. But, because of the distance the ball travels, they can also be the most destructive. John Daly is familiar with both sides of the coin. His mammoth hitting has brought many a golf course to its knees, but sometimes it is Daly himself who is brought to his knees by the trouble a disobedient driver can find. So this chapter deals not so much with the technical side of good driving, but more the strategic and positional aspects of this critical part of the game.

Faults from the fairway

Striking woods successfully off a fairway depends on a sound
technique and an easy rhythm. Problems
arise when you force the shot by either hitting the ball too
hard or trying to lift it off the turf.
Let the club do the work.

Q When I'm using a wood on the fairway I find it hard to get the ball airborne, and often squirt the ball low and out to the right. What am I doing wrong?

A You're probably trying to hit the ball too far. If you thrash at the ball instead of letting the club do the work – woods are designed for distance – your left side and hands are too far ahead of the clubhead just before impact.

From this position, it's impossible for the clubhead to catch up with the hands at impact. With your weight on the left side and the clubhead lagging, you chop down on the ball with an open blade. But because your hands are so far ahead, the blade is also delofted. This combination sends the ball flying low and out to the right.

Easy rhythm and tempo

For a good strike and a straight shot you must swing with an easy tempo and have faith that the club does what it's designed to do – don't thrash at the ball. You must also stay balanced throughout the stroke and stay behind the ball at impact. This ensures that you strike the ball at the bottom of the arc with a smooth action.

X LEFT SIDE AND HANDS TOO FAR AHEAD OF BALL

X CLUB CHOPS WITH OPEN FACE

SHOT FLIES LOW AND RIGHT

✓ BALANCED ATTACK

✓ STAYS BEHIND BALL AT IMPACT

Q I strike my woods well off the tee but tend to either thin or top the ball when I try to hit off a fairway. Why?

A The reason for your inconsistency off a fairway is that you probably have too much weight on the right side into impact. The tendency is to try and lift the ball off the turf rather than let the natural loft of the clubface do the work.

This means you lean back as you swing down and through impact so that the club catches the ball on the up. You may get away with it when the ball is sitting on a tee peg, but from a fairway it spells disaster. You don't strike the ball at the bottom of your arc and so either thin or top the shot.

TOO MUCH WEIGHT ON RIGHT SIDE

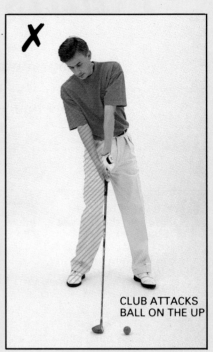

CLUB ATTACKS BALL ON THE UP

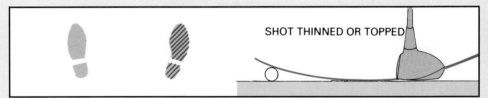

SHOT THINNED OR TOPPED

Balanced strike

It's crucial to stay balanced with the correct weight distribution to hit properly flighted woods from a fairway. On the backswing your weight should slightly favor the right side.

Coming down into impact your weight should shift towards your left side so that as you strike you're balanced behind the ball with your weight evenly distributed. As you swing through your weight moves on to the left side. This transfer is essential for a free flowing swing but must never be excessive.

WEIGHT WELL DISTRIBUTED

CLUB CATCHES BALL AT BOTTOM OF ARC

Playing for position

Although park and heathland courses are usually designed to look and play at their best in summer, you can turn less attractive winter conditions to positional advantage.

On this exposed par 4 of a heathland course, the pin is 346yd (317m) from the tee.

Two small bunkers directly in front guard the raised-level green.

The first of a row of trees is 235yd (215m) from the tee. As it's winter, the ground is soft, so your ball is unlikely to run underneath them – which is possible in dry conditions.

The rough is fairly light, unlike the thick, heavy growth of high summer.

The first fairway bunker is 190yd (174mm) from the tee. The second is 20yd (18m) further on.

Conditions are frost free; recent rain has left the course damp and soft rather than sodden. A light breeze drifts across the fairway from the right.

SAFE SHOT
Stay on right of fairway
Tee off safely right with a 3 wood, so that you miss the fairway bunkers and stay short of the trees.

For your second, aim right of the greenside bunkers with a short iron – the breeze will help. This right-hand position gives you a short pitch into the pin, around the bunkers, which sets up a good chance of par.

First and second shots
Grip: normal
Stance: normal
Ball position: first shot opposite inside of left heel; second shot between left heel and center of stance
Weight distribution: even
Swing: full
Swing path: normal
Club: first shot 3 wood; second shot 7 iron

Third shot
Grip: choke down slightly
Stance: normal
Ball position: center of stance
Weight distribution: even
Swing: half
Swing path: normal
Club: wedge

MATCH WINNER
Drive right for position
You can safely drive down the right, with the help of the breeze, without running into the trees – the ground is soft, so the ball should sit down quickly. The trees are bare – even if you do stray too far right, your ball's path to the green should not be hampered.

You are left with a short pitch and run to set up a birdie – as you have driven right, you can ignore the greenside bunkers and use the full width of the green.

First shot
Grip: normal
Stance: normal
Ball position: opposite left heel
Weight distribution: even
Swing: full
Swing path: normal
Club: driver

Second shot
Grip: normal
Stance: slightly open
Ball position: center
Weight distribution: even
Swing: full
Swing path: slightly out to in
Club: wedge

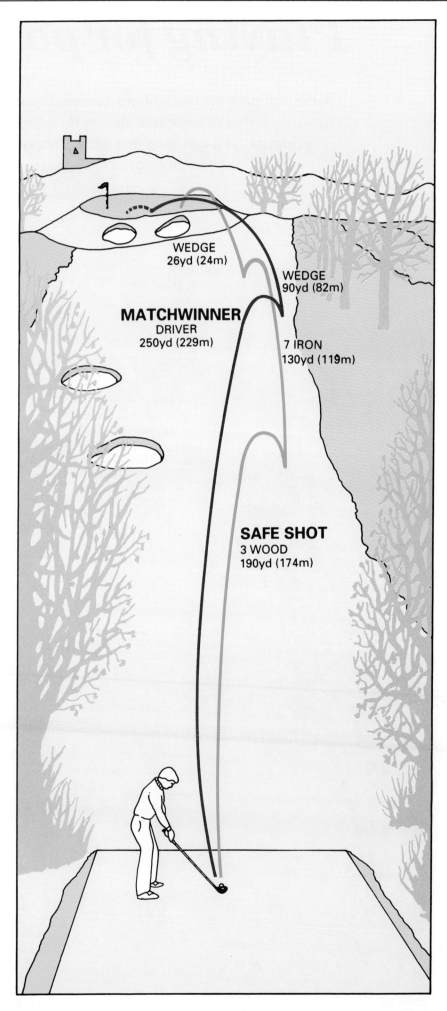

WEDGE
26yd (24m)

WEDGE
90yd (82m)

MATCHWINNER
DRIVER
250yd (229m)

7 IRON
130yd (119m)

SAFE SHOT
3 WOOD
190yd (174m)

Clearing a gully

**From the tee, most golfers want to hit the ball as
far as possible. Some holes are designed
to lure you into doing just that – when it's bound to
lead you into certain trouble.**

A strong wind blows from
left to right on this
exposed links.

A deep hollow beginning
200yd (183m) from the
tee, with steep slopes on
either side, lies in front of
the green.

dunes and heather

Any short approach shots
that don't roll back down
the slope may be snapped
up by the pot bunker in
front of the green.

The fairway narrows in
front of the gully – there
are mounds to right and
left at this point.

A wide tractor path pits
the surface of the gully.

At 310yd (283m) the hole
is a relatively short par 4.
However, the plateau
green is small, making it
difficult to land and hold
the ball there.

thick gorse

The ground is hard and
dry, so the ball is likely to
run.

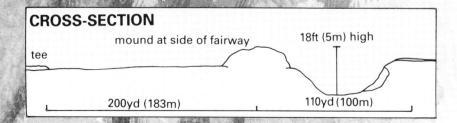

CROSS-SECTION

mound at side of fairway

18ft (5m) high

tee

200yd (183m)

110yd (100m)

SAFE SHOT
Stay accurate

Keep the tee shot on the fairway to avoid the dense rough on either side. Hit a smooth fairway wood down the middle, leaving 140yd (128m) to the green.

Select a medium iron for your next shot. Your priority is to clear the gully, so a club more than you would normally take for the distance is a good choice. The less the loft, the more the ball rolls, so even if your ball bounces in the gully there is at least a chance that it could run up the slope to the green. From the gully every shot is a lottery, as you can't see the pin.

First and second shots
Grip: normal
Stance: normal
Ball position: opposite inside of left heel for first shot; between left heel and center of stance for second
Weight distribution: even
Swing: full
Swing path: normal
Club: 3 wood for first shot; 5/6 iron for second

MATCH WINNER
Lay up short

If you have confidence in your ability to control the ball well, play a 2-iron 190yd (174m) to the top of the ridge, leaving you with a clear view of the pin. Next, hit a full 9 iron to clear the gully and set up a birdie.

A big drive is a bad idea because it leaves the ball at the bottom of the slope. From there you can't see the flag.

As the ground is dry and hard, it's tricky to lift the ball up and over the slope. Even if you do that successfully, you have to stop the ball quickly so that it doesn't overshoot the small green.

First and second shots
Grip: normal
Stance: normal
Ball position: opposite inside of left heel for first shot; center of stance for second
Weight distribution: even
Swing: full
Swing path: normal
Club: 2 iron for first shot; 9 iron for second

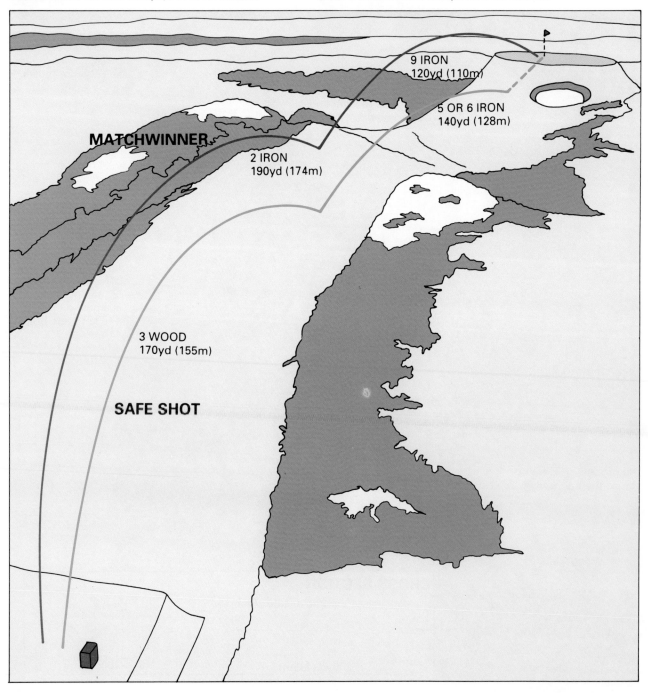

Drive with slope

On this dry, sloping heathland course strokes can be gained or lost depending on how you play from the tee. To avoid disaster you must use the conditions to your advantage.

A slight breeze blows from your right.

On this 315yd (288m) par 4 hole, the pin is 300yd (274m) from the tee.

Two fairway bunkers trap balls landing on the left side. The first bunker is placed at 160yd (146m) and the second 180yd (165m) from the tee.

The ground is firm giving the ball plenty of run on landing. The fairway slopes from right to left with trees on either side.

The hole dog-legs slightly around to the left. Careful alignment is required when you tee up.

SAFE SHOT

Drive to right of fairway
As you address the ball aim to the right of the fairway away from the trees and bunkers. The ball should land on the slope and roll down slightly towards the second bunker.

Take a favorite club. Knowing the ball will hit and stay on the fairway allows you to tee off with confidence. Your next shot requires a short iron to the green.

Tee and approach shots
Grip: normal
Stance: normal
Ball position: opposite left heel for drive; midway between center of stance and left heel for approach shot
Weight distribution: even
Swing: full
Swing path: in to square to in
Club: 3 or 4 wood for tee shot; 8 iron for second shot

MATCH WINNER

Long draw with roll
If you are driving well go for a high draw off the tee which avoids the trees and bunkers and almost reaches the putting surface. You gain maximum distance with this shot as the breeze makes the ball travel further and the dry sloping ground gives plenty of run towards the green on landing.

A good draw leaves you a chip and run on to the green with an opportunity for a birdie.

Drive
Grip: normal
Stance: slightly closed
Ball position: opposite inside of left heel
Weight distribution: even
Swing: full
Swing path: very slightly in to out
Club: driver

Second shot
Grip: slightly lower than usual
Stance: slightly open
Ball position: center of stance
Weight distribution: even
Swing: half
Swing path: in to square to in
Club: wedge, 7 or 8 iron

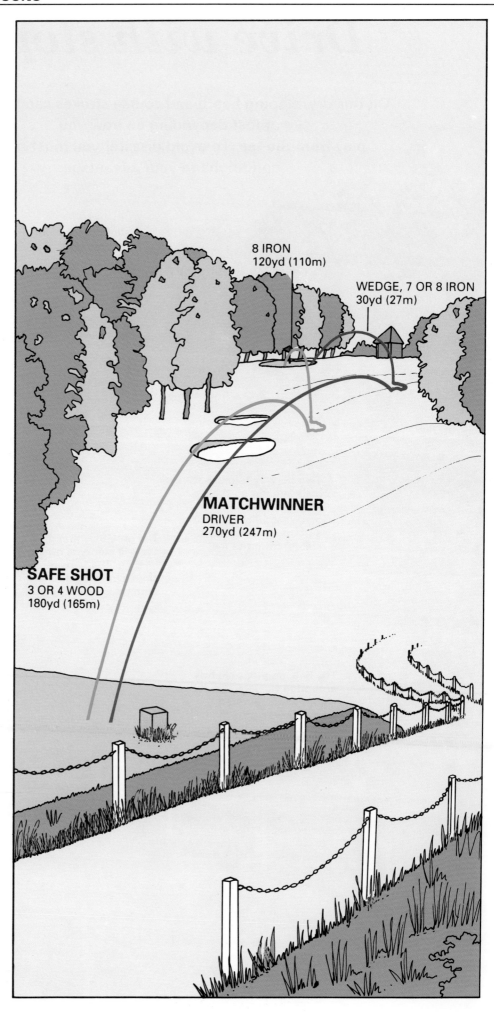

8 IRON
120yd (110m)

WEDGE, 7 OR 8 IRON
30yd (27m)

MATCHWINNER
DRIVER
270yd (247m)

SAFE SHOT
3 OR 4 WOOD
180yd (165m)

Planning from the tee

Consider your options before you tee off on this long and
challenging par 4. Position is
all important – your first and second shots
are both threatened by sand.

A gaping greenside bunker stands guard ready to trap any short approach shots.

The first bunker is 190yd (174m) from the tee, the second 210yd (192m) and the third 240yd (220m).

Long shadows produced by late evening sunshine make distances and club selection difficult to judge.

The dry sunny conditions have made the ground firm but the watered greens are holding well.

The hole is a 423yd (387m) par 4 on a parkland course.

SAFE SHOT

Short of fairway bunkers

Weigh up your options and visualize where you want your shot to land. In these dry conditions avoid using a driver – lay up short to prevent rolling into the bunkers. Trust the yardages – don't be fooled by the shadows. Women can use the same tactics – but make sure you have enough club.

After your tee shot you have another long iron to carry the fairway bunkers. Your approach must clear the large bunker and stop quickly on the watered green for a respectable bogey or chance of par.

First and second shots

Grip: normal
Stance: normal
Ball position: opposite inside left heel
Weight distribution: even
Swing: full
Swing path: normal
Club: 3 iron

Approach shot

Grip: normal
Stance: normal
Ball position: center of stance
Weight distribution: even
Swing: three-quarters
Swing path: normal
Club: wedge or 9 iron

MATCH WINNER

Take two to the green

There's no point in playing short of the bunkers – from behind them you would need to hit a wood 240yd (220m) to carry the greenside bunker.

Be positive: picture your drive landing on the fairway between the third bunker and the trees. This leaves you with a high long iron approach to the green. Take care with club selection as the shadows make judgement of distance difficult.

Two easy putts on the green give you a solid par 4 with a birdie chance.

Drive and approach

Grip: normal
Stance: normal
Ball position: opposite inside left heel
Weight distribution: even
Swing: full
Swing path: normal
Club: driver for first shot, 4 iron for second

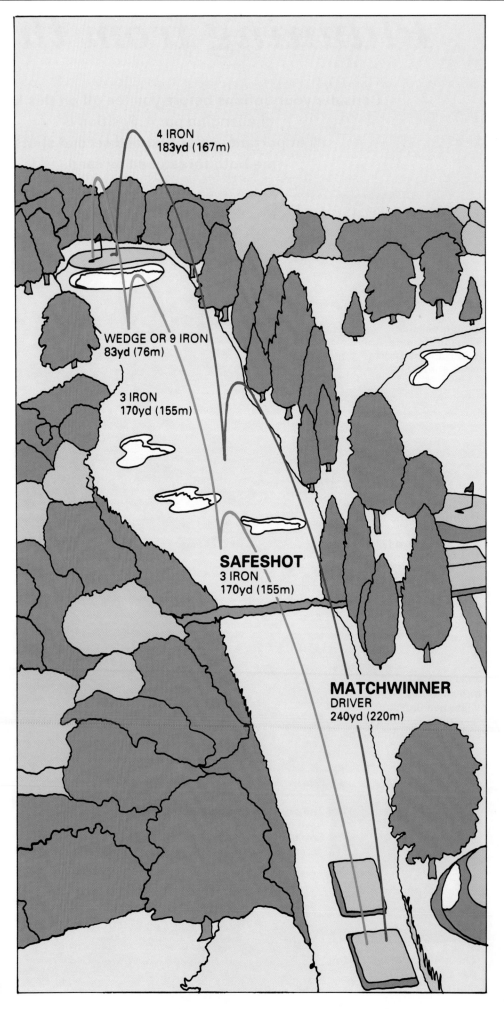

4 IRON
183yd (167m)

WEDGE OR 9 IRON
83yd (76m)

3 IRON
170yd (155m)

SAFESHOT
3 IRON
170yd (155m)

MATCHWINNER
DRIVER
240yd (220m)

Position from tee

With a wandering burn and a strong wind ready to catch
a slice on this seaside links hole,
a well placed drive helps relieve pressure and leaves you
on course for par or even a birdie.

Winds gust from left to right on this coastal site.

A small pot bunker gathers any loose approach shots.

Though the ground is dry, expect unpredictable bounces from bumps and hollows in the narrow fairway.

Three fairway bunkers await a miss-hit drive.

A burn flanked by rough and out of bounds winds down the entire right side of the 365yd (334m) par 4 hole.

A bad hook or pull from the tee is lost in thick clumps of gorse.

SAFE SHOT
Safe fairway landing

Don't automatically reach for your driver – with trouble lurking all round, go for accuracy rather than distance. From the tee take a club you're confident will keep you on the fairway – the wind on your back increases the chance of a slice. You must be firm of purpose and pay no heed to the burn. In particular, relax your muscles – they tighten under pressure – and focus your mind on making a good shoulder turn for power.

From mid fairway play safely left of the burn but go short of the greenside bunker. Allow a good margin for error – bumpy ground may throw up a cruel bounce. A neat chip and run with an 8 iron leaves a chance of par.

First and second shots
Grip: normal
Stance: normal
Ball position: opposite inside left heel
Weight distribution: even
Swing: full
Swing path: normal
Club: 5 wood first shot; second shot 5 iron

MATCH WINNER
Draw from the tee

A line close to the fairway bunkers offers the best chance. Be precise and allow for a poor bounce from bumpy ground. A little draw from the tee should hold up in the wind. From the left side hit a low punch shot or play a slight fade to bounce towards the pin.

First shot – driver
Grip: normal
Stance: slightly closed
Ball position: opposite left heel
Weight distribution: even
Swing: full
Swing path: slightly in to out
Club: driver

Second shot – 8 iron
Grip: slightly lower than usual; hands well forward at address
Stance: normal
Ball position: center of stance
Weight distribution: just favoring left side
Swing: three-quarter
Swing path: normal
Club: 8 iron

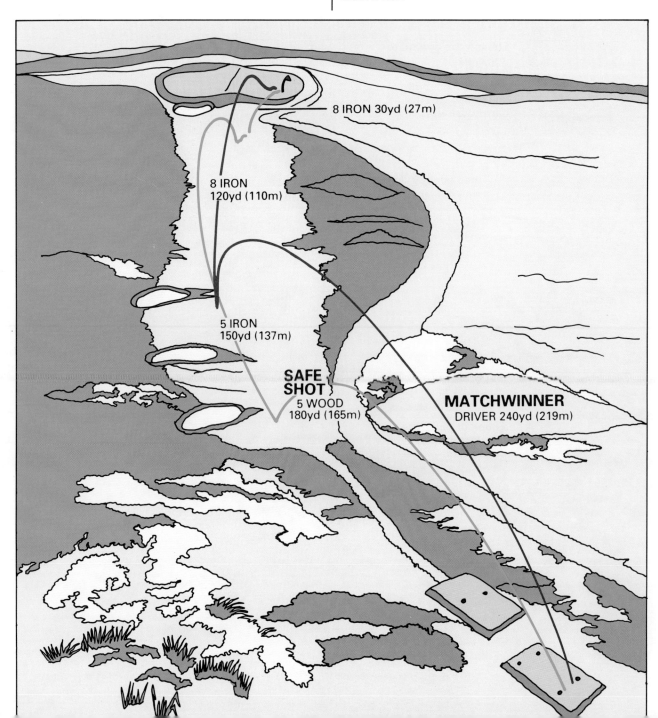

8 IRON 30yd (27m)

8 IRON
120yd (110m)

5 IRON
150yd (137m)

**SAFE
SHOT**
5 WOOD
180yd (165m)

MATCHWINNER
DRIVER 240yd (219m)

Driveable par 4

On most courses there are some holes which might be regarded
as birdie chances. This short par 4 measures
only 276yd (252m). Take care though – trouble lurks
if you adopt the wrong strategy.

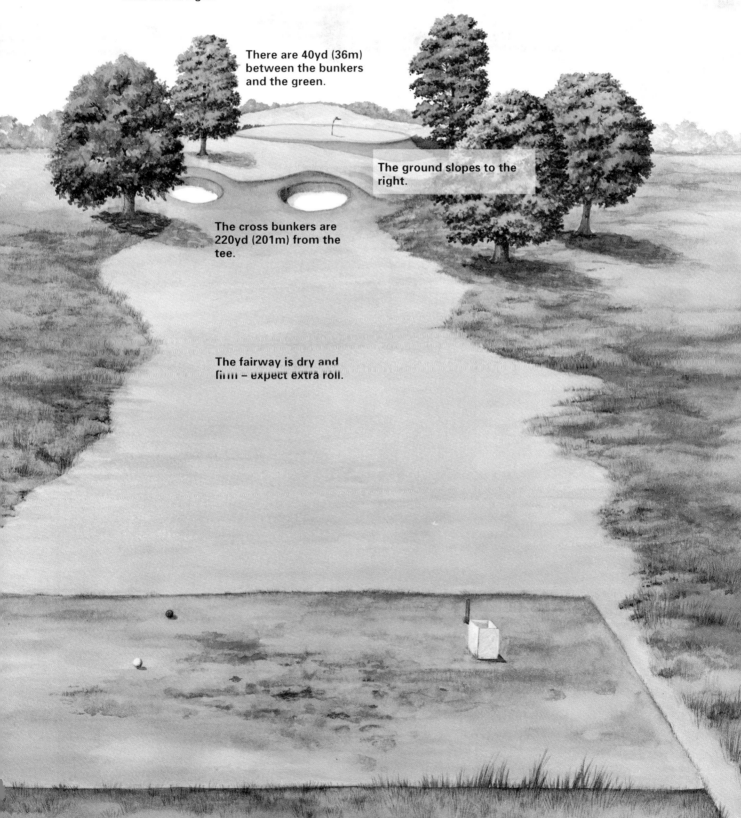

There is a slight breeze
from left to right.

There are 40yd (36m)
between the bunkers
and the green.

The ground slopes to the
right.

The cross bunkers are
220yd (201m) from the
tee.

The fairway is dry and
firm – expect extra roll.

SAFE SHOT
Mind the bunkers
Even a golfer of modest ability would expect to make 4 on a hole measuring 276yd (252m).

However, like all good golf holes there is more to this little par 4 than the card suggests.

The cross bunkers are likely to have a magnetic attraction for a stray tee shot.

If your best drive goes around 200yd (182m) the cross bunkers are not in reach. However, with the dry ground you might end up in the sand.

Take your favorite lofted wood or long iron and aim to place the tee shot dead center and short of the bunkers. Even if your drive drifts a little you should still finish on the fairway leaving a wedge shot of 100yd (90m) to the flag.

Don't be too ambitious with the pitch. Play for the left side of the green and let the wind drift your ball back towards the mark.
First shot
Grip: normal
Stance: normal
Ball position: opposite inside left heel
Weight distribution: even
Swing: full
Swing path: normal
Club: 5 wood or 3 iron
Second shot
Grip: normal
Stance: normal
Ball position: center of stance
Weight distribution: even
Swing: full
Swing path: normal
Club: pitching wedge

MATCH WINNER
Go for eagle
If you are a long hitter and carry the ball around 240yd (220m), you have a good chance of reaching the green with your tee shot.

If you have been hitting your tee shots well, this is the moment to pull out the driver.

The ground is dry so you can expect the ball to run more than usual.

Aim for the left side of the green allowing the wind to carry your ball back towards the flag.

Driving a par 4 puts extra pressure on your opponents and leaves you with an outside chance of an eagle.
Grip: normal
Stance: normal
Ball position: opposite inside of left heel
Weight distribution: even
Swing: full
Swing path: normal
Club: driver

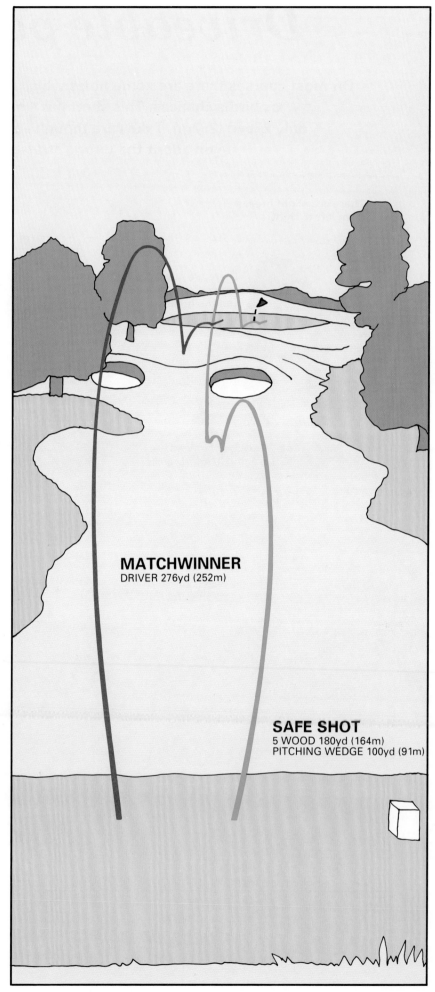

MATCHWINNER
DRIVER 276yd (252m)

SAFE SHOT
5 WOOD 180yd (164m)
PITCHING WEDGE 100yd (91m)

SELF-HELP
FOR
YOUR SWING

Intelligent course management is the invisible secret to low scoring. It may not manifest itself in, the same spectacular way as a 300-yard drive or a 60-foot putt, but it's just as important, if not more so. The strategies you adopt on the course determine whether good ball-striking is converted into a good score, or just an average one. Similarly, clear, sensible thinking can convert an indfifferent ball-striking round into a good score. Jack Nicklaus, the ultimate thinker, is the finest exponent of this art. "The Golden Bear" would be the first to say that yes, a great swing is an asset, but only if it is combined with a smart brain. This chapter can help you make good decisions on the golf course.

Correct your swing shape

Q I'm making good contact with the ball, but I keep hitting it either straight right or, more often, snapping to the left. What could be wrong?

A You need to look carefully at the shape of your swing – it sounds as though you are attacking from the inside on an in-to-out path. Study steps 1-4 below.

CORRECT SET UP

IN LINE WITH FEET

TAKEAWAY TOO FAR ON THE INSIDE

1 Even if you're set up perfectly, swinging on the wrong plane and path is certain to lead to shots that don't fly straight. But if your set-up is good, you have more chance of swinging with the correct shape.

2 Taking the club too far back on the inside leads to an off plane backswing, which in turn causes problems on the downswing. The correct takeaway puts the club in line with the feet and parallel to the ground.

CLUB PARALLEL TO TARGET LINE

CLUB OVER THE TOP POINTS RIGHT

IN-TO-IN

HOOK

IN-TO-OUT

3 The incorrect inside takeaway leads you into an off line top of the backswing position – the club points right of target. From this over the top position you swing down from too far on the inside. A good top of backswing position – the club parallel to the target line – helps you to swing down on the correct path.

4 Swinging down from too far on the inside means you attack the ball on an in-to-out path. The combination of the wrong path and a square clubface sends the ball hooking to the left. The push happens if your blade stays open at impact. Straight shots come from an on plane downswing and an in-to-in attack.

Q I feel as if I'm set up and swinging well but I keep slicing the ball to the right or sometimes hit a pull shot. Why?

A This is another effect of bad swing shape. You're probably attacking the ball on an out-to-in path. Check steps 1-4 below.

CORRECT SET UP

CORRECT ON-LINE MOVE

TAKEAWAY OUTSIDE THE LINE

1 Your ball positioning, posture and alignment may all be perfect, but you could be swinging on the wrong plane and path. Both the slice and the pull result from an out-to-in path.

2 If you pick the club up outside the line on your takeaway – instead of moving it back on line – you automatically put your backswing on the wrong plane.

CLUB LAID OFF AT THE TOP

CLUB PARALLEL TO TARGET LINE

IN-TO-IN

SLICE

OUT-TO-IN

3 An outside takeaway leads you into a laid off position at the top of the backswing, with the club pointing left of the target line instead of being parallel with it. Unless you loop the club severely you stand no chance of attacking the ball from the inside on the downswing.

4 As a result, you swing down from outside the line and attack the ball on an out-to-in – not the correct in-to-in – path. If the blade is square the ball starts left and then curves away to the right. If the clubface is slightly closed you hit the pull shot.

Off striking

There are few flaws more annoying than striking the ball
badly – it can be very baffling.
Players who do strike the ball off the heel or toe struggle to
cure the fault, but it usually
takes only a minor correction to fix the problem.

Q Why do I keep hitting a feebly struck shot that curls slightly left and lands well short of the target?

A This shape of shot is produced by a strike off the toe of the club. One possible cause for this off-center strike is poor weight distribution during the swing

If you address the ball with too much weight on your heels – even if your posture is good – it leads to an unbalanced backswing. As you take the club away you naturally rock on to your heels and straighten your back.

From this upright top of backswing position it's almost impossible to swing down on the correct plane and path. You probably attack the ball on a path that's inside the correct one, and so strike the ball with the toe of the blade.

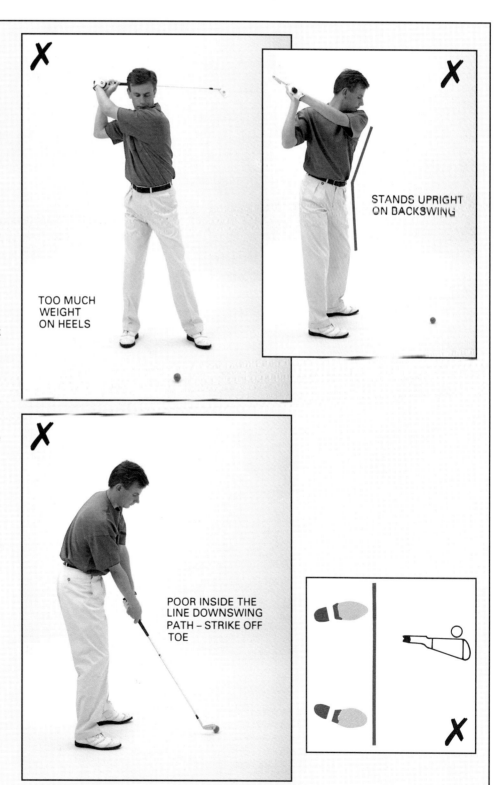

TOO MUCH
WEIGHT
ON HEELS

STANDS UPRIGHT
ON BACKSWING

POOR INSIDE THE
LINE DOWNSWING
PATH – STRIKE OFF
TOE

CROUCHES ON BACKSWING

TOO MUCH WEIGHT ON TOES

CLUB ATTACKS FROM OUTSIDE THE LINE – STRIKE OFF HEEL

Q I'm frustrated because I don't seem to hit the ball out of the middle every time and often hit a weak fade short of my target. What am I doing wrong?

A The poorly struck left-to-right shot is a product of a hit off the heel of the club. This could be a result of setting up with too much weight on your toes.

Even if your posture is good at address, when you take the club away the tendency is to lean forward and move into a crouched top of backswing position.

You have now little chance of returning the blade on the proper path to the ball. You tend to swing down outside the correct line and so strike the ball with the heel of the club.

CLUB ON CORRECT PLANE AND PATH

WELL BALANCED

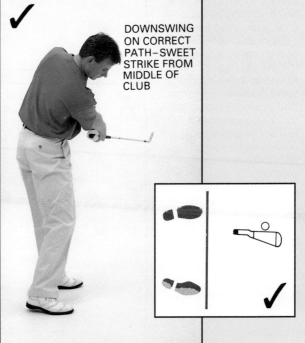

DOWNSWING ON CORRECT PATH – SWEET STRIKE FROM MIDDLE OF CLUB

Balanced backswing

If your weight is well distributed at address – so that it's difficult to either rock forward on to your toes or back on to your heels – you have a good chance of staying stable throughout your swing.

From a balanced stance you should be able to move easily into good top of backswing position with the club on plane. This gives you a great chance of swinging down on the correct path and attacking the ball squarely with the middle of the face.

Power failure

**Using your hands and arms correctly is vital for powerful striking as well as for hitting the ball straight.
You need to co-ordinate a good arm swing with dynamic wrist action for consistently potent shotmaking.**

Q **I seem to turn well into a tight, coiled backswing position, but still can't generate power. Why?**

A It's quite possible that everything that should happen just before impact comes too early. You waste any potential power gained from a coiled position if you flail the arms and use your wrists too soon.

If you start the downswing by flicking the wrists, the club can't move into the ball at speed. All energy is lost and the hands stay passive into impact. Your downswing is all arms and the clubhead moves down in line with the hands – this produces a very weak hit.

Hitting late

To create the necessary power – without ever forcing the downswing – you must use the wrists and your arms in a co-ordinated movement. The relative positions of the clubhead and hands at the top should be kept until at least halfway through the downswing.

This creates a lag effect where the blade trails behind your hands. The angle between your arms and shaft should be held until your hands are almost opposite your right thigh. Then and only then should you start to work with your wrists.

Leaving any work with the wrists so late means that the clubhead has to travel very quickly into impact to strike squarely. This creates the speed to hit powerfully.

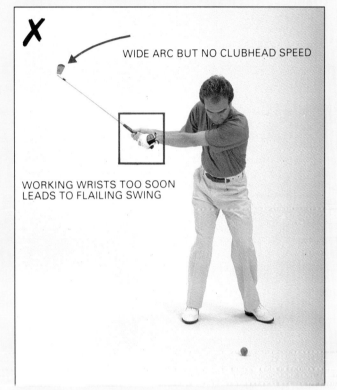

WIDE ARC BUT NO CLUBHEAD SPEED

WORKING WRISTS TOO SOON LEADS TO FLAILING SWING

ANGLE BETWEEN ARMS AND SHAFT AT TOP OF BACKSWING HELD ON DOWNSWING

HANDS ALMOST AT IMPACT POSITION, BUT CLUB STILL LAGS, WHICH CREATES POWER

Q I am continually choosing an iron that I think is right for the distance, but the ball often falls short of my target. Why?

A Clubhead speed through impact is all important for a powerful strike. Lack of speed is caused either by swinging on a narrow arc or having too passive wrists.

If you take the club away with plenty of wrist break you create a very narrow swing arc. You naturally swing down on the same arc and you can't generate the amount of clubhead speed that a wide arc produces.

This downswing leads to a flicking action through the ball and there is no sign of a full extension – another must for powerful striking.

If your wrists are too passive throughout the swing and you are all arms, it's impossible to generate clubhead speed even though your swing arc is wide. The club attacks the ball on a too shallow path and you strike with a slapping action.

ARM SWING CRAMPED AND TOO WRISTY – CLUBHEAD ON NARROW ARC

FLICKING ACTION LOFTS BALL HIGH BUT WITH NO POWER

WRISTS TOO PASSIVE – WIDE ARC BUT NO SPEED

WEAK THROUGH BALL AND NO RELEASE OF HANDS

Released and free

Your hands and wrists need to be uninhibited during the swing to allow the clubhead to swish freely through the ball. For the crispest and most powerful strike, use your wrists late in the downswing so that the clubhead lags behind your hands until the last possible moment.

Combine this free, late hitting downswing with a full extension and a proper release of your hands. This wide through swing arc is critical to straight and powerful hitting.

ARMS AND WRISTS COMBINE TO CREATE POWERFUL LATE HIT

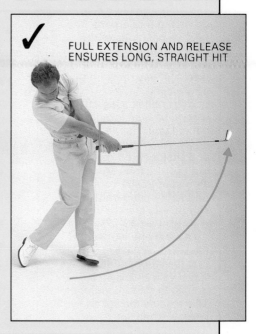

FULL EXTENSION AND RELEASE ENSURES LONG, STRAIGHT HIT

Backswing blunders

Each part of the golf swing must link to the others for a
consistent action. The takeaway dictates
the backswing, which in turn affects the downswing and
throughswing. So your backswing has to be correct if you're to
deliver the blade powerfully square at impact.

Q I work hard at getting my backswing on plane and have a smooth rhythmical action. I hit the ball straight but seem to lack a little power. What may be wrong?

A Your action can be perfectly on plane throughout the swing – so it might look good to someone standing behind you – but this doesn't guarantee a powerful strike. If your backswing arc is too narrow you can't generate any real clubhead speed through the ball, as the tendency is to swing down on the same arc.

A narrow backswing arc is produced from a poor extension of the arms on the take-away combined with too much use of the wrists. You tend to pick the club up quickly with the arms tucked in. The swing arc becomes too cramped.

Widespread power

To create a wide arc you must take the club back in one piece – so that your hands, arms and clubhead move away together for the first 18in (45cm) of your swing.

Keep any wrist cock until later in your takeaway. And then hold the relative positions of the hands and shaft all the way to the top to ensure you keep the swing wide. The high handed position at the top leads naturally to a good downswing with the clubhead on a powerful wide arc.

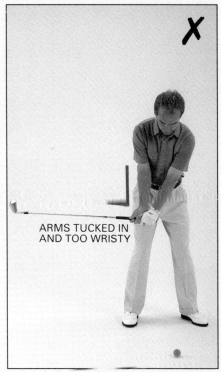

ARMS TUCKED IN
AND TOO WRISTY

CLUB PICKED UP
TOO QUICKLY AND
SWUNG ON A
NARROW ARC

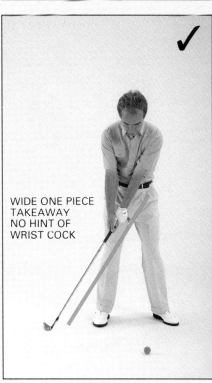

WIDE ONE PIECE
TAKEAWAY
NO HINT OF
WRIST COCK

BACKSWING PATH
ON WIDE ARC

Q I've heard of golfers being long and wild, but I seem to be short and wayward, even though I feel as if I'm swinging well. What might I be doing?

A Lack of power comes from a lack of clubhead speed through the ball and one way to lose power is with a short backswing. From a three quarter position you have very little time to generate clubhead speed.

Usually when a backswing is unintentionally short, your body turn is poor and your shoulders don't move round fully. This poor top of the backswing position leads to problems on the downswing. More often than not, you swing down weakly and from slightly outside the line. This is the cause of your waywardness and lack of power.

Full turning back

To create the necessary power and control to knock the ball long and straight you need to make a full swing with the correct shoulder turn.

Concentrate on moving the club away on a wide arc and bringing the left shoulder round underneath your chin. The shaft should be parallel to the ground – or slightly short of parallel with the more lofted irons.

This coiled position gives you a solid base from which to unleash a powerful attack. The full shoulder turn means that you have a greater chance of swinging down on the correct path. Your shots should become longer and straighter.

BACKSWING TOO SHORT ✗

✗ POOR TURN

DIFFICULT TO GENERATE POWER ON DOWNSWING

✓ FULL SHOULDER TURN

CLUB PARALLEL AT TOP ✓

✓ POWERFUL ON LINE ATTACK

Backspin bungles

Seeing your ball bound through a green with no backspin is a frustrating experience – especially after a good looking shot. A change of technique, or a refresher course, should see you create more backspin and find extra control.

Q I have great difficulty holding greens in summer, especially with my medium and long irons. Why?

A The shape of shot dictates how much backspin you create. If you usually play with a right-to-left shape, you produce drawspin. This means that when the ball lands it kicks on instead of pulling up – don't forget that a draw gives you extra length off a tee.

So if you set up aligning slightly right of parallel and swing fractionally in to out, you have little chance of stopping the ball on a firm green. Your short irons hit the ball high enough to be able to stop the shot, but the lower flight of the mid and long irons and the drawspin make holding shots very hard.

Play for the fade
The fade is the shape of shot that creates the most backspin. A fader's action swings slightly out to in and across the ball, cutting it up into the air. The shot has no hint of drawspin so lands softly and bites quickly – especially useful for holding mid and long irons on firm greens.

Align a fraction left of target but keep the blade square. Swing as normal – along the line of your feet – and your attack naturally becomes slightly out to in. This creates the back and left-to-right spin that aids your control.

X

ALIGNING RIGHT OF TARGET

SWING FROM IN TO OUT

X SHOT RUNS THROUGH GREEN

BALL DRAWN – TOPSPIN NOT BACKSPIN

✓

SET-UP ALIGNING LEFT

OUT-TO-IN ATTACK

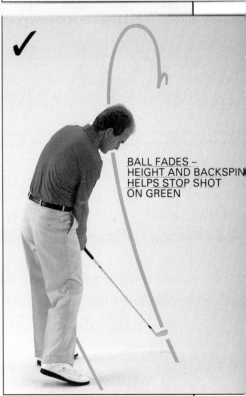

✓

BALL FADES – HEIGHT AND BACKSPIN HELPS STOP SHOT ON GREEN

POOR WRIST ACTION – ALL ARMS ✗

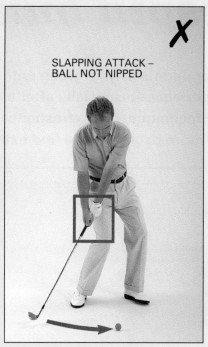

SLAPPING ATTACK – BALL NOT NIPPED ✗

STIFF FOLLOW-THROUGH – SHOT ROLLS THROUGH ✗

Q I see lots of golfers stop their wedges stone dead, but I can't seem to. My shots keep rolling on by the flag. Why?

A Your action is probably stiff and forced. If your swing is mostly arms with little or no wrist break, it's difficult to strike the ball with the proper nipping action.

By holding the wrists solid throughout the back and downswing, you can't attack the ball on the correct path or generate good clubhead speed.

Your blade strikes the ball with a slapping action rather than clipping it off the turf. The ball shoots forward on a lower trajectory than it should and with little backspin. The shot has no bite and runs on past the flag.

CONTROLLED BACKSWING – GOOD USE OF WRISTS ✓

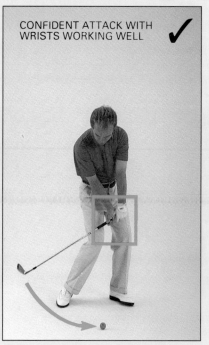

CONFIDENT ATTACK WITH WRISTS WORKING WELL ✓

BALANCED FINISH – SHOT FIZZES THROUGH AIR AND BITES QUICKLY ON GREEN ✓

Nip with the wrists

To play a neat, spinning, fast stopping wedge, your wrists need to be free yet controlled. Take the club away into a nicely balanced backswing position with a good hint of wrist cock. This enables you to attack the ball on a downward path and accelerate through the ball with a crisp late hit.

A fast yet rhythmical attack with good use of the wrists means you nip the ball off the turf with as much backspin as possible. A full release into a controlled finish position ensures you don't quit or guide the ball at the hole. The shot should take one hop and then pull up – so you can afford to be bold and pitch it right up to the hole.

Mechanical mayhem

The correct swing principles and techniques are important to know and master. But being too caught up in theory can be disastrous to your game. A relaxed mind and body are essential to put all that know-how to good use.

Q The whole of my long game is inconsistent, although I'm confident with my grip, aim and alignment. What could be going wrong?

A The trouble with many golfers is that they over theorize, and concentrate too hard on the basics they've been taught. If you have several little points to think of when you set up – grip, aim, feet shoulder width apart, knees flexed – you stifle your natural abilities.

Your mind becomes cluttered with swing thoughts, and your address and action are stiff and mechanical. Often you grip the club too tightly, and your stance is cramped and rigid. It is then impossible to make a flowing, uninhibited swing, and your body gets into poor positions – maybe laid off at the top with no shoulder turn. The results are weakly struck, off line shots.

Free and flowing

It is very important to know how to set up and swing properly, but you must not be preoccupied by it. The correct address position should become natural in time, so that once you have set up you are focused only on the shot. As you set up, concentrate on your aim and alignment, then relax.

Never clutter your mind with any more than two swing thoughts. This way, your body reacts naturally as you start to swing. A comfortable and relaxed posture automatically leads you into a free and flowing swing where your body can get into good positions.

STIFF, ROBOTIC ADDRESS

BODY MOVEMENT FULL OF TENSION – POOR TOP OF BACKSWING POSITION

RELAXED, TENSION-FREE STANCE

EASY TO TURN FULLY INTO PERFECT COIL

Q I take time to set up properly over a putt – blade square, hands and wrists firm and a sturdy body position – but I still keep missing ones I should hole. Why?

A A good, sturdy stance is vital for putting, but you should never be too rigid or robotic. Even if you align perfectly and set your blade square, you can hit a poor putt by being too mechanical. By striving to putt with a pendulum action – no wrist and swinging solely with a tilting of the shoulders – your body can become too tense.

Your grip on the club also becomes too tight – often you can see the whites of your knuckles – and it is difficult to take the blade back smoothly and on the correct path. A pull, push or jab is often the result.

ALIGNED CORRECTLY BUT BODY TENSE ✗

✗

WORK HARD ON READING PUTTS AS WELL AS CONCENTRATING ON STROKE

WHOLE BODY RELAXED ✓

GRIP LIGHT BUT WRISTS FIRM ✓

Smooth and relaxed

It's probably more vital to be relaxed over a putt than for any other type of shot. There should be as little tension as possible in your hands, shoulders and legs.

Let your arms hang freely down and take a feather hold on the putter. This makes it a lot easier to take the blade back smoothly and on line, and to stroke the ball at the hole.

However, concentrating on a relaxed posture and a good stroke can itself be distracting. Just making a perfect swing doesn't guarantee success. Work hard on reading the green so that you can judge the weight and line of the putt correctly.

Senior setbacks

**Losing length – particularly from the tee – is probably the most
frustrating problem that confronts the senior golfer.
But take heart – a few basic changes are often all you need to help
you keep in touch with your more youthful counterparts.**

Q Physically I still feel in fairly good shape, but I just can't seem to hit the ball as far as I used to. Why could this be?

A Your loss of power may stem from adopting a young man's grip. A neutral hold on the club may serve you well when you are young, strong and supple. But as you grow older, this grip can make it difficult to generate power, unless you are extremely strong.

This makes the temptation to throw your upper body into the swing almost too much to resist. But an increase in effort seldom converts into yards and meters. Rather than giving you more distance, you lose length – and accuracy to boot.

Give yourself strength
Strengthen your left hand grip so that you can see three knuckles – this helps you regain lost distance. Make sure your right hand remains in a neutral position.

Provided the clubhead travels on the correct path through impact, you gain extra distance because it's easier to draw the ball with a slightly stronger grip. You should also be able to deliver the clubhead square to the ball more consistently.

Once you start to dispel the fears of losing length, you can concentrate on swinging the club in a controlled way, rather than thrashing at the ball. Always aim to finish in a balanced position. The ball may have long gone, but it helps you to swing within yourself throughout.

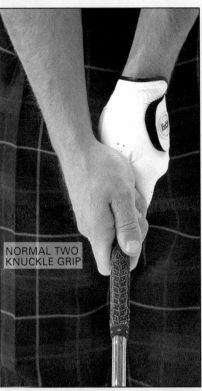

NORMAL TWO KNUCKLE GRIP

X

FORCED STROKE IN ATTEMPT TO FIND LOST LENGTH

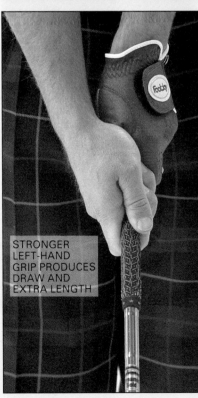

STRONGER LEFT-HAND GRIP PRODUCES DRAW AND EXTRA LENGTH

EASY SWING – BALANCED FINISH

✓

X

STIFF LEG
ACTION – POOR TURN

X

NO DRIVE WITH
LEGS – LOSS OF LENGTH

Q My natural shot has always been the fade, but in recent years this has developed into a slice which is costing me distance and accuracy. I don't feel my swing is different, so what could be causing the problem?

A Faults are often hard to detect because golfers drift into bad habits over a long period. This is probably what's happened to you – your slice is simply an exaggeration of your once controlled fade.

This can stem from a slight lack of suppleness which causes you to swing on an upright plane with not enough shoulder turn. The club is outside the line at the top of the backswing, and therefore travels on an out-to-in path through impact.

Stiff legs add to your problems because you cannot properly transfer your weight – this makes the loss of distance even more dramatic.

✓

FULL SHOULDER
TURN – LEGS
WORKING WELL

✓

GOOD USE OF LOWER BODY
AND FULL RELEASE
GIVE GREATER POWER

Turn key

A major step towards eliminating your slice, and therefore regaining lost distance, is to make a full shoulder turn. From the top of the backswing you're well placed to attack the ball from inside the line.

Don't worry if the club doesn't reach horizontal – provided your turn is good, it's better to be slightly short at the top than to strain yourself.

Your legs can help you far more than many golfers assume – they are the stabilizers in the swing so don't leave them out of the action. Your left knee should point in at the ball on the backswing and your right knee should drive towards the target on the downswing.

Focus on hands and arms

The golf swing is like a precise piece of machinery – all the moving parts must work together at the correct speed and time. It's vital to understand the role played by the hands and arms in the swing – and use them properly – if you're to swing well.

A correct grip ensures that you return the clubface square to the ball. Grip pressure is also important. Too tight a grip restricts your forearms and shoulders, while too loose a grip gives you no chance of controlling the club properly – a poor strike results.

You should feel lively tension in the muscles which run along

CLUBHEAD SPEED
The hands and arms move much more slowly than the clubhead, yet it still tears through the ball at great speed. This speed – achieved by correctly tuning the hands and arms with the body – is the reason why top players hit such long distances.

HAND AND ARM ROLE

① SET THE TONE
To start your swing, let your hands, arms and shoulders move away together. Good preparation helps you achieve this – correct set-up and proper grip pave the way for a smooth swing.

② BODY SWINGS THE CLUB
Now your big back muscles take over and start to dominate the backswing. Your hands and arms are passively pulled through. Try to feel as if your body swings the club – don't let your arms swing your body.

③ FULL SHOULDER TURN
Turn your shoulders fully to complete a proper backswing. Your left arm is comfortably straight and you should feel live tension in the muscles between your hips and shoulders – this is the source of the power as your swing gathers momentum.

④ HIP TURN DROPS ARMS
Your left hip starts the downswing, which automatically drops your hands and arms down to the mid point – in effect, your hands take a free ride. At this stage your hands and arms are loaded with positive tension, providing huge power.

the insides of your arms. These inner arm muscles link with other muscles to shape the swing.

The hands and arms are also partly responsible for the waggle. The back waggle prepares you for the swing path, while the forward waggle helps you deliver a square blade. The instinctive adjustments you make when waggling promote comfort and the relaxed tension you need.

MOVE AS ONE

A common fault for most high handicappers is swinging with just the hands and arms. Remember that the only way to make a full turn and a complete backswing is to move your hands, arms, left hip and shoulder away together. No single part of your body starts the swing.

Your hands and arms don't act independently until the mid point of the downswing. They've been pulled there automatically by your upper body and legs from the top of the backswing – at this stage the hands and arms have no duty except holding the club. Hip and shoulder coordination has done most of the work, loading your

One-handed swing
To develop feel for the role of the hands – left for control, right for power (for right handers) – try swinging a 7 or 8 iron with your left arm only. This exercise shows how the left hand keeps the clubhead in the groove of the correct swing path.

Now try swinging the same club with your right hand only – it should be almost impossible to keep the club on the correct plane, but easier to apply power.

LEFT HAND AND ARM CONTROL CLUB

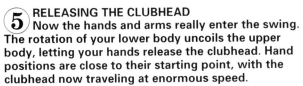

5 **RELEASING THE CLUBHEAD**
Now the hands and arms really enter the swing. The rotation of your lower body uncoils the upper body, letting your hands release the clubhead. Hand positions are close to their starting point, with the clubhead now traveling at enormous speed.

6 **HANDS AND ARMS PULLED ROUND**
As your upper body keeps turning, your hands, arms and head are pulled upwards as the momentum takes you through to the finish. Your left arm folds as the right side drives through the ball and you swing the club into a poised, well balanced finish position.

WAGGLING WITH THE HANDS

① **PREPARING YOUR BODY**
The waggle does more than relieve tension – it prepares the muscles you're going to use for the shot. The movement comes from the hands, not the shoulders.

hands and arms with power.

Both hands work together as you strike – problems occur if one overpowers the other. The right hand releases the power – rather like skimming stones at the seaside – but the left must control the clubface, keeping its speed steady through impact.

② **LEFT HAND DOMINATES**
Your left hand dominates the waggle. The clubhead moves away from the ball along the intended line of the swing. This keeps your body relaxed and poised.

IMPACT

At impact, the back of your left hand faces the target. You thin the ball if you release the club too early – the right hand takes over and flicks the club up. Keep your left hand active – never let it become lazy.

Your hands and arms are fully stretched just after impact, when the clubhead is travelling at top speed. This speed carries your arms through to the finish – their momentum pulls you round to face the target.

③ **LIVELY TENSION**
Your hands return the clubhead to the ball – three or four waggles should be enough to set you feeling comfortable for the swing. Don't dally over the ball – you're likely to lose concentration and delay play needlessly.

Finding the sweet spot

There's a sweet spot on every club in your bag – from the driver down to the putter. It's positioned in the middle of the clubface, precisely where the club-maker intended you to strike the ball.

Many of the game improvement clubs on the market today are designed to increase the size of the sweet spot. Peripheral weighted clubs have the weight distributed evenly around the clubhead. This gives you a greater margin for error – shots struck slightly off center produce better results than similar shots from a standard blade. But there's nothing to beat the feeling of a solid hit from the center of the clubface.

All too often the sweet spot is difficult to find. Even the great Ben Hogan believed he struck only half a dozen shots he was pleased with in a round of golf. Hogan's standards were higher than most, but you can expect to find the sweet spot more often if you know what to look for.

ADDRESSING THE BALL

At address make sure you ground the clubhead with the sweet spot directly behind the ball. A useful tip is to draw a vertical line on the clubface of an iron, dissecting the sweet spot from the top of the blade to the sole. The line indicates where you should position the ball at address. It's an elementary point but one that is neglected by golfers of every ability.

If the clubhead is placed incorrectly behind the ball – towards the heel, for example – you need to make a compensatory move in the swing to achieve a strike from the middle of the club. This makes life very difficult. Good shots are still possible, but are likely to be

---

pro tip

Making your mark
It's very simple to check precisely where on the clubface you're striking the ball.

Rub chalk or crayon on some of your practice balls. After every shot look at the mark left on the clubface – this indicates exactly where the ball has been struck. Wipe the clubface clean between shots so there is never more than one mark on the club.

Select a mid iron for this practice drill and always use a tee peg – this ensures that lumps of mud or grass don't come between clubface and ball.

▲ MARK OF SUCCESS
Professionals hit far more shots than the average golfer, most of them from the middle of the club. The chrome plating on the face takes such a battering that it wears out after a while – the mark of excellence is that the worn patch falls on the sweet spot. Hitting the ball from the sweet spot is vital if you're to strike regularly with authority. This applies to all clubs – whether you're pitching with a 9 iron or attempting to hole a short putt.

◄ AID TO BETTER PUTTING
Many types of putter have a line on top of the clubhead indicating the position of the sweet spot. This helps you place the putter correctly behind the ball at address and you can find the sweet spot more often. It's easy to paint a mark on your putter if there isn't one already. This boosts your confidence as well as your putting stroke.

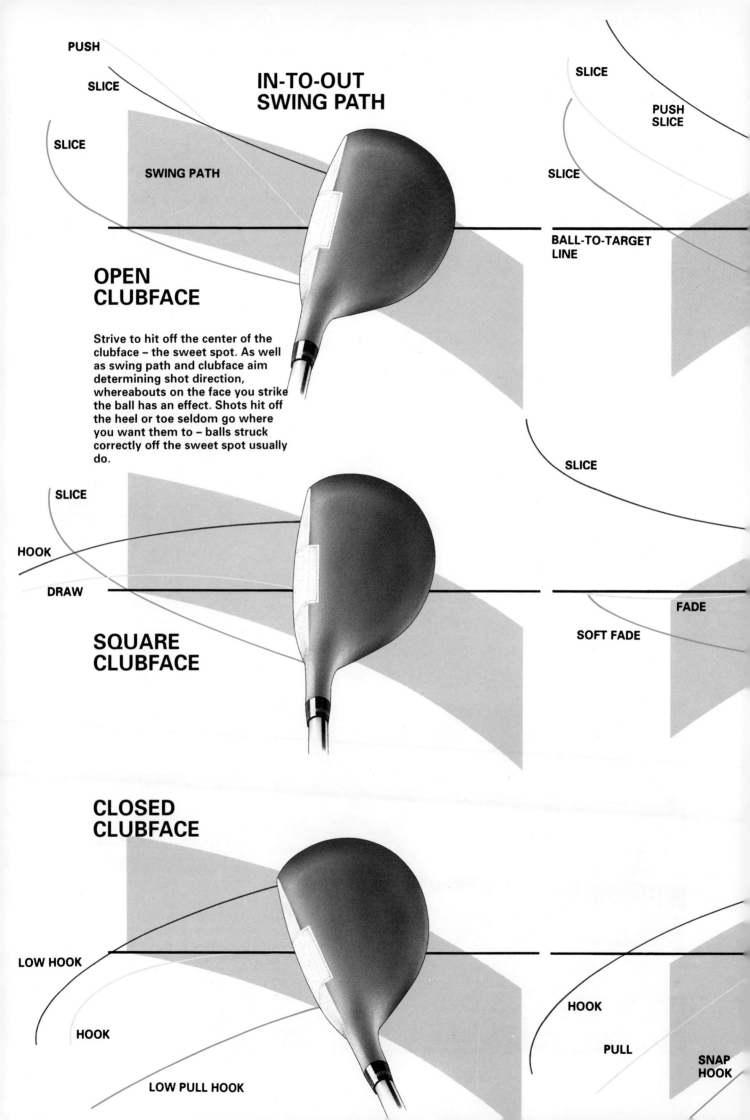

PUSH

SLICE

SLICE

**IN-TO-OUT
SWING PATH**

SWING PATH

SLICE

PUSH
SLICE

SLICE

BALL-TO-TARGET
LINE

**OPEN
CLUBFACE**

Strive to hit off the center of the
clubface – the sweet spot. As well
as swing path and clubface aim
determining shot direction,
whereabouts on the face you strike
the ball has an effect. Shots hit off
the heel or toe seldom go where
you want them to – balls struck
correctly off the sweet spot usually
do.

SLICE

SLICE

HOOK

DRAW

FADE

SOFT FADE

**SQUARE
CLUBFACE**

**CLOSED
CLUBFACE**

LOW HOOK

HOOK

HOOK

PULL

SNAP
HOOK

LOW PULL HOOK

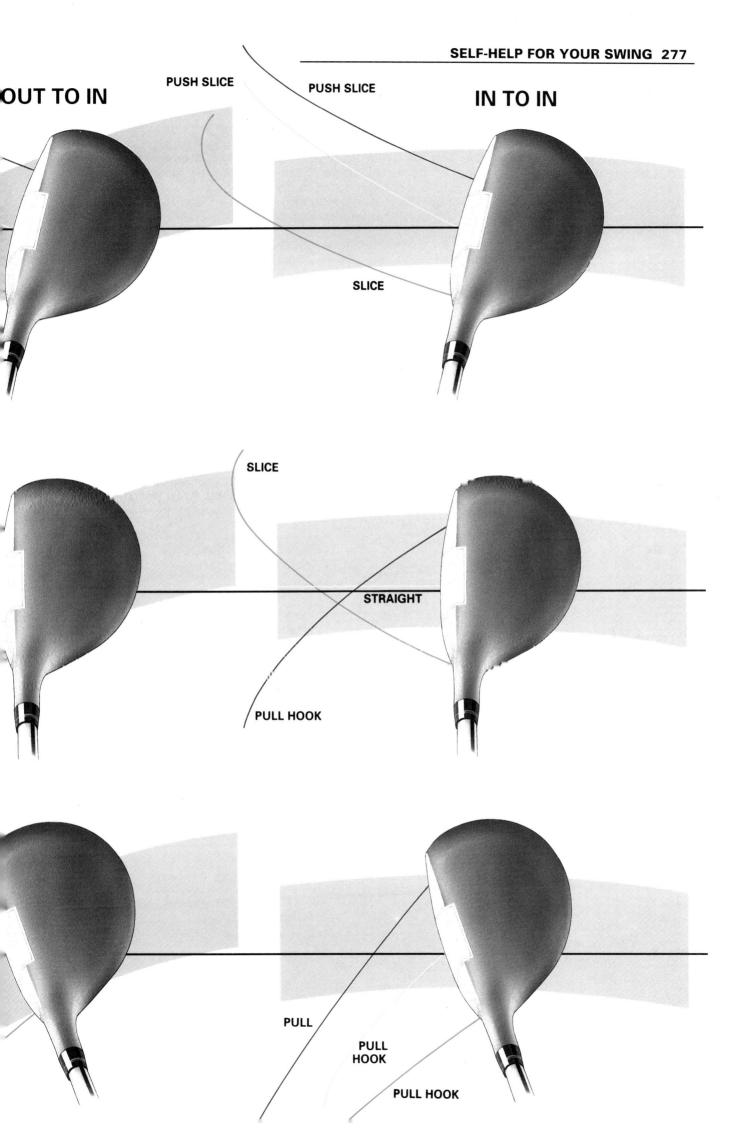

OUT TO IN

PUSH SLICE

PUSH SLICE

IN TO IN

SLICE

SLICE

STRAIGHT

PULL HOOK

PULL

PULL
HOOK

PULL HOOK

few and far between.

The clubhead must travel on an in-to-in path through impact if you want a consistent strike from the middle of the club. A strike from the sweet spot combined with the correct swing path produces a shot to savor.

There's only so much you can achieve through having a natural eye for a ball. A fault in your technique is bound to let you down – particularly under pressure. If the clubhead travels across the ball-to-target line, the chances of the sweet spot meeting the ball are slim. When they do come together it's with a glancing blow.

PUTTER SWEET SPOT

Striking the ball from the sweet spot is just as important in putting. If you consistently stroke the ball from the middle of the clubface, more of your putts threaten the hole than fall short.

Compared to the full swing your putting stroke requires very little body movement. The putter head is seldom more than 12in (30cm) from the ball, but miss-hits still occur. The result can be just as destructive as a poorly struck full shot – you immediately put yourself under pressure and may risk taking 3 putts.

There's only one situation where you should consider not striking the ball from the sweet spot – a slippery downhill putt. Strike the ball towards the toe of the putter – this deadens the impact and so still lets you accelerate the putter into the back of the ball. You make a positive stroke but avoid racing the ball a long way past the hole.

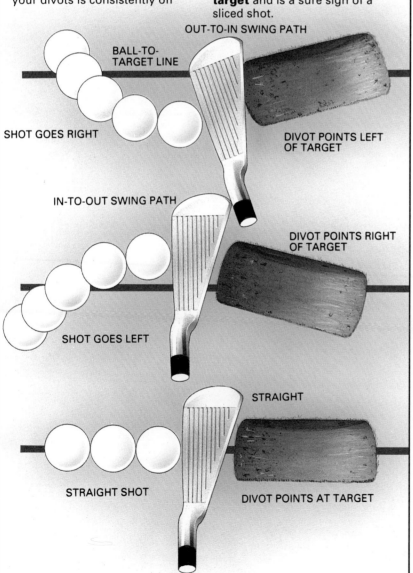

Learn from your divots
The path of the clubhead through impact is critical. Before you replace a divot, study the mark left in the ground – you can learn a great deal about the shot. From a good straight shot the divot mark should **point directly at the target**. If the direction of your divots is consistently off line, you need to take a close look at your swing. A divot mark pointing **right of target** suggests the clubhead is on a severe in-to-out path through impact – a hook is the likely result. An out-to-in path creates a divot mark pointing **left of target** and is a sure sign of a sliced shot.

OUT-TO-IN SWING PATH
BALL-TO-TARGET LINE
SHOT GOES RIGHT
DIVOT POINTS LEFT OF TARGET
IN-TO-OUT SWING PATH
DIVOT POINTS RIGHT OF TARGET
SHOT GOES LEFT
STRAIGHT
STRAIGHT SHOT
DIVOT POINTS AT TARGET

Putter tip
If you're not sure where the sweet spot is on your putter, a simple experiment leaves you in no doubt.

Hold the middle of the shaft in two fingers and allow the putter to hang down naturally. Bounce a golf ball on different parts of the clubface. When the ball hits the sweet spot the putter swings straight back – contact off center makes the putter twist slightly in your hand.

Rub a little chalk on the golf ball to leave a mark precisely on the sweet spot – you can then paint a more permanent reminder on the top of the putter to help you when you next go out on to the course.

Swing lengths

S wings differ from one player to another, but there is one fundamental every golfer should strive to achieve – you must make sure the club is horizontal, or very close to it, at the top of your backswing.

This is particularly true when you use the driver and your long to mid irons – it's the best position from which to maintain control of the club. A slightly shorter backswing is perfect for the lofted clubs in your bag – it helps increase your accuracy and clarity of strike.

Check the position of the club to make sure you're not overswing-ing. Your left wrist should be firm at the top, resisting the momentum pulling the clubhead too far back. Many golfers overswing in an attempt to hit the ball huge distances. But this is one of the major causes of wayward shots, particularly the snap hook.

Instead of achieving a solid position, the club points down towards the ground and waves out of control. This makes it hard to bring the club back on the correct path and your timing is thrown. Shorter shots in all directions are usually the result of your added exertion.

If you're on the practice green trying to correct an overswing, have someone else with you to give you advice – the backswing often feels shorter to you than it really is.

If it's a persistent fault that you

PARALLEL LINES
If your build allows you, it's important the club is parallel to the ground at the top of your backswing. It's easy to check – all you need is a mirror in front of you. Whether you take the club back too far, or not far enough, your game can benefit enormously from just a slight alteration.

PERFECTING A FULL SWING

①RIGHT FROM THE START
The driver has a fearsome reputation, but if you adopt a sound position at address you go a long way to hitting your drives consistently. Place your feet shoulder width apart for a solid stance, with the ball opposite your left heel. It's important that your left arm and the shaft form a straight line.

②CREATING WIDTH
Move your arms and the club back in one piece to pull your shoulders, upper body and hips round away from the ball. Notice how wide the club is swept back to create extension on the backswing. The tempo is smooth – there are no sudden movements which may throw the club out of plane.

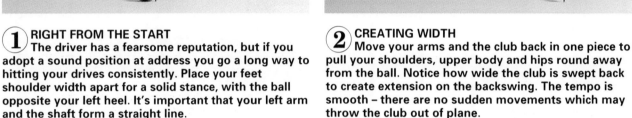

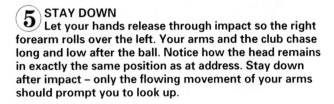

⑤STAY DOWN
Let your hands release through impact so the right forearm rolls over the left. Your arms and the club chase long and low after the ball. Notice how the head remains in exactly the same position as at address. Stay down after impact – only the flowing movement of your arms should prompt you to look up.

⑥PERFECTLY POISED
Your left leg remains firm and provides support as almost all your body weight transfers on to the left side. The vertical grid lines serve to highlight the perfect weight shift. The follow-through is perfectly balanced with the body facing the target – there's no toppling back or falling over to one side.

③ SOLID AT THE TOP
At the top of the backswing the club is just fractionally short of horizontal – the shoulders are fully turned. It's a strong and perfectly controlled position with a little more than half your weight on the right side. The left wrist is firm to guard against a potentially destructive overswing.

④ HAND SPEED
You reap the full benefits of a wide backswing as the body unwinds like a coiled spring. You're able to generate power as the hands deliver the clubhead at tremendous speed into the back of the ball. The shallow loft of the driver ensures you propel the ball forward on a low and penetrating flight.

simply cannot rid from your game, check with a professional that your clubs are right for you. Lighter clubs may be more suitable as they don't put such a strain on your arms and wrists at the top of the backswing. Too much weight makes it difficult for you to maintain control of the club.

AVOID SHORT CUTS

If your backswing stops well short of horizontal, you should look to lengthen it providing you're supple enough. The extra width in your swing helps generate clubhead speed, adding yards and consistency of strike to your shots.

Age and build have a significant effect on your golf – particularly on the length of your backswing – so remember to swing within yourself. Don't risk pulling a muscle every time you hit a shot – you succeed only in damaging yourself as well as your score.

Many golfers struggle to complete a full backswing because of a lack of movement from the chest down. If the hips and legs are too

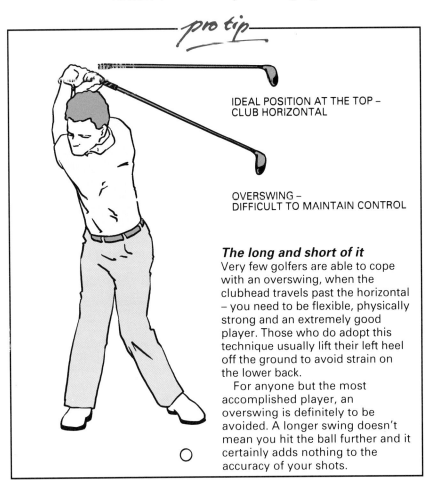

pro tip

IDEAL POSITION AT THE TOP – CLUB HORIZONTAL

OVERSWING – DIFFICULT TO MAINTAIN CONTROL

The long and short of it
Very few golfers are able to cope with an overswing, when the clubhead travels past the horizontal – you need to be flexible, physically strong and an extremely good player. Those who do adopt this technique usually lift their left heel off the ground to avoid strain on the lower back.

For anyone but the most accomplished player, an overswing is definitely to be avoided. A longer swing doesn't mean you hit the ball further and it certainly adds nothing to the accuracy of your shots.

CONTROL FROM CLOSE RANGE

(1) JUDGE HOW FAR
For a less than full shot, your main thought must be to swing the club back far enough so you can generate enough clubhead speed coming down. But don't go so far that you aren't able to accelerate into the ball without overshooting the target. With 50yd (45m) between you and the target, little more than a half swing with a sand wedge is required.

(2) STEEP UP AND DOWN
Breaking the wrists quickly on the backswing helps you strike down steeply into the bottom of the ball. The back of the left hand leads the clubhead into impact. The strike is firm but controlled – there should be nothing hurried about your swing. Even for a shot of this distance your weight must transfer on to the left side.

(3) HIGH FLYER
The followthrough is shorter than for a full shot but still has many similarities. Your hands and arms pull your body up into a comfortable position – there's no abrupt halt to the movement. Most of your weight is supported by the left side and balance is absolutely spot on.

rigid, it's impossible to make a smooth free flowing swing. The backswing becomes a series of sudden jerking movements which create little extension away from the ball. Rhythm vanishes and the result is a succession of short shots, most of them sliced.

MASTER THE HALF SHOT

When you're faced with a less than full shot, you must still strike the ball with authority. The distance you hit the ball is determined by the length of your swing. Concentrate on making your backswing the same length as your followthrough.

Many golfers fail to master the half shots because they forget about the length of their swing.

The most common error is to swing the club back too far. But this makes it impossible to accelerate on the downswing and still hit the ball the correct distance. You slow down into the ball to compensate and the result is disastrous.

Playing a pitch with too short a backswing is likely to cause you similar misery. The downswing becomes a frantic lunge at the ball as you try in vain to generate enough clubhead speed. More often than not the ball scuttles along the ground and seldom finds the green.

EXCEPTION TO THE RULE

Some professionals have swings which aren't taken straight from

the textbook, but their success is despite their unorthodox action, not because of it. Copy them at your peril!

Tom Watson has always played with an overswing – the club often travels well past horizontal. Sandy Lyle swings his driver, and every other club, without even coming close to horizontal at the top. But both players are supremely gifted, very strong and, most importantly, in complete control of the club throughout the swing.

When you feel your swing is grooved to the correct length, be careful not to drift back into old habits. Make sure you regularly check the position of the club at the top of the backswing – it's a part of your game you must never neglect.

Understanding spin

Spin helps you maneuver the ball around obstructions, keep your shots high or low, stop the ball quickly or chase it forward with plenty of run. On certain parts of the course, reducing the amount of spin can work in your favor, too.

There's some form of spin on the ball every time you strike a shot – from the tiniest tap-in putt right up to the towering long drive.

It can be divided into two main categories – backspin and sidespin. There's good and bad in both, so learn to understand how and when to apply the two types of spin. You can then make it work *for* you rather than against you when you're out on the course.

Introduce into your repertoire the shot with **backspin** and you immediately improve your ability to score. Well judged backspin gives you that extra bit of control over the ball.

Backspin is most evident on a well struck iron shot, particularly if it's into a receptive green. The ball takes one hop forward on landing and usually sticks like glue on the second bounce.

SPIN ELIMINATOR
Sidespin can help you in many situations. But when you're standing on the tee armed with your driver, the less sidespin you put on the ball the better. Grooving into your game an in-to-in swing path is a major step towards achieving this goal. You reduce the amount of sidespin which causes the ball to fly straighter through the air. The low penetrating flight and small amount of backspin give the shot plenty of run on landing.

STRAIGHT DOWN THE LINE
A correct backswing sets you up in ideal position to hit a good shot. Draw the club back low and slightly inside the line so that it points parallel to the target at the top – this is the position you should always strive to achieve.

You can continue the swing along the same path without the need to make compensatory moves. The clubhead travels from in to in through impact – perfect if you're looking to put the correct amount of sidespin on the ball and consistently hit straighter shots.

SWING PATHS THAT CAUSE SPIN

Backspin is no mystery if you use the right technique. It's generated by striking crisply down into impact – the more lofted the club the greater the backspin you can apply.

Correct ball position is essential to ensure the clubhead travels on a downward path into the bottom of the ball. The strike is clean – only after impact does the clubhead make contact with the ground to create a divot. If mud or grass come between the clubface and the ball you destroy any hope of generating backspin.

The ball should be central in your stance for a shot with a lofted iron. If it's too far forward the clubhead has traveled past the bottom of its arc and is on a path upwards at impact. The result is usually a weak strike that generates almost no backspin.

The required angle of descent to hit a solid shot with a longer club – such as the driver – is quite shallow. The ball is struck nearer its equator. This sweeping action, combined with the straighter clubface, means there's less backspin.

While backspin is lacking in shots with the long clubs, there's potentially lots of **sidespin**. When under control, sidespin can help you in all sorts of situations – it enables you to shape the ball through the air, either with a draw or a fade.

HEADING FOR THE SLICE
An overhead view shows the relationship between your backswing and the path of the clubhead through impact. If you take the club away from the ball outside the line, it points left of target at the top of the backswing. Because it's difficult to correct

faults during the swing, the club usually continues on the same path, cutting across the ball from out to in. If the clubface is open – which is likely on this swing path – a slice is the depressing result. Square up the clubface and you reduce the spin on the ball and hit a fade.

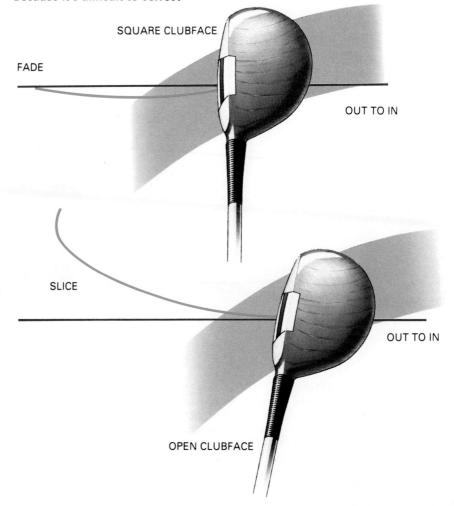

SQUARE CLUBFACE

FADE

OUT TO IN

SLICE

OUT TO IN

OPEN CLUBFACE

AIMING RIGHT AT THE TOP
If you take the club back too far inside the line it's almost certain to point right of target at the top. Unless you make a last second adjustment the club continues on the same path and travels severely from in to out through impact. This imparts too much sidespin on the ball and often leads to a big hook. If the clubface is square at impact the result is a draw.

But beware – too much sidespin is dangerous, and can destroy your score in the space of just a few holes. A slice happens when the clubhead travels from out to in through impact and is the worst fault. A hook is marginally the lesser of the two evils because the clubhead at least approaches the ball from inside the line.

Learn to manipulate shots both ways by subtly adapting the ball position and your swing. Always bear in mind that the longer the club the easier it is to apply sidespin. You need to work harder at shaping a shot with a pitching wedge than you do with a 5 iron.

To hit **a draw** the clubhead must approach the ball from inside the line. Position the ball fractionally further back than normal in your stance. This hoods (closes) the clubface so that it aims straight at the target.

Take the club back low and slightly inside the line. Allow your hands to release through impact – the clubhead imparts the small amount of sidespin that causes the ball to move right to left in the air.

For most golfers **the fade** is easier to hit. The ball needs to be positioned about 1in (2.5cm) further forward than normal in your stance. Take the club straight back along the ball-to-target line. On the downswing try to delay the release of your hands through im-

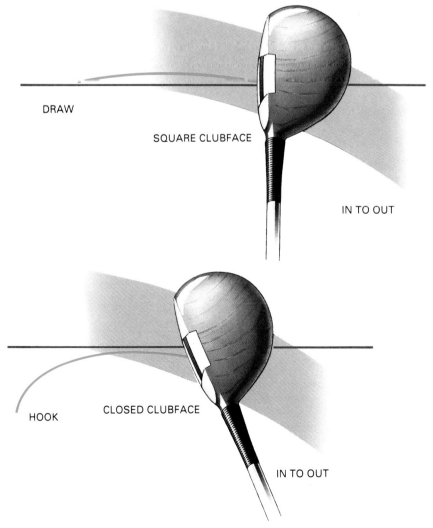

DRAW

SQUARE CLUBFACE

IN TO OUT

HOOK

CLOSED CLUBFACE

IN TO OUT

SPIN COMPARISON

FULL WEDGE
One of the golden rules of golf is to keep your swing the same, regardless of the club you have in your hands – it's the variation in loft and the length of shaft that determine the type of shot you hit and how much backspin you generate. With a pitching wedge the ball should be central in your stance so that the clubhead meets the ball on a steep path downwards. The loft produces a high trajectory and the strike generates backspin. Both combine to stop the ball quickly on the green – close to the flag if all goes according to plan.

MID IRON EFFECT
The position achieved through impact is identical but the shot is altogether different. The ball is a little further forward in the stance than with a lofted iron, so the clubhead approaches the ball on a shallower angle of attack. Combined with a straighter clubface this produces a lower, more penetrating flight. There's less backspin on the ball so don't expect the shot to stop quickly on landing.

pact. The back of your left hand should face the target for a bit longer than a draw.

Try to be aware of your hand action throughout the swing for both shots. An excellent way to cultivate this feeling is to hit half shots on the practice ground. Swing slowly, concentrating on your hand movement and the path of the clubhead. As you grow in confidence increase the length of your swing and experiment by hitting draws and fades as well as straight shots.

SHORT SHOT SPINNER

Spin doesn't apply only to the full shots. Use it to help sharpen your touch around the greens. Some chip shots cry out for backspin, others are best played with plenty of run on the ball.

If there's no trouble between you and the flag, it's usually best to avoid backspin. The more the ball is running at the hole the greater the chance of holing the shot. Choose a club in the region of a 7 iron and let the loft do the work. Play the shot with an extension of your putting stroke.

When there's very little green

APPROACH SHOT
PITCHES CLOSE

BALL SPINS BACK
AWAY FROM HOLE

The drawback of spin
If you ever go to a tournament or watch professional golf on television, you'll be familiar with the sight of the ball spinning back as though pulled by a piece of elastic.

There are times when this is desirable – for example if the flag is tucked in behind a bunker with trouble through the green. But think twice before you adopt the

same tactics where it's not absolutely necessary. Too much backspin can sometimes do you more harm than good.

If you use a balata ball and a wedge with square grooves, it's easy to lose control over your approach shots. A solid strike into a receptive green can result in the ball coming back towards you at an alarming rate.

to work with, backspin is a precious quality. With a more lofted iron, position the ball central in your stance with your feet, hips and shoulders aligned left of target. Make sure the clubface points straight at the flag. Play a hands and arms shot, sliding the clubhead underneath the ball. The shot

floats high, lands softly on the green and checks on the second or third bounce.

On this sort of shot the lie also determines how the ball reacts on landing. If the ball is sitting down it's very difficult to generate backspin – a good lie widens your options.

Understanding swing paths

The clubhead travels a long way during the golf swing – the path through impact is the most critical point. However, it's one of the less obvious features of the golf swing because the clubhead travels so fast – over 100mph on a full blooded drive.

The swing path is one of the factors that dictate the direction and shape of your ball through the air. It's important to understand how to control your swing path and the effect it has on your shots.

PATHFINDER

For full shots an in-to-in swing path is ideal, helping you regularly strike the ball straight.

To achieve swing path consist ency, you have to adopt a techni-

cally sound address position. For a straight shot make sure you align your feet, hips and shoulders parallel to the ball-to-target line. This encourages you to make a good backswing.

It's natural to swing along the line of your body, so if your alignment is even slightly askew, you position the club on an incorrect path as soon as you make the first move. You're then faced with the difficult job of trying to compensate for the fault in mid swing.

If you fail to correct the fault before impact, the clubhead cuts across the ball and you generate spin. The result is a shot that curves through the air.

While your set-up is extremely important, remember that it's only the foundation of a good shot. You

have to swing the club correctly before the job is done.

The direction you take back the club determines its path on the way down. The clubhead should travel away from the ball on a wide arc and fractionally inside the line for the first 18in (45cm) of the

PATH TO SUCCESS
While you see many different styles of swing in a professional tournament, all good players have one move in common – they make sure the clubhead is on the correct path when it meets the ball. With your driver the clubhead must travel from slightly inside the line into the back of the ball. With a square clubface, the result is a straight drive with no sidespin on the ball.

✓ PERFECT PATH

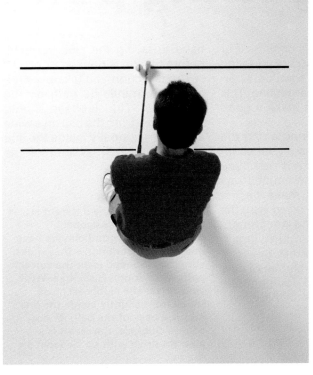

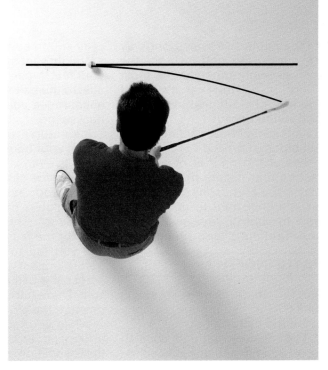

①CORRECT ADDRESS
Get it right at address. With a 5 iron, make sure your hands are ahead of the clubhead with the ball positioned between your left heel and the center of your stance. Align your shoulders parallel to the target line.

②SET A WIDE ARC
Sweep the club back slightly inside the line and low to the ground to set the club on a wide arc away from the ball. Your shoulders are already beginning to turn.

---

pro tip

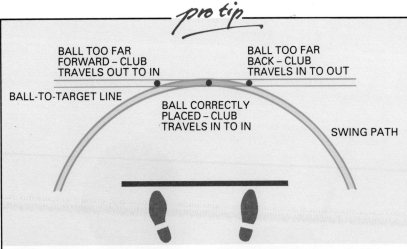

BALL TOO FAR FORWARD – CLUB TRAVELS OUT TO IN

BALL TOO FAR BACK – CLUB TRAVELS IN TO OUT

BALL-TO-TARGET LINE

BALL CORRECTLY PLACED – CLUB TRAVELS IN TO IN

SWING PATH

Ball position

As well as the swing there are several other factors which determine the path of the clubhead through impact. The position of the ball in your stance is one of them.

For a shot with a 5 iron, the ball should be midway between your left heel and the center of your stance. This promotes an in-to-in swing path when the clubhead meets the ball.

If the ball is too far back in your stance and you make a perfect swing, the clubhead arrives at the ball on an in-to-out path. This makes it very difficult to return the clubface square to the ball – the result is often a push.

If you position the ball too far forward and make exactly the same swing, the clubhead travels beyond its ideal path before making contact with the ball. At impact the clubhead is on an out-to-in swing path. Depending on the angle of the clubface you could hit one of two poor shots – a slice if it's open or a pull if it's closed.

backswing. This means you don't have to make adjustments to achieve an in-to-in path through impact.

The shaft of the club should point parallel to the ball-to-target line at the top of the backswing. This means you have successfully completed the first half of the swing. You need a friend alongside to advise you if the shaft is pointing where it should be.

DELIBERATE CURVE

There are times when a lot of spin is called for – to hook or slice your ball round a tree for instance. In these situations a knowledge of swing paths helps you out of a tight spot.

To hit an **intentional slice** you need to align left of target. Position the ball further forward than normal in your stance and take the club back outside the ball-to-target line. The clubface should be square to the target – this is open in relation to the swing path.

The clubhead travels out-to-in to create the sidespin and gives you the necessary curve from left

(3) STRAIGHT DOWN THE LINE
A correct start to the swing pays dividends at the top as the club points parallel to the ball-to-target line. Notice the position of the right hand – underneath the shaft to provide support for the clubhead.

(4) ON LINE
From a good position at the top you can swing down without making adjustments. The clubhead approaches the ball from slightly inside the line, returning to square at impact, and back inside again. Notice how the back of the left hand faces the target.

(5) HAND SPEED
The right hand takes over as the forearms roll over through impact – this action releases the clubhead through the ball. Your head is pulled up by the movement of your arms – not by an early glance up.

(6) BODY TURN
Your shoulders travel more than 180° from the position at the top of the backswing to completion of the followthrough. This shows perfectly the vital role of the upper body – coiling on the way back and unwinding on the way down and through.

✗ IN-TO-OUT SWING PATH

1 NORMAL ADDRESS
The address position is good with shoulders and feet aligned square to the ball-to-target line. But you can still lose control of your swing from a correct stance.

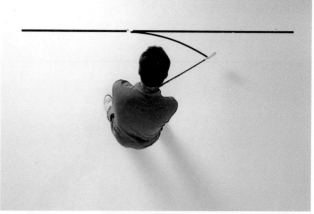

2 FIRST MISTAKE
The early part of the backswing positions the club on an incorrect path. The clubhead is taken back too far inside the line reducing the width of your swing arc.

3 RIGHT OF TARGET
At the top of the backswing the club points way right of the target line. This is a direct result of taking the club back too much inside the line and continuing on the same path.

4 DOWN ON THE INSIDE
The first movement down drops the club too close to your body. It's now too late to correct the fault – your hands are moving too fast for the brain to react quickly enough.

5 INSIDE OUT
The severe in-to-out path is best viewed from above. The clubhead travels inside the line towards the ball and way outside just after impact. An open clubface means the ball flies right of target – a push.

6 GOOD FINISH
It's possible to achieve a good followthrough position even with an in-to-out swing path. Unfortunately the damage is already done.

✗ OUT-TO-IN SWING PATH

① SQUARE AT ADDRESS
The foundations of a good shot – good alignment, grip and ball position – are in place, but the swing has yet to start.

② PICK UP
On the first part of the backswing you take back the club way outside the line and on too steep an arc. This is never a good start because it restricts shoulder turn – a crucial part of the swing.

③ LEFT AT THE TOP
The poor backswing results in lack of shoulder turn and also causes the club to be laid off at the top – pointing left of the intended target. This is a very weak position.

④ THROW AWAY
You throw the club outside the line which creates an ugly loop down towards the ball. From this position it's impossible to get the club back on the correct path. Your swing is heading for disaster.

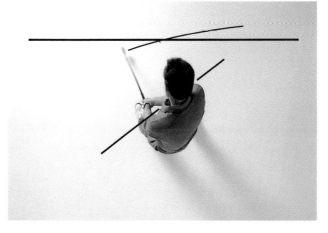

⑤ WIDE OPEN
Through impact the clubhead cuts across on a severe out-to-in path. The shoulders are way open, as are the hips. These moves are typical of the slicer's swing.

⑥ POOR FINISH
An out-to-in swing path seldom results in a classic followthrough position. The hands finish too far away from the body and the balance is far from perfect. This swing is certain to cause a lot of sliced shots.

to right on the ball.

The swing path required to hit an **intentional hook** is opposite to that for a slice. The club has to approach the ball in a severe in-to-out path, so your alignment should be a little right of target with the clubface aiming straight at the flag – in relation to your body this looks closed. Position the ball centrally in your stance.

Take the club back well inside the line so that it points right of target at the top. This enables you to attack the ball from the inside – essential if you want the ball to move right to left.

Once you master the art of deliberately hitting a hook or slice, you can go a long way to curing this normally undesirable shot when it creeps into your game at a bad moment.

Your swing path is just as important on less than full shots. You must be aware of this if you're to build a wide range of shots into your approach play. You can only play some chip shots if the clubhead is on one particular path.

APPROACH PLAY

To achieve a high floating trajectory on an **approach shot** the clubhead must travel slightly out to in across the ball. This generates height and spin which combine to land the ball softly. The shot cannot be played as effectively any other way.

The same is true of a **greenside bunker shot**. Sliding the clubhead through the sand from out to in is one of the fundamental rules of short range bunker play. It's the best way to maintain control over the ball. Never attempt to generate draw spin on this type of shot.

A **low chip and run shot** is best played with an extension of your putting stoke. The clubhead should travel from slightly inside the line, reaching a square position at impact, and inside the line again on the way through.

Keep wrist movement to a minimum to help make sure contact is pure and crisp. Once you start to strike the ball consistently, you're able to judge the weight of your chips more accurately.

A loose, wristy action introduces too many moving parts into the stroke. This technique is prone to error, particularly under pressure in a competition.

Putting along a path
The putting stroke is short compared to the full swing, but the path of the clubhead through impact is just as vital if you're to succeed.

From short range the straighter the putter swings back and through the better. But as you move further away from the hole, achieving an in-to-in swing path becomes vital. Keeping the putter head on a straight line for a long putt is unnatural and bound to cause terrible problems. You need only try it once to know it's ungainly.

Spend a few hours on the putting green to study the path of your putting stroke. It's one swing path that the human eye can easily detect.

Hand craft

When Ronan Rafferty was asked at a tournament to name the most common fault among club golfers, he had no hesitation in targeting the grip as the main offender. Rafferty feels he could improve his partners' grips in almost every pro-am he plays.

While you see many different swings at a professional tournament, you seldom come across an accomplished player with anything less than a perfect grip.

It takes time, but if you improve a faulty grip, your golf prospers. This helps you to realize your full potential, because your game is then free from a very damaging flaw.

However, if your grip is bad, you make it difficult for your hands to operate as a single unit. Once your hands start fighting each other, the ball can – and often does – fly in any direction.

CREATIVE HANDS

A good grip is fundamental to successful golf, but bear in mind that a little creative use of your hands can help you in other areas – often to escape from trouble.

SHOW OF HANDS
As your only contact with the club, your hands have a unique role to play. Moving a long way during the golf swing, they must work in harmony to make sure the clubhead is in the correct positions from start to finish. Poor hand work is a very damaging practice. If you make mistakes in this area, no amount of skill or effort can rescue you from disaster.

✗ DEAD HANDS

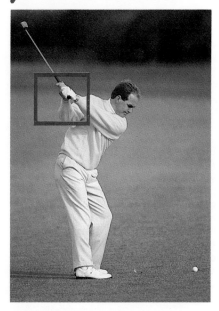  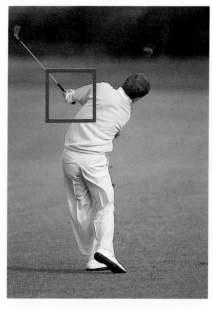

RIGID HANDS – STIFF WRISTS
One of the most common forms of poor hand action is stiffness – a fault that makes it impossible to generate clubhead speed. This often stems from gripping the club too tightly at address, which in turn leads to a stiff-wristed backswing. As a result, the position at the top is poor – the club is laid off and your hands are much too flat.

HEAVY HANDED
If your backswing is stiff-wristed, it's very difficult suddenly to bring your hands to life on the downswing. This makes it difficult to strike the ball correctly. The clubhead cuts across the line from out to in and the hands fail to release. There can be only one result from an action like this – the ball carves out to the right.

FLAT FOLLOW-THROUGH
The follow-through position usually reflects the action that goes on before that – in this case extremely poor. The right hand fails to roll over the left and still the arms have very little life in them – the final position is very flat and ungainly.

✓ LIVELY HANDS

 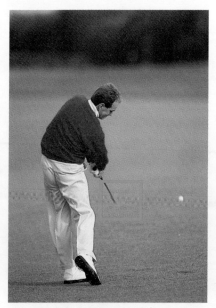 

SQUARE AT THE TOP
When your hands and arms move correctly on the backswing – and in harmony with the rest of your body – the position at the top is perfectly square. The right hand is underneath the shaft of the club and the back of the left hand and clubface are at a similar angle.

CLUBFACE COMPARISON
The most relevant point to note is the angle of the clubface. In a correct swing the toe of the club points skyward through impact – this is known as the release. The bad position in the poor sequence shows the clubface held open – an indication that the hands have failed to work.

HIGH HANDS – HIGH REWARD
The comparison between a lively, powerful follow-through and a stiff-wristed action is dramatic. Your hands should finish high – with the right rolling over the left – pulling the upper body into the correct position. Also notice how the angle of the clubface and the back of your left hand remains constant.

pro tip

 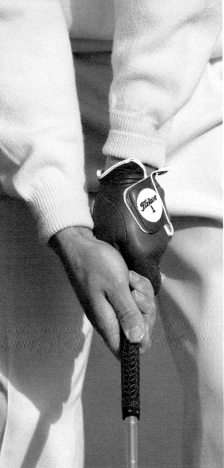 

Importance of grip
Because the grip is something you cannot change in mid swing, it must be correct at address. If not, you're heading for a bad shot.

A **neutral grip** is the safest way to hold the club. In the mirror you should see two knuckles – the middle finger and index finger – on each hand. Return your hands to this position at impact and the blade should be square.

A **strong grip** is probably the lesser of two evils. The telltale signs of this fault are seeing more than two knuckles on the left hand and fewer on the right. While a small minority of pros adopt this method – Fred Couples and Bernhard Langer to name just two – it tends to lead to a hook because the hands roll more easily through impact.

A **weak grip** is the worst fault of all. You can barely see any knuckles on the left hand, and unless you're mightily strong, it's difficult to return the clubface square at impact. The blade tends to lay open on the downswing and you struggle to release your hands – the result is often a push slice.

Experiment with a weaker left hand grip when you play the cut-up chip shot. This tiny alteration helps you hold the clubface open throughout the swing and, most importantly, at impact. Make sure you break your wrists slightly on the backswing, but keep them firm on the way through.

This is a stroke you may have to play over a bunker, or any other place where you need to stop the ball quickly. If the clubface closes at impact the shot is ruined – a weaker left hand grip reduces the chances of this happening.

Although recommended by some teachers, be wary of altering your grip when trying to hit the big hook or slice – shots you may wish to attempt after a wayward drive.

These strokes are best judged by letting your set-up do the work for you – for instance, aligning right of target, with the clubface square, when you want to hook the ball. If you change your grip as well, you introduce yet another variable to a game in which there are enough already.

Putting is another area where hand action is often misunderstood. Certainly your hands should work in harmony – the more they work as a team the better. But how you position them on the grip, and how much you use your hands and wrists during the stroke, is entirely up to you.

Controlling the putting stroke from the shoulders is a popular method – here the hands and wrists have very little independent movement.

However, if you find a wristy putting stroke works don't change it for convention's sake.

ROLL PLAY

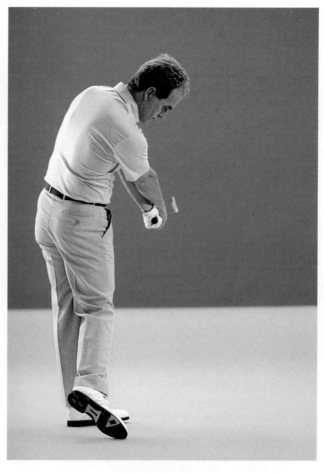

SIMULATE THE DOWNSWING
If your hands aren't working around impact, you need to breathe life into them to see an upturn in your game. A simple half-swing exercise can help you achieve this far better than your normal full swing can ever do. As you take the club back, roll open the clubface and stop when the club is parallel to the ground. This is in fact the position you should return to on the downswing, with the toe pointing skyward.

RELEASE THE CLUBHEAD
Make sure your right hand overtakes the left through impact. Once again the toe points skyward – a sign that the hands work properly and a powerful release takes place. In a good swing this occurs naturally as a result of correct moves on the downswing. However, if you're an habitual slicer, and you don't release properly, you may struggle in this area. A simple drill such as this gets you used to the feeling. You can then work at grooving the move into your swing.

Identical hands
The clubs could not be more different – driver and pitching wedge. And the shots are equally contrasting – high floater and low driller. But look at the position of the hands at impact – exactly the same.

While certain aspects of your technique change with each club you use – ball placement and width of stance for instance – the position of your hands remains the same.

The back of your left hand must face the target at impact. As long as your grip is fundamentally sound, this ensures the clubface meets the ball at the same angle as address – square, if your set-up is correct.

Left side control

Ben Hogan once said that golf is a left handed game played by right handers. This sums up the importance of the left side and highlights why this part of your body should control the swing.

It also explains why many golfers tend to throw the right side into the swing when trying to hit the ball too hard – the right shoulder being the worst culprit. It happens because – for most players – the right side is naturally stronger than the left.

LEADING ROLE

Therefore, it's important you're aware of the role your left side has to play. While you may have a swing trigger that helps start the backswing, it's your left arm that makes the first significant move away from the ball, gradually pulling the shoulders and upper body into a coiled position.

This may be the best method because it reduces the tendency to hinge the wrists too early on the backswing.

The one notable exception to the rule is Seve Ballesteros. He regards his right hand as the ignition key and feels this is the best way to control that vital early part of his backswing.

It's worth experimenting if you're not sure which hand should be the more dominant on the takeaway. If you do favor the Spanish maestro's method, be careful that your wrists don't hinge too soon – there must be width in your backswing.

DOWNSWING DRIVE

With every full shot in golf you should hit against a firm left side, because this is the part of your body that provides support through impact.

Your firm left side sets up the resistance against which you release the clubhead into the back of the ball. A firm left side also helps ensure the clubhead travels on the correct path.

NO RESISTANCE

If your left side collapses on the downswing, there's no resistance for you to hit against and the clubhead is dragged across the line from out to in.

This creates cutspin which inevitably leads to a loss of power. This in itself is damaging enough, but you also lose control of the clubhead at a time when you simply cannot afford to do so.

① AGAINST THE WALL A block of wood standing against the left foot at address highlights the role of your left side during the golf swing. First take note of the space between the piece of wood and your left hip – this is a critical area.

② SLIGHT SWAY A gentle sway away from the ball is recommended on the backswing because it means you transfer your weight correctly. The tell-tale sign is that the left hip turns towards the ball and moves just a fraction to the right.

③ LEFT SIDE DRIVE The downswing is where the left side really takes charge. The legs drive and the left side clears, remaining firm and supporting most of your body weight at impact.

✗ BAD BACKSWING

① WRISTY TAKEAWAY
The danger with letting your right hand start the take-away is that you tend to be too wristy. The swing lacks width and your problems have only just begun.

② TOO UPRIGHT
Unless you can make dramatic compensations for the bad start, the club travels on a very upright plane and outside the line. Your left arm is not in control.

③ PROBLEMS PROGRESS
You can see how one problem leads to another. A lack of extension away from the ball results in a poor turn and therefore a weak position at the top.

---

pro tip

Taking sides

The one-armed swing cultivates strength in your hands and arms – a vital feature of a good repeatable golf swing. It also teaches you the sensation of swinging the club freely and feeling the weight of the clubhead throughout. This exercise effectively puts your left side in charge.

Take a mid iron and swing the club back only as far as you can control it – until your hand is about waist high is far enough. Allow your wrist to hinge as you would with a normal swing – it's this cocking and uncocking of the wrists that helps generate clubhead speed.

Grip lightly and try to feel the weight of the club as you make the downswing. Striking is more difficult with one hand, so tee the ball up slightly.

Complete this exercise several times and then switch to half swings with your right arm.

✓ GOOD TAKE-AWAY

1 LEFT IN ONE PIECE
Study the relative positions between a good backswing and a poor one – it's easy to spot the difference. If you sweep the club away from the ball, with your left arm and the shaft in one piece, you immediately create width.

2 BODY TURN
A compact one piece take-away pulls your left side round towards the ball – this activates the upper body coil so vital to a good golf swing. If you fail to do this, there's every chance that the club travels outside the line on a very upright plane.

3 COPYBOOK LOOK
A full turn means the left shoulder finishes under your chin and your left knee points in at the ball. This is how your left side should look at the top of the backswing. From here you can uncoil your body and drive your legs towards the target – the secret to generating power without effort.

A swing too far
The one-armed swing is a useful practice tip, but only if you perform it correctly. This exercise can be quite damaging if you carry it out badly.

Very few golfers are able to make a full one-armed swing while maintaining complete control of the clubhead – you need very strong hands and arms. At some point the upper body has to join in to provide support. This introduces parts that you wouldn't otherwise use in the golf swing – usually those which have a damaging effect.

Never swing into a position that feels a strain. Remember – if it hurts, it probably isn't doing you any good.

LEFT-SIDED SINS

◄ **FIXED ADDRESS**
A fixed block of wood helps illustrate the major swing faults that can crop up on your left side. At address, take note of the gap between the left hip and the block of wood.

▶ **DAMAGING TILT**
The reverse pivot is a serious fault because your weight moves on to the wrong side during the backswing. The left hip actually moves towards the target, the shoulders and hips fail to turn – you generate very little width on the backswing.

◄ **MIND THE GAP**
An equally damaging fault is transferring your weight too far on to the right side. A severe sway makes the gap extremely wide between your left hip and the block – from here it's very difficult to return consistently to the correct impact position.

▶ **NO DRIVE – NO POWER**
Either one of these untidy backswings can lead to toppling on to the right foot through impact. This happens when you fail to drive your left side towards the target – it's a damaging fault because you cannot strike down on the ball.

Index

long 88
tufts 43, 82
gravel **103-4**
green:
  breaking 126, 209
  condition of 68
  downhill to **223-4**
  holding 265
  inspecting 194, 224
  judging distance **195-6**
  plateau 193-4, **227-8**
  raised **217-18**, 223-4
  saucer **175-6**
  split-level **221-2**, **233-4**
Green, Hubert 204
greenside recovery **101-2**
grip **11-12**, **293-6**
  hitting left 61
  neutral 295
  pressure 88, 271
  putting 204
  senior golfer 269
  strong 61, 295
  weak 52, 56, 66, 295
gripping down:
  ball above feet 43, 79
  long bunker shot 185, 186
gully:
  planning **215-6**
  gorse **193-4**
  greenside **229-30**

H
half shot 282
hands **271-4**, **293-6**
  faults 54, 62
  practice drill 57-8
  warming 168
hard ground **167-8**
hard pan 40
hats 178
hazards:
  cross hazards **169-70**
  psychology **145-8**
  see also bunker; water hazards
head movement 67, 185, 188
headwind **77-8**
heather 123, 179-80
heathland course 69, **123-4**, 179-80
  avoiding trees **151-2**
  downhill lie **109-10**
  winter conditions **243-4**
heavy, see sclaff
heel, striking with 260
heels, weight on 259
high shot:
  approach shots 292
  draw 166
  from gravel path 104
  over trees 106
hole, inspecting 232
home course 196
hook **31-2**, 59, 61, 63-4
  alignment 14
  ball placement 16
  from heather 123
  intentional 292, 295
  posture 13
  from sidehill lie 79
  sidespin 285
  swing plane 257

I
impact:
  clubhead speed 68, 95, 97, 262
  drive 280-1

drive through drill 61
fairway wood 141
faults 51, 60, 61, 64, 67
hand position 274, 296
pitch shot 215
position 11
in rough 86-7
splash shot 147
square 64
irons **184-98**
  faults 36, 38
  power hitting 262
  practicing with 20
  tee height 39, 131

J
Jacklin, Tony 172
junior golfer 58, 63

K
knees 270
  playing from 236

L
Langer, Bernhard 184, 204
late strike 261-2
lay-up 178
left, hitting **59-64**
  see also pull; hook
left side 67, 71, **297-300**
legs 270
links course 71, **161-2**
  gorse **193-4**
long grass 88, 114
long holes:
  par 3 133, 144
  par 4 138, 144
  par 5 144
long iron 38, 185-90
loose impediments 116
low shot:
  chip and run 152, 226, 292
  to green 224
  into headwind 77-8
  under trees 118, 152

M
McNulty, Mark 204
manufactured stroke 180
matchplay competition 24
mechanical action **267-8**
medal competitions 22-4
mental attitude:
  hazards **145-8**
  heathland course 124
  par 5 hole 139
  positive approach 145, 147-8, 166, 194
  quitting on shot 67
  tee shot 128
mid iron, backspin 286
mounds **155-6**, 159

N
nerves 41, 58, 190
Nicklaus, Jack 120, 204
9 iron 70
Norman, Greg 29, 54

O
Oakmont, 3rd hole 147
off striking **259-60**
1 iron, tee shot 150, 198
overshooting green **69-72**

P
par 3 hole **131-4**

long 133, 144
mid-range 133
over water **159-60**
penal **165-6**
pre-shot routine 134
short 132, **181-2**
par 4 hole **135-8**
  long 138, 144
  medium length 138
  short 135-8, **253-4**
par 5 hole **139-44**
  danger hole 143
  long 144
  spacious 142
parkland course, damp **121-2**
paths **103-4**
penal hole, par 3 **165-6**
percentage play **157-8**, 172
pin, see flag
pitch 218
  control 214-15
  from divot 116
  downhill lie 110
  faults 67, 122, 216
  forced shot 69, 214
  swing length 282
pitchfork 23
pitching wedge:
  hard sand 90, 92
  long grass 88, 114
  spin 286
planning, see strategy
plugged greenside lie **93-8**
posture **13-14**
  avoiding slice 49
  distance 66
  uphill lie 83
  see also stance
power **261-2**, 263-4, 269
practice 18, 26-7, 218
  see also exercises
practice ground 23, 25-7
practice range **19-20**
pre-shot routine:
  drive 136
  grip 56
  short game 215
preferred lie **173-4**
pressure shots 41, 54
prize giving 24
professionals 204, 282
psychology, see mental attitude
pull **43-4**, 49, 59, 63-4
  ball placement 16
  low shot 78
  putting 209-10
  swing plane 258
pull hook 63
punch shot 226
  avoiding push 42
  ball placement 15
  fade 162
  right-to-left wind 42
push **41-2**, 55, 57-8
  ball placement 16
  swing path 290
  swing plane 257
putter 90
  sweet spot 275, 278
putting **203-4**
  dew **231-2**
  downslope 126, 278
  faults 64, 68
  grip 204, 295
  par 5 hole 143
  pendulum 203

practice 23, 27
relaxed 268
short putts **209-10**
swing path 292
in wind 209

Q
quitting on shot 67, 122, 201

R
rain, see wet weather
raking 92
relaxing, see tension
reverse pivot 57, 300
rhythm 26, 81, 215
right, hitting **55-8**
  see also push; slice
rough **81-2**, **85-8**
  downhill lie **109-10**
  flyer 72
  greenside recovery **101-2**
  restricted backswing 99
rules, local 22

S
sand, hard **89-92**
sand wedge 98
  avoiding shank 35
  long grass 114, 234
  soft sand 92
  taking too much sand 200
saucer green **175-6**
sclaff **45-8**, 65, 67
  see also fat hit
senior golfer **269-70**
set-up, see address
shadows 130, **195-6**, 249-50
shank **35-6**
shoes 22
short game **213-16**
  hitting left 63-4
  practice 213
  spin 286
  swing length 282
  see also approach shots
short hitting **65-8**
  approach shots 68, 216
  into wind 77
  irons 262
  senior golfer 269
short holes:
  par 3 132, **181-2**
  par 4 135-8, **253-4**
sidehill lie **79-80**, **111-12**
  ball above feet 43, 79
  ball below feet 80, **109-10**, 177-8
slice **33-4**, **49-54**, 55-7
  alignment 14
  ball placement 16
  fade turning into 270
  intentional 288-92, 295
  posture 13
  sidespin 284-5
  swing path 291
  swing plane 258
  wet weather 75
slopes:
  fairway **247-8**
  teeing off from 129
  see also downslope;
    sidehill lie; upslope
snap hook 62, 279
snow 168
solid ball 71
spin **283-6**
  backspin 71, 87, 97-8,

Picture Credits

Photographers:
All pictures by Eaglemoss/Phil Sheldon; Phil Sheldon Golf Picture Library:
2-3, 4-5, 6, 8, 10, 18, 30, 74, 120, 184, 200, 240, 256, 301;
Yours in Sport: 147(b)

Illustrators:
Lynn Chadwick: 103, 107, 109, 111, 113, 115, 117, 165, 167, 169, 171,
173, 175, 177, 179, 181, 193, 195, 197, 227, 229, 231, 233, 235, 237,
247, 249, 251, 253; **Elizabeth Dowle**: 105; **Eaglemoss**: 100, 102, 118,
155(b)-156, 158, 170, 174, 176, 178, 180, 182, 198, 219-220, 222, 236, 238,
244, 245(b), 246, 254, 286, 288; **Eaglemoss/Mike Clark**: 116(t), 157, 159,
161, 163, 225, 232(b), 234(b); **Eaglemoss/Nigel Duffield**: 116(b), 194, 196,
234(t); **Eaglemoss/Mitchell Gaynor**: 53(b), 104, 106, 110, 112, 114, 160,
162, 164, 166, 168, 192, 226, 228, 230, 250, 252; **Eaglemoss/Paul Kellett**:
108, 224, 248, 273; **Kevin Jones Associates**: 28, 45, 68, 90, 92, 131-133,
137-138, 142-144, 172, 232(t), 276-278, 284-285; **Robert Lobley**: 99, 101,
155(t), 223, 245(t); **Robert Lobley/Ian Fleming Associates**: 153-154, 191,
221, 243; **Chris Perfect**: 24(r), 53(t), 54, 56-57, 62-63, 128-129, 134, 179-152,
216-218, 281.